A Girl Called Judith Strick

A Girl Called

COWLES BOOK COMPANY, INC. / NEW YORK

Judith Strick

By JUDITH STRICK DRIBBEN

FOREWORD BY GOLDA MEIR

To
the fighters for freedom
who died, as well as
those who survived,
in the struggle
against Nazism.

I wish to express my deep gratitude to my cousin, Mrs. Pauline T. Silver, who by her endless work and insistence induced me to bring this book to publication.

To my heart surgeons, the late Professor Hanoch Milwidsky and Professor Joe Borman, who prolonged my life, making possible the writing of this book, my sincere gratitude.

CONTENTS

FOREWORD

No sensitive reader would dismiss this book as simply one largely autobiographical account of the agony of European Jewry during the Hitler period. Judith Dribben has given us something uniquely hers that is at the same time a powerful comment on the history of the Jewish people in the fourth and fifth decades of the twentieth century.

It is a girl's voice that speaks to us—a gallant, resourceful, and dedicated girl whose survival, the reader becomes convinced, was in very great measure due to the strength of her spirit. Reading these memoirs of the years 1941–1954, we watch the amazing development of a young girl student from the large, warm community of Pinsk— the Pinsk that I remember so well from my own childhood days and that has been almost effaced from the earth.

We follow her through incredible danger and suffering and heroism in the underground; in encounters with the Gestapo; in prison; in Auschwitz; in the Soviet Army; in the fight for Israel's independence —and, magnificent culmination, at work in the desert kibbutz of Sde Boker.

That destruction and death did not break her spirit; that she could live again in her people's land and help to make the land live; that she could, after these storms and perils, turn to the life of the soil— all these are not only stages of an extraordinary life, but the stages of the history of her people, from the terrible prelude to national revival in Israel.

This is a book stamped with memories of death but restorative of faith in life, and it is good that its author—now a member of Moshav Orot—has written this record for all of us to read.

Golda Meir

I

HARDENING STEEL

1

Autumn is usually a beautiful season in Poland and the Ukraine. The people call it "golden autumn." The trees are in a glory of yellow, orange, rust, and red. The branches of the fruit trees are heavy with yellow and red apples and red-cheeked pears. The air is tender and the evenings still warm and full of starlight and shadows.

During the blackout the stars and the moon could be seen more clearly than through the bright city lights.

In the evening hours Legion and Academy avenues were crowded: soldiers on the way to and from the Eastern Front, girls younger than I—I was seventeen—and merchants selling candy and cigarettes and sometimes their own sisters.

The best cafés, restaurants, and cinemas were closed to the local population, with big placards in German and Ukrainian, "For Germans Only."

On the corner, in front of the big hotel and nightclub called George's, there was a mirror. I could see in it a young girl's face, framed in curls. She wore a bright-flowered summer dress and high-heeled red shoes, and held a lace handkerchief. The painted lips smiled.

Trying to walk slowly, freely, and gracefully, I mixed with the crowd and began my search for a "target." The "target" had to be one or two Germans in uniform, from combat units, of medium rank. A young soldier in a blue air force uniform tried to stop me, but I gave him a contemptuous look.

Then I had to avoid a group of five infantry privates. A hurrying army sergeant major paid no attention to me. Three drunk civilians passed by, talking noisily and cursing in Ukrainian.

After a while I noticed an *SS Scharführer* (SS sergeant)—a tall, long-faced, and nasty-looking young fellow. His left cheek bore an old, ugly scar. He walked slowly, turning his head after every woman who passed. On his breast were pinned several medals, among them the East Medal, and the Iron Cross hung under his collar. Here was a good target for an experienced "hunter."

I followed the man closely, then overtook him and turned back to look into his face. My heart hated and despised him, but my painted lips smiled and my eyes had an inviting look.

The German showed some interest. I walked ahead, then stopped as if to fix my shoe. He approached. I dropped my handkerchief. He picked it up and after a few seconds his hands touched mine.

"*Fräulein,*" he said in a harsh voice, "you lost your handkerchief."

"Oh, thank you! How nice, *mein Herr*!" I answered in German.

"You speak German. How wonderful." He smiled happily.

"It happens to be my mother tongue," I said proudly.

"Are you German?" he asked. "A local national?"

"Yes, *Scharführer,*" I answered, "we have been German for many generations, although we have lived on foreign soil."

"I would like to introduce myself. I am Hans Jurgen from Dresden. As you see, an *SS Scharführer,* veteran of the Polish, Balkan, French, and Russian campaigns."

"I am greatly honored," I answered politely. "I am only a student. My name is Annemarie. My family used to live in Tarnopol."

"What do you mean, used to live?"

"What do I mean? Don't you understand? I was studying here in Lvov, and the Bolsheviks deported them. They wanted to go to western Poland but they probably ended in Siberia or some other terrible place."

"The Bolsheviks are really savages. And so you remained alone."

"Yes, and I have to survive in these awful times. Luckily your armies came to our rescue."

"Certainly. We are ready to give our lives to serve you, my dear Annemarie." He pressed my arm.

I knew that the subject would soon change and I was more eager for it than my companion, though for different reasons.

After a while he took my arm. I looked at my watch. The hour of curfew was a long way off.

"It's a real pleasure meeting you, Hans Jurgen, but I'll soon have to go home. The curfew, you know."

"Could I come with you? At least take you home?"

"You could take me home, but please don't ask to come in, because I want you to know I am an honest girl. My housekeeper would hear and think who knows what. I would never talk to a strange man, but you are a faithful German officer, a hero of so many combats. I admire you so much."

I had in my pocket my false documents and identification cards for any eventuality. You never knew when these Germans might suddenly like to see your papers. The "document plant" could furnish several sets of genuine-looking documents, posting orders, and even German army or police identity cards. The Star of David had been discarded.

I gave him a smile. "I can't refuse you, dear Hans. Maybe the housekeeper is out."

Hans swallowed the bait. Forgotten all the warnings about underground fighters and about strange women, even if they were German.

We jumped into an overcrowded streetcar and got out at the last stop in the eastern outskirts. I led my cavalier through dark lanes, around small houses, orchards, and vegetable gardens. When I was sure he would never find the way back, we climbed up a hill toward a lonely little house surrounded by tall pine trees, with an orchard nearby.

It was dark. I allowed Hans some familiarities.

"How nice it is here, and how lovely you are, Annemarie."

Then he pressed me strongly to him. I could feel his hard and muscular body, and the specific smell of soldiers: smoke, leather, gunpowder. The skull and crossbones on his cap, as he bent down, made me tremble with disgust, but Hans interpreted this in his own way.

I could see the door of the house above his face. I caught his hand and squeezed it.

"Sh-sh," I whispered. "Follow me. It certainly was fate that brought us together. But you know, Hansi, I am afraid to love a frontline soldier. You'll go off and forget me. You'll be in so many places where there are so many nice girls . . ."

"Annie, my only one, it's Russian bullets and shells you should fear, not other girls. In three days I'm going back to the central Eastern

Front and I'll tell you something, I hope we will be in Moscow very soon."

"Come." I took his hand as we approached the door.

I deliberately stumbled on the steps. Then I knocked on the door. The German gave me a push.

"Let's wait a minute," I whispered, "to see if anybody's inside."

There was absolute silence.

I turned the key in the lock twice, slowly. Inside the house it seemed even darker than outside.

I pulled at Hans's arm. We went in. I walked on ahead, with Hans feeling his way in the dark although I was holding his hand.

Suddenly two dark forms jumped at him and quickly overpowered him.

"This is an SS sergeant with an East Medal. Take care of him. I'll be downstairs in a few minutes."

I entered a small room lit by an oil lamp. There was a mirror on the table. I looked much as usual. Only my eyes gave off sparks of cruelty, my eyebrows almost met, and my forehead was furrowed. I wiped the lipstick off and suddenly felt cleaner.

Then I walked down the stairs leading to the cellar. This was a small, narrow, windowless room. The door was covered with felt, with a heavy blanket over it. An electric light bulb hung from the low ceiling, casting a yellowish glare over the room and throwing grotesque shadows on the walls. I looked at Hans, bound and gagged there. There was fury on his face when he saw me.

I said hello to Alex.

"That's a good rabbit you caught. An SS uniform, plus documents, and an honest Parabellum at his side. He should know a lot of interesting things, about the front, for instance." Then, turning to Hans, he said, "Now, if you'll promise not to make any noise and tell us everything we want to know, we'll take out the gag."

Alex's friend pointed a gun at Hans. "One sound and you're in hell." I ungagged him.

"You goddamned whore!" He was shaking with fury and fear. I slapped his face.

I couldn't overcome my own cruelty. Here was someone who could have killed me, who had killed so many people . . . and he was in our hands.

We went on with the usual investigation. Hans was a hard fellow and didn't want to tell us about his unit or what he knew of troop movements on his section of the front. He didn't believe he was going to die.

"Who are you?" he asked in a low voice. "Gangsters? I know nothing. I'm only a soldier at the front."

"We are not gangsters. We are those your special orders warn you against. Do you understand now?"

"No," he said, "I don't understand. The fellows who fight us are bandits and criminals, so our commander says. Look, I have no money. Let me go. I leave for the front tomorrow."

"Damned fool!" Alex said. "*You're* the criminals, you, your friends, your family, all the Germans. If you're a Christian you have a chance to pray before you die, because you'll never get out of here alive."

Hans's face became ashen as he finally understood. Different feelings contended for expression on his face. Then he started howling. "Don't kill me. I am not a bad German. I'll show you my officer, he is a real son of a bitch. He tortured people in the east, gave orders to set fire to a village with people in the houses. We shot those who escaped. Why kill me? I want to live. Have mercy . . ."

I turned away. We didn't have mercy.

I went back to the little room upstairs. I was overcome with weariness and disgust. I stretched out on the low couch, threw off the high-heeled shoes, and tried to forget about everything. But after a few minutes thoughts started running through my mind against my will. So, that's my eleventh dead German. Eleven Germans less. Eleven uniforms more. Several pistols. I know it's only a drop in the sea, but . . .

And now I know. They have killed him downstairs. He will not be back tomorrow. They'll report him AWOL, then as a deserter or missing, but it will be incorrect. We'll report it differently: "One enemy sergeant caught in a trap and liquidated; pistol, SS uniform, and papers seized."

I jumped from the couch. Alex came in, drying his hands and face with a towel.

"I like to wash after a dirty job," he said. "Ivan will be ready soon. He is digging."

Digging under the heavy heap of potatoes at the side of the cellar. Then the body will slip into the lime and disappear. An iron cover will conceal it. Over that, the lumber, and then potatoes on top. Only darkness will remain, and warm, damp cellar air. This wasn't the kind of grave Hans Jurgen, SS sergeant from Dresden, would have chosen for himself, but in our time people didn't choose their graves.

"You're getting very good at your job," Alex said to me. "I'm curious—when will they decorate you? By the way, aren't you hungry? Have a sandwich."

Until I bit into it I didn't realize how hungry I was.

"You'll sleep here. It's too late for you to go home."

"I would, but my mother will be crazy with fear."

"Do you want me to go over and let her know?"

"No, Alex, I've got to go home."

"I'll take you to the streetcar on my motorcycle."

When I jumped down from the streetcar and ran toward the street where we lived, it was just ten minutes before curfew. As I wasn't wearing the Star of David, I walked on the Christian side. On the little back staircase I had a hiding place for my real papers and the Jewish armband. I changed my papers, put on the armband, and was home.

My mother looked up at me. "You come home so late. I am really anxious sometimes."

"I'm sorry, mummy, but I have to."

She didn't ask any more questions. She probably guessed what I was doing, because she'd been a revolutionary herself under the czarist regime. She understood there was an underground and, fair as only a former partisan could be, she didn't ask any more.

2

Only yesterday there was peace. Now there was war. Awakened by bombs, we listened as the windows rattled. I dressed quickly and ran outside. On the street, some people looked frightened, others showed malicious satisfaction. And what would you expect of the population of Lvov early on the morning of June 22, 1941?

I was a curious girl, and in spite of warnings I ran to the center of the city. People were running into houses there as three planes with black and white crosses dived with a frightening noise. Stukas. . . With a sharp whistle, the first bomb landed in the road about twenty yards away. A strong hand pulled me into a house as machine gun strafing broke out; a stern-faced infantry officer had dragged me to safety. Just then an explosion shook the house. Dust, plaster, stones, and shattered glass fell around us. We ran back into the street; now the three upper stories of the house were burning. A fire engine's siren was almost lost in the noise of antiaircraft guns, exploding bombs, and diving planes. A rescue squad wearing Red Cross armbands carried out a wounded woman.

"Go home!" urged the officer. "But look—and remember what you see." His eyes were full of hate. "This is death against life."

I ran fast up Castle Mountain, where we lived. My appearance frightened my family and, when I looked into a mirror, I saw a pale face covered with dust, disheveled hair white with plaster, a pair of hard, hating eyes. From that moment I knew that I would hate the enemy.

Through the window I saw a truck in front of our house. Russian women and children were getting in, the driver helping with their belongings.

I ran to my parents' room. "Let's escape," I cried. "Don't you see they will come and kill us? I have already seen wounded people, and even some dead. I don't want us to die."

Mother was startled. "Are you out of your mind? Why should we go to starve in Russia? We will stay here and see. After all, they cannot kill everybody." At that time well-to-do people feared the Russians more than the Nazis.

My father agreed, so I ran out again—it was impossible to stay at home. I climbed to the top of our mountain, from which I had an excellent view of the city. Looking down from a clump of poplar trees, I could see the black-cross bombers dive over the city below. I watched the explosions, the fires, the ruins.

Then one of the bombers was hit. Black smoke gushed from it and it crashed somewhere in the outskirts of the city. Now fighter planes were engaging the bombers and dispersing them.

When I returned home, everyone was in the shelter, even my father, who had helped my eighty-four-year-old grandmother down. The cellar was dark and narrow, divided into little compartments for the tenants. People had brought down their belongings and it looked like a gypsy camp. Suddenly I hated the place—it reminded me of a grave. I felt a powerful aversion to death and rebelled at the thought of being killed or buried alive.

In the afternoon I was called by the block commander to join the crew looking for incendiary bombs and giving first aid to the wounded. I felt very important with my green armband and binoculars. The bombardment lasted all that day and night; about midnight, the Stukas attacked again in waves. The whistle of the bombs and the howling of diving planes were more frightening than the actual explosions.

I was at an attic window when a dive-bomber howled and a bomb whistled directly over my head. As I flew downstairs a new explosion shook the house. I thought, this is it. I threw myself on the ground and covered my head as I heard another deafening roar. When the noise stopped I saw a dark shadow among the courtyard flowers. The bomb was there. I covered my head again and waited for an explosion. There wasn't any. A half hour later I reported to the block commander. He did not believe it was a bomb, but next morning we saw the tail of a 550-pound bomb sticking out of the flower bed.

That was the first time I escaped death. Was it sabotage by an anti-Nazi worker in the bomb factory or just chance that saved my life?

With the sunrise, the Stukas came in another big wave. A huge black cloud rose over our mountain. When I looked down through the heavy smoke, I saw the railway station burning and the alcohol factory in flames.

For seven days and nights the bombardment continued, almost uninterrupted. During the last three days the city was also bombarded by artillery. The Russians had left on the fourth day, and now there was no one to sound an air raid alarm. The antiaircraft guns disappeared. A Yak fighter was rarely seen. The black crosses dropped their explosives on a defenseless city.

On the way to my uncle's family in another part of the city, I saw electric wires hanging from broken poles. Pictures of Soviet leaders and slogans on dirty red cloth and paper were piled up in the deserted streets. Many houses were destroyed. Only hungry dogs and cats moved about, searching in vain for garbage.

At Theater Square, I noticed smoke and flames coming from the building, once much feared, of the Russian secret police—the NKVD. I could see guards at the gate, but they walked slowly away as the fire ate its way along. Evidently the Russians were destroying their secrets. Two Ukrainians watched from a doorway. One of them laughed and said, "There must be a God in heaven if we have lived to see the Red dogs pull out."

My uncle told me there had been many clashes between the Russians and local armed men. From a rooftop near St. Anna's Church, fire was opened on a Russian unit passing by. The soldiers attacked the house, set it afire, and shot anyone they found there.

After five days we realized the city was a no-man's-land. The Russians had pulled out. The Germans were somewhere on the outskirts. There was no law or order, no civic authority. The shops were closed. Luckily people had learned, since 1939, to keep stocks of food. We baked our own bread until the gas supply gave out, and then the electricity. There was a little water, though many pipes had been destroyed. There was wood everywhere, so there was no difficulty about cooking.

Rumors spread fast. The Russians had shot all the prisoners in the three big city prisons; escapees told how guards had walked from cell to cell with machine guns. Ukrainian nationalists organized a pogrom in the Jewish quarter. There weren't many dead but they pillaged everywhere, injured many, raped women young and old, compelled several hundred Jews to carry out the massacred victims.

Ukrainian flags appeared on many houses, and the colors, blue and yellow ribbons, in many buttonholes. Proclamations on walls announced in big letters "Ukraine for the Ukrainians" and called for revenge on the enemies of the Ukrainian people—Communists, Poles, and Jews. A quickly organized militia soon appeared, with the "right" to arrest people, search homes, and countermand all previous orders. But this Ukrainian sovereignty did not last long, and no one knew whether German rule would be better, although non-Ukrainians believed that any rule would be.

Then the artillery fire ceased and we heard that the Germans were entering the city. My mother said, "I remember how they came in 1918. They entered Rovno like proud Romans. They rode on horses, with shining helmets. They restored order. They were kind and decent."

"But, mother, these are Nazis," I burst out. "Do you think they will be kind to us Jews?"

In the afternoon a long line formed in front of the bakery—were they selling bread? I ran up. A young German soldier in a green uniform, a swastika on his arm band, stood before the door with a machine gun and shouted, "First the Ukrainians, then the Poles and other Aryan Christians. Jews out of here!"

I knew I did not look Jewish. I took my place in line and decided to get some bread anyway.

An old man came forward and addressed the soldier in good German. *"Mein Herr,* the people say they are satisfied to stand in the line as it is now formed." And he bowed politely.

"You fool, shut your damned mouth. I am giving orders here, not you. Tell them to do as I said."

The man translated. The line readjusted itself a little.

"No Jews here?"

"No, this is a Christian street," the old man replied.

So I got bread that afternoon, but I knew that in the future it would be a problem, and there would be many others.

On a brief walk through town, I saw army camps whose inmates had changed for the third time in the last twenty-one months. I looked with curiosity at the Germans. Most of them looked strong, young, healthy, with full faces and thick necks. Some were talking, or walking with girls. As a new army enters a community there are always some females ready to welcome it.

In one place I saw trucks, armored cars, and a few camouflaged tanks. Here the men wore black uniforms and somehow looked different. When I noticed the skull and crossbones on their hats, I knew them for the SS. Hatred filled me and I quickly left the place. Across from our house, in a meadow surrounded by trees and underbrush, another unit was stationed. Here there was a field kitchen, and about a dozen soldiers, completely naked, were enjoying an improvised shower. They were giggling and splashing water, paying no attention to the surroundings or the people. We did not exist for them. We were nothing, so there was no need to be embarrassed before us.

Later, my mother and I walked a few blocks to see some friends. Three soldiers came toward us, talking idly. They almost walked over us. Then one, with a fresh boyish face, yelled, "You swine, don't you see we are German soldiers? Get out of our way!"

We turned to the wall and let them pass, but I clenched my fists. "I could kill them," I whispered. Mother looked at me, frightened.

"What are you talking about?"

"Before they kill us. There's only one language they'll understand. You remember what the Yugoslavs did—we heard on the BBC."

"Just relax. One person cannot carry the world on her shoulders. Don't do anything foolish. Hide your feelings and wait."

"Mother, this is only the beginning—"

"My dear, it is clear that this is only the beginning. And you are just a little bird in a cage. Be clever. Wait and see."

I understood her. Only yesterday I had been a girl of seventeen, a happy college student, studying law and administration, enjoying sports and the arts. Only yesterday I had had a date; we had walked in the park, listened to music, picked flowers, and eaten ice cream.

Now there was war, and I knew I would fight the enemy as life fights death.

3

In 1941 eastern Europe was blessed with a beautiful summer, a good season for war, as the Nazis made their way into Russia.

The New Order was established quickly. Announcements and orders of the military government followed one another on the city's walls. All flags except the flag of the Third Reich disappeared; this applied to the Ukrainian emblem, the three-pronged "pitchfork." The first order established the German military *Kommandantur* as the only governor. The city was renamed Lemberg, its name under the Austrian monarchy.

Foreign citizens had to register. Jews were ordered to wear a white band with the blue Star of David on the left arm. Eight o'clock was curfew.

Soon after the Germans entered, the population, under threat of execution without trial, had to surrender all arms, military equipment, radios, and radio equipment. We had no chance of hearing news from the free world.

The Germans occupied all hotels and the best houses and villas, giving the occupants only a few hours to leave. Jewish residents were ordered to take nothing with them. Uniformed Germans took everything they wanted from houses. They pillaged most from Jews. Germans were sacred; anyone who infected a German with venereal disease was executed.

It was a bad year, this 1941. We did not know that the next one would be worse. Soon, "volunteers" were required for German industry. Not enough volunteers offering themselves, people were taken by force. Food disappeared. The rations were a bit too much for quick starvation, but not enough to live on. The black market flourished and the price of food rose astronomically.

People were caught like animals, forced to work in Germany, in army installations, railroads, municipal plants, wherever ordered.

A staggering "contribution" of twenty million reichsmarks was demanded of the Jewish population. The reasons were explained in a bulletin signed by the military governor of the district. It stated that the Jews were responsible for the outbreak of World War II, and consequently the Jews of Lemberg would have to pay twenty million marks for the damages caused by war operations to the city and the Aryan population, and for the efforts and expenses the Germany army had to expend to bring order to this city and district.

Many people disappeared. Attractive young girls never came home. It was said they were taken to special pleasure establishments for the troops. There were rumors that the men were taken to work camps, or to horrible jobs at the front burying the dead or clearing minefields. Everyone was chasing a job where a "good card" could be obtained. The good cards were the ones that protected the owners from being taken by other "employers." The best cards were those with the seal of the German army, Gestapo, or police, or from factories producing for the war effort.

Other rumors spread about trains blown up on their way eastward, about Germans who disappeared. Someone must have reported to the Russians the location of the SS theater, for it received a direct hit from bombs while jam-packed with SS officers and soldiers attending a special performance. It was clear that some underground group was active. This news raised hope in my heart and a longing to do something useful.

The first shock over, we knew what to expect from these German conquerors. They mistreated old people and then beat them to death in a school courtyard. They forced people to work and, as they worked, kicked and beat them. The Sand Hills outside of town became an execution place. Yet the prisons filled up fast, as people were jailed for ridiculous reasons or for no reason at all.

Once the Gestapo had established its offices and two prisons, the number of arrests increased.

Traitors in the local population denounced people to the Gestapo, exposed their activities under Polish or Soviet rule. Many private accounts were settled in this bloody way. Yet a strange thing happened. The resistance-minded people did not feel that they were Poles, Ukrainians, or Jews. They became brothers with a common ideal.

Many people were thoroughly confused, particularly the youth. What had been considered wrong and unjust under the Polish regime became right and just under Marxist ideology. What had been right, decent, and moral became, under the Soviet rule, wrong, bourgeois, decadent. Under Nazism, the Slavonic people became an inferior race, and the Jews and the gypsies "outlaws."

Yet we believed that the Allies were stronger and that the Berlin-Rome-Tokyo Axis must eventually be defeated. We also believed that truth must defeat the lie, that the desire for freedom was stronger than terror and fear.

They resisted successfully in Czechoslovakia. They resisted in France. They resisted in Yugoslavia, and also in Holland, where they pushed Germans into the canals.

We knew all this from our forbidden radio. The news from England and Russia was concise and factual. We tried to listen in spite of jamming by the Germans.

At about 9:00 P.M. there was a pounding on the door. I opened it. In the doorway stood three men, a German policeman, a Ukrainian policeman, and the Ukrainian caretaker. They had a list of names.

"We want the Jew Alexander Strick," the Ukrainian policeman said.

The caretaker seemed greatly honored, escorting this mixed police patrol, and looked at me insolently.

"Why now, after the curfew?"

"We need some men for a job," explained the Ukrainian policeman, looking away. "It is only for a couple of hours."

At that moment my father came into the hall. "I'll be ready immediately," he said in his polite and gentle way.

I was seized by a terrible suspicion. "Let me go with my father," I said to the Ukrainian in his language.

"What does she want?" asked the German.

"I wish to go with my father," I said in German.

"No!" the German yelled.

"Where are you taking him?"

"I don't know," the German replied and turned away.

Father left his watch and documents behind. He looked so confident, his blue eyes showing no fear. He kissed all of us good-bye and left with his escort. The gate made a noise closing. Father turned back and waved his hand. That was the last time I saw my father. He did not come back that night, the next morning, nor any other day.

In our house lived a young Ukrainian by the name of Yashka, a drunkard and idler. No one knew how he made a living.

The morning after they came for my father Yashka asked to see my mother. They talked awhile in the kitchen and then he left with a package. He told my mother that the men were being kept in the courtyard of one of the Ukrainian police buildings, and he pretended that he could get my father released with the help of a friend he had there. Mother gave him a coat and watch, and waited for his return.

He had mentioned the Ukrainian police station, so I went there and asked a young armed policeman for permission to see an officer. He directed me to the guardroom, where the sergeant was surprisingly polite, even after he saw the Star of David on my arm.

When I entered the office I stopped, stunned. The police officer was one of my classmates from the university, a young, intelligent, and very decent Ukrainian from Tarnopol.

"Peter," I began, but stopped short.

"Finish what you were saying, Ditta," he said politely. He had an uneasy look but immediately regained his composure.

"Peter, where could my father have disappeared? They took him away last night."

Peter's face changed. "Last night? I'll find out and let you know. By the way, where are you living now, and *how* are you living now?" There was a strange eagerness in his voice.

"You find out about my father and I'll come again. It will be better that way."

"Don't you trust me anymore?"

"No! I never thought you could wear that uniform and sit there!"

"There are reasons for that." He lowered his voice. "Imagine if there were only bad Ukrainians serving in the police force these days . . ."

"But how do I know you are not one of them?"

"I am one of them," he replied mockingly, "but I want to help you, and I need you. I always liked you. Listen, give me your address. I must see you again."

Somehow I was not afraid of him. "All right, Petya." I used his nickname. "I'll see you again. I hope you will have some good news for me." I gave him my address.

"I'll tell you something. Do you know what day it was yesterday?"

"No idea. Just another day," I said.

"No, my dear. Yesterday was the anniversary of Petlyura's death."

Petlyura was a celebrated Ukrainian nationalist and organizer of pogroms, killed in 1926 in Paris by a Jew called Swarzbart, who thereby avenged the deaths of his family. The anniversary of Petlyura's assassination provided an excuse for new pogroms.

The revelation made me feel weak. I understood now why the German had turned away. I was filled with misgivings.

On my way home I thought of Peter's remark. They might torture the poor men. Maybe kill them. Play cat-and-mouse with them before they killed them. I was shaking with anger, and only at the last moment did I get out of the way of three German soldiers.

Until the beginning of August I worked only when called or caught by soldiers or police. There was the problem of feeding our family after father's disappearance. My older brother, Michael, was somewhere with the Russian army. We were four: grandmother, mother, my fifteen-year-old brother, and I.

Since the "anniversary" night my mother had lost much of her drive and courage. I could see more gray in her dark hair. She could still get food by selling our clothes or other belongings, but I became the only possible source of livelihood.

One day I went to the building of the Jewish Council. Some of our acquaintances worked there and had jobs to distribute.

A principle of the German rule was to govern, not directly, but through artificially created bodies with very limited rights and freedom of action. In some countries politicians and statesmen were ready to collaborate, but in Poland and in the Russian territory occupied by the Germans there were no leaders ready to set up a government for the Nazis. Certainly there were traitors, collaborators, agents, but not even the Fascist group in Poland wanted to work with the Germans.

In keeping with this principle, the Jewish Council—*Judenrat*—was created to carry out the orders of the German authorities: to control the Jewish population; to deliver manpower on demand; to collect taxes; to ensure food, hospitalization, and sanitation; to keep order by means of a Jewish police. A local lawyer, an elderly and highly respected man by the name of Dr. Parnas, agreed to assume the difficult task of president of the Jewish Council.

The council was assigned a big five-story building, and it began to organize the life of the Jewish population. In some ways the population liked having its own rulers, a place to go with complaints or for help. There was no doubt that the local Jewish leaders sincerely wanted to be the true servants of their oppressed brothers in those evil days.

One of the important departments was called *Besorgungsamt*—the Delivery Office. Any German who wanted anything—jewels, furniture, rugs, clothing, furs, or special foods and drinks—came and ordered it. The office was obliged to fulfill these orders by any means available.

So it happened that many times officials of the all-powerful *Besorgungsamt* walked from house to house, chose the desired objects, and just carried them off. At first people demanded payment, but later nobody cared, as they realized that the only thing of value was life itself.

The council tried to organize hospitals, a cheap or free kitchen, a food supply, and some social services. But the belief that the Jewish police was a means of ensuring order and some elementary security did not last long, for soon the Germans began using them to seize people for forced labor, or to hand over people wanted by the Gestapo or the German police. Many decent Jews, believing they were doing a service to their own people, accepted various Jewish Council and Jewish police jobs, but others kept away from this organization, thinking it best to avoid contact with the Germans.

Peter kept his promise. One evening he knocked on the door, greeted my family politely, and asked me to go for a walk with him.

The evening was dark, with no traffic. Peter led me past the last house, where the street turned toward the mountain.

"No one can see us here," Peter said. "So listen. All I was able to find out was that on Petlyura's anniversary about ten thousand men and women were brought to the yard of the Leckiego Prison."

"But why a prison?"

"This one has a courtyard surrounded by a high wall. They were brought there and naturally were mistreated by the German and Ukrainian policemen. Later they were put into big trucks."

"Were they taken to the Sand Hills?" This was the usual place of execution.

"No," Peter said firmly. "It has been checked. They did something more complicated. It's quite certain they did not intend to kill all those people, at least not that same night."

"Tell me the truth. I want to know everything. It's better than to live on false hopes."

"I swear to you, they didn't kill them that night. As far as my information goes, some, mostly men, were put into an eastward-bound train. So there is hope that they took them for work near the front or the supply lines. The rest left in four trucks in different directions. The trucks belonged to a German transport unit. I'm sorry to tell you they left the city twenty-four hours ago. It was too late to inquire of the drivers."

Although I was dismayed by the news, I detected something in Peter's words. How could he have gotten this information so fast? Again I wondered whether Peter belonged to an organization. Or was it only his police connections.

"So what am I to think, Peter? Should I believe that my father is alive somewhere?"

"I don't know what to tell you. I don't have enough connections yet to be able to find out everything. But it's better not to expect too much. You know already what they are."

"I know they are Fascists and murderers. If you knew how much I hate and despite them and their helpers! I would give half my life to be able to kill them, sabotage them, do them real harm."

Peter's face was close to mine. I could see a sarcastic expression in his eyes. "That's what you think? Very interesting. And that's all you do. You get angry and talk about doing terrible things. Don't you know such talk could cost you your life?" He laughed.

"What do you mean, Peter? I thought I could trust you."

"That's what bothers you!" Peter sounded surprised, and I had the impression he was choking with laughter.

"What's so funny? Maybe I'm mistaken, but it seemed to me you might be the man to help me find the right way." I stopped because I thought I had said too much.

To my distress, Peter's smile turned into laughter.

"That's feminine logic. You just said that you hate the Germans and their helpers and would kill them if you could. Then you say to me, the Ukrainian police officer, the anti-Semite, the collaborator, that I could show you the right way to become an agent and informer for the Germans, for the Gestapo, and for my own Ukrainian police! You could even make a little money and receive a useful work card."

How could I have been so stupid, I thought. How could I have been deceived by his gentleness? I got angry.

"Don't make so much noise." It sounded like an order, but I didn't shut up, only lowered my voice.

"I'm sorry I talked to you, you dirty collaborator. Maybe you have already killed and tortured people, and told me a sweet story, the devil knows why. I wish I had never known you. I'm ashamed to be here with you. Take me home."

"Have you finished?"

"Perhaps."

"Come on, I'll take you home," Peter said, and we walked back without speaking, until we reached the gate.

"Anyway, I thank you. You came as promised and brought me the news."

"It's all right." Again there was hidden laughter in his voice. "It was a pleasure to meet you and to do something for you. And by the way," he bent down and whispered in my ear, "maybe we'll meet again, the *right* way. Would you like it?"

"Certainly," I whispered. "I knew it, but when and where?"

"Leave it to me," he said, putting his hand on my shoulder. Then he quickly walked away.

I entered the house and answered my mother's questions. Why should I hide what Peter had told me? It still sounded better than our suspicions. The only difficult question for me to answer was, what was I doing in the company of a Ukrainian police officer?

The next day I went to the Jewish Council building to inquire about work. There were announcements about work for women and girls: "Tomorrow at 8:30 A.M. fifty girls and women for cleaning and kitchen work for the army and police," or "Tomorrow at 7:00 A.M. ten strong girls for general work for the police."

I decided to work for some army or police unit. I couldn't sit in an office, fill out papers, or perform such tasks as collecting money or requisitioning the property of other people. What I wanted was to face the enemy, to penetrate army units, to study what was going on there. Maybe this would be of some use later, when Peter came to see me again.

Next morning I left early. Mother gave me some clearheaded advice —not to display my knowledge of German. She probably thought that would protect me from all contacts with soldiers and from being molested.

At 7:00 A.M. a police sergeant, a big blond fellow, appeared.

"I want ten good, clean, strong girls," he shouted, but his face was not mean.

In a moment he had about twenty girls around him clamoring for the job.

"I'll make the choice myself," he announced. He looked the girls up and down.

"You, and you, and you. Not you, you have no apron, and you look dirty. When did you last comb your hair?"

I was happy when he pointed at me.

"Are you really a Jew?" he asked. "You don't look Jewish."

"What does he want?" I asked another girl. She explained.

"Tell him I am a pure Jew."

The sergeant ordered us to line up in couples and to follow him. He walked proudly, as if he had a very important mission: to bring ten girls to work!

We reached a big building that had been a high school. An elderly-looking sergeant major explained our duties, to clean the building, to keep everything spotless, and not to fool around with the men. We would get food at noon and in the evening before leaving, but there would be no money.

I was assigned to clean four places: the canteen, the sergeant's room, and two offices, including the hall and the stairs to the next story. I noticed how pedantic the Germans were about work. The sergeant major said anyone who was dirty or behaved badly would be thrown out immediately. We were promised work certificates after three days.

I got used to the work and the place after several days. I had my own way of behaving toward the Germans—always proud and never afraid of them.

One morning some Germans saw me on the stairs. Richard, a blond and fresh young man who spoke Ukrainian, stopped me.

"Last night we set your synagogue afire! Didn't it burn wonderfully, Hans?"

"The Jewish God is burnt to ashes."

"Don't be stupid," I said. "You're unable to burn God, even the Jewish one. And setting synagogues on fire is not our idea of European culture."

I walked away toward the canteen, my refuge. There I saw Staff Sergeant John, a good-hearted elderly man. He was kind, this little old father from Berlin. Many times I found in my bag a package of butter, sugar, cigarettes. Sometimes he did it openly, saying that my work was worth more than two bowls of soup a day. Once he gave me five marks and laughed, saying that a German should not give the imperial money to a Jew, but he did not care. Many times a day he would take out a photograph of a plump woman with two children and look at it longingly. Sometimes he sang "Home, Home"—a German song—while the others sang "We Fly Against England"—a hateful war song.

Once I asked him, "How is it, John, you are so good while the others are so evil?"

"I am not good. I try to be a little human, that's all. And some of them are crazy. Young boys get spoiled easily. Oh, you good old Germany, the damned house painter leads you and us straight to hell."

About the middle of August there were new orders for the Jewish population. In ten days the Jews must leave their apartments, except in one section of the city. The Christians had to move out of that section. The Jewish quarters, not yet a closed ghetto, consisted of the poorest and worst areas on the outskirts of the city. They were always damp and muddy.

In the better quarters, the Jews had to leave all their furniture. They could take only their clothes and personal belongings. The German and Ukrainian police helped them to travel light by relieving them of anything they fancied.

We were lucky. There were not many Jews in our street on Castle Mountain, and we could take our most valuable things with us. We moved to an apartment on a street close to the edge of the Jewish quarter. Around the corner lived my mother's brother and his family.

The Germans didn't allow fewer than six people to occupy a medium-sized room. We were four, so a couple of old friends moved in with us. The apartment had three rooms, a hall, a kitchen, and, luckily, two bathrooms. One room was occupied by a mother with a lovely black-haired daughter, two brothers, a nurse, and a single man. In the third room lived the owner of the apartment, an old woman with her daughter and a married grandson, an elderly single woman, and an old man.

The apartment was located on the third floor, which was considered lucky. For when the Germans or Ukrainians came, they usually started on the first floor and sometimes did not reach the third. However, you could never be certain. They could start at the top floor.

I could help pack our belongings only in the evening. The following evening I joined my family in the new apartment. At first I was confused by the noise and the presence of so many people.

My mother had some news for me. Before the family moved, a Ukrainian police car had stopped across the street and Peter had emerged. He had asked for me and had not left until my mother told him where I was working. Then, in his car, he had followed the cart with our belongings until it stopped safely in front of the new house. My mother had noticed that he looked up at the house as if he wanted to remember it.

Did it mean that Peter remembered me and his promise, and also wanted to protect our property? And how had he known when we were told to move?

Next morning I went back to work. The two rooms were empty and later, while going to the kitchen for hot water, I noticed that the huge building was almost deserted. Passing the canteen, I saw John inside.

"Tell me, John, there aren't many of your people around. May I ask you something?"

"They are away on a maneuver. What do you want?"

I told him the story of my father's disappearance and asked him if he could find out what had happened to all those people.

"You should know," he said sadly after walking to the door and glancing around, "it is bad enough when Germans take away a Jew, but it is worse when those Ukrainian sons of bitches join them. I don't know what happened, but I can surmise. It couldn't be anything but bad."

John walked away, cursed between his teeth, and knocked down a chair. I went back to my work.

The offices were empty. I had an idea that made me shiver. Why shouldn't I examine the various papers and files? Maybe I'd find something important I could tell Peter about. I left the door wide open, spilled water on the floor, and put the mop and scrubbing brush against the wall. The long hall was empty and silent. If anyone came up the stairs I would hear his heavy nailed boots.

I opened the file marked "Daily Orders." There was a list of places guarded by the battalion and the times and routes of the patrols. I read them carefully. Knowing the city well, I was able to retain them in my memory: mostly strategic places like military depots, prisons, radio stations. Then came the apartments of army commanders, police, and other officials, with names and addresses.

I knew there were many kinds of police in the German system, and here was my opportunity to familiarize myself with them.

There was the Gestapo, which dealt with all political affairs, espionage, underground activities, and Jews in hiding.

Then the *Schutzpolizei,* or Public Police, with regular police tasks such as maintaining order in the streets, checking and identification of people and vehicles.

Then the *Sonderdienst,* the Special Service, an organization re-cruited from the SS, with such tasks as dealing with local German nationals, fighting guerrillas and partisans, expropriating, and trans-ferring or extirpating the population.

Then there was the *Kripo,* the Criminal Police, dealing exclusively with daily crime.

Then the *Feldgendarmerie,* the Military Police.

The Ukrainian auxiliary police, who gave the Germans a better understanding of local problems, language, and customs.

The Jewish quarters were under the Jewish police. They had control over the Jewish population and took their orders from the Germans concerning arrest or transfer of Jews.

The other files contained personal papers and correspondence, but nothing secret or important. Printed orders next attracted my attention. One page was devoted to special precautions concerning the local population and possible underground activities against the Germans. There were reports that single soldiers and policemen had disappeared in mysterious circumstances in occupied countries; that isolated patrols or outposts had been assaulted by "bandits" who disarmed them and took away their uniforms and documents; that uniformed as well as civilian Germans had been found murdered; and that the same had happened to local people faithful to the German authorities.

A wave of hope and satisfaction surged through me. So it was not just a rumor. The facts of an existing and active underground were printed in black letters on white paper!

I had to interrupt my reading because there was a sound of heavy steps rapidly approaching in the hall. At once I began wringing my mop and peacefully scrubbing the wooden floor. But my heart was beating so fast and loud that I thought anyone entering the room would hear it. The steps stopped somewhere in the hall.

"This is going to be my school here," I said to myself, "the school of nerves, of searching for valuable information, of learning how to spy."

4

The nights were long and dark. Through the open window I could see narrow Jachowicza Street and a small strip of autumn sky.

There was darkness outside, and fear, and menace. At any time a German or a German collaborator could emerge from the darkness, enter your house, mistreat you, pilfer. Many trembled when they heard the sound of nailed boots or pounding at the gate, a knock on the door.

I was not afraid of them and that was why I always opened the door if I was at home. Home now was a small, crowded apartment shared by about fifteen people of different ages and both sexes. But who cared? It was supposed to be temporary.

It was pleasant to sit alone at the window at night. People were talking in their sleep. Jews crowded in the narrow apartments didn't sleep peacefully. They were tired but unable to find rest even in sleep.

Then I thought about Peter. How much I admired him. He had brought me into the underground. I would never forget him and the others: Alex, Ivan, Stephan, Nadia. They were all Ukrainians or Poles. They should have been collaborating with the Germans. They should have been anti-Semitic, but they were not. How fearless they were. They spied, sabotaged, and yet they were such fine, good-hearted young people. Everyone in our group had taken the oath of the underground, from which there was no way out. I remembered how I repeated the words of the oath after Peter's strong, clear whisper, trembling with excitement such as I had never felt before.

"Joining the ranks of the fighting underground against the German Nazi occupiers and invaders, I vow and promise solemnly to be ready to fulfill any order of my superiors, to be ready to renounce everything for this sacred fight, even give my life, health, and freedom. I will never betray by action or word this organization, my fellow partisans, or any information, even under threat and torture. I will carry high our pride and love of freedom and independence. And if I fail in my actions and betray by weakness of soul or body, my name will be despised by freedom-loving people; contempt and most severe punishment will be my just reward."

These solemn words of the oath had remained in my mind. We were working for the general cause of the Allies. I knew we were connected with the Russian secret service, underground spy nets, and partisan headquarters. At the same time we had connections with some similar Western nets and undergrounds. At that time I did not know the details and I never desired to find out more than my direct duties and tasks required. I knew we were acting against the Germans. That was enough.

I had my dreams, but they were not the usual dreams, of love or professional advancement. I dreamt, for example, of being sent to Berlin to kill Hitler, or at least Göring or the ugly little Goebbels.

Why didn't we arrange something *big*? Instead of the small change of sabotage, kidnapping and liquidating little soldiers, spying on railroads or on local garrisons. Why shouldn't we organize ourselves in the forests where the Germans didn't dare to penetrate? No, I was wrong. The commanders knew better. Every machine is composed of many parts and cannot run properly without the smallest cogs.

I remembered how I brought in my first German. It was a big event —not like searching for information about troop morale or reading papers in the police battalion office. This was a real enemy, taken alive, without noise or violence, by a young slip of a girl who knew why she hated Germans.

Later Peter and I were standing under those straight, tall pine trees in the courtyard. I was extremely excited. For the first time in my life I had caused the death of a man. I had brought him to die—that dark-haired Walter, that little SS corporal with the skull and bones on his cap and collar. Then I said to Peter, "I killed a German this evening," and I tried to smile.

"There isn't anyone who could understand you better," Peter replied and put an arm around my shoulder. "Maybe you think I like this bloody slaughter. I would prefer a thousand times to meet them face to face on the battlefield, but there is nothing we can change. Somebody must do this job, so dirty and unpleasant and dangerous. We are here and we have to do it."

The German authorities next ordered the president of the Jewish Council to take a census and to supply twenty thousand Jewish residents. The president refused and told the governor and the Gestapo chief to do it themselves. Their answer was a pistol shot, and another lawyer replaced the dead Dr. Parnas, who had dared refuse.

At about this time Police Battalion 310 was sent east. For me it meant the loss of a good job and the protection of the German police seal on my work card. My good friend John took my address and promised to find me other work.

Meanwhile I was lucky enough to get a temporary job with the Hungarian army. There were Italian, Hungarian, and later Romanian troops stationed in the city.

I worked in the kitchen of a cavalry unit. Hungarian is a difficult language, but the chief cook knew a little Russian and German, so we could understand each other.

One evening a girl from the second floor knocked on our door, thereby giving the alarm: a German on the stairs. This was the way the tenants warned each other. One of our people came in, frightened, saying a big German policeman was on the staircase. I went out. It was pitch-dark, and I bumped into someone. I recognized John.

At my knock, one of the women opened our door and, seeing the German policeman, at once retreated.

"Come in, please," I said.

But John looked surprised and sad. "I think we'd better go outside. I never knew that people get so scared when they see a German."

"They have their reasons, and it is not written on your forehead that you are a good man, John. Don't blame them."

"I don't blame them. I am very ashamed."

After a while I persuaded him to enter the apartment. I called my mother and introduced John, who, to our extreme astonishment, bent down and kissed my mother's hand.

"You see, madame," John said, sitting on the only chair in the room, "one German takes away your husband and another kisses your hand and cares enough to get a job for your daughter. The world has gone crazy. Where are the good old times?"

Later, after a few strained remarks, John gave me the address of two German sisters, officials in the food department of the mayor's office.

"They are good girls and have plenty of food and money and a big apartment. They are too lazy to clean it and to cook for themselves, so with my introduction you can have the job."

The policeman at the gate of the mayor's building looked up at me crossly. "You want to see the Schultze sisters? What the hell do you want from them?"

"I have been sent by Staff Sergeant John, from the police, about work."

The guard reached unwillingly for the phone. After a brief conversation, he said, "Go ahead. Room thirty-one."

Behind a desk sat a dark-haired woman in her thirties.

"Good morning," I said politely. "I have been sent by Staff Sergeant John."

"Oh, yes, I know about you." The woman seemed pleased and nodded at me.

"I want you to start work in our apartment as soon as possible. Could you come tomorrow morning?"

"Certainly."

"We are only two sisters in the apartment, but we entertain a great deal. Can you cook and bake? How about your housework? John said you were clean and honest."

"Yes, I can cook and bake and keep your apartment in good condition. I can wash and iron, and I am clean and even honest."

"I am sure you are, and John's word is good enough. Could you take all these stockings home and mend them by tomorrow? I have nothing to wear, everything laddered, and it's difficult to get new stockings now. By the way, we are not supposed to pay you money, but we will give you food. Of course, you will eat at our place during the day, and we would like you to stay overnight when we have guests. Don't worry, we will pay you well if we like your work. Well, I have plenty to do now and lots of people to phone . . . some on official business and some men friends . . ." She sighed deeply and started combing her hair and repainting her lips.

"Here are the stockings." She took them out of a drawer. "Listen, I might forget, so tell me your name and I'll make out a work card for you. John told me it would be difficult for you without it."

I walked home with the stockings and the precious paper with the swastika seal. I expected something from this new job. "We entertain a great deal," Miss Schultze had said. Whom could they receive but Germans—maybe uniformed ones and civilian officials? It could be interesting.

The third-floor apartment on Pelczynska Street, not far from the Gestapo building, consisted of three rooms plus a kitchen, bathroom, and big hall. On the entrance door there was still the old nameplate "Family Weinbaum," this typical Jewish named carved handsomely on a copper plate. Over the plate was pinned a little card, "Grete and Cilly Schultze," written in German Gothic.

When I reported for work, the younger sister showed me the house and explained my duties. The older sister was away.

After Cilly had left for work, I took a good look at the house. I found many photographs of soldiers and a drawer full of letters. The big cupboard in the bedroom was in complete disorder. Mixed with cheap sexy underwear were some really fine garments with Paris labels. There were cartons of Yugoslav, Bulgarian, Polish, and German cigarettes.

In the living room cupboard were vases from Holland, wooden carvings from Norway, bottles of French champagne, and choice wines from Italy and Greece. In the kitchen, sausages, a goose, several chickens, butter and milk, sugar, and all kinds of produce filled the refrigerator and the medium-sized room to bursting.

In the hall I found a big suitcase filled with fine linen embroidered with the initials of the former Jewish owners.

I was delighted with the Philips radio. "Little wooden box, you can help me. You can connect me with the voices of our Allies." I tried

to find the BBC wavelength. It was jammed. However, I knew that
with patience and time I would be able to get the Allied stations.

Afterward I had to hurry with my work. In one drawer I found a
curious assortment of objects. Sleeping pills. A beautiful lace handkerchief. Prophylactics. A bottle of French perfume. A long thin dag-
ger. A photograph of a handsome man in uniform fitted into a round
medallion. A box of pills made in Germany "for intimate care and
against contamination by venereal disease." A little golden cross and
several hairpins.

I prepared a good dinner and waited for the sisters to come home.
When the door opened, I saw Cilly coming in with an army captain,
a tall, broad-shouldered young man. Cilly hadn't mentioned how much
food I was to cook, but I had prepared plenty and had filled myself in
the meantime.

Instead of "good evening," Cilly said, "We are hungry. Is supper
ready?"

Her companion entered the living room in his muddy boots and,
without taking off his greatcoat, threw his cap on the rug and stretched
out on the couch.

"Bring me a drink," he ordered, "but a strong one."

I mixed some pure alcohol with cognac and served it in a tall glass.

It was getting late and I had a job to do that night. I showed Cilly
the prepared meal and then went off because of the curfew hour.

At that time the streetcars were forbidden to Jews except for going
to work and coming back home in the afternoon. There was nothing
to do but walk. I had not gone far before Peter's police car drew up
beside me.

Peter took me home. I told him about my new job and he agreed it
was promising.

Peter took my hands and gently stroked my hair and forehead.

"I would like to say so many tender things, but I can't, my dear.
'The muses are silent among arms.' We were born in an evil time.
Instead of enjoying our youth we have to kill, and steal secrets, and
live dangerously. Yet how wonderful life could be—perhaps that is
why we can do all this?"

Peter pressed his cheek to mine. It was only a moment, but it
meant more to us than hours and days.

I watched his shadow disappearing in the darkness of the late November evening, and for the first time I felt afraid—for Peter.

The next morning at work, the first thing I saw was a green cap and army greatcoat. I knocked on the bedroom door. Cilly called out, "Come in." I opened the door and saw two heads, Cilly's and a man's lying on the pillow. Instinctively I drew back and closed the door.

"What's the matter with you, girl?" Cilly was choking with laughter. "Perhaps you have never slept with a man."

I heard the man's vulgar laugh, also.

I began preparing breakfast. I could see Cilly's friend walking to the bathroom and could hear him bellowing German marches under the cold water.

Cilly came into the kitchen in a wrinkled nightgown.

"Breakfast for a hungry and tired couple," she said shamelessly and yawned. "Make some ham and eggs, oatmeal, strong coffee with cream. And don't forget the butter, cheese, and jam. I'll take a bath and dress."

After they left I discovered a one-mark bill folded on the kitchen table. Here was my first tip! It struck me as so funny that I laughed out loud, standing there in the middle of the kitchen alone.

A moment later an ironic thought passed through my mind—well, mother and father, you have brought me up carefully and given me a high school and university education. You have taught me languages, music, and love of the arts—just so I could become a maid for two German tramps and serve uniformed Fritzes.

One afternoon two infantry officers came to the Schultze apartment, all frozen, in ragged and dirty uniforms and overcoats, winter field caps, scratched boots. They installed themselves around the stove in the living room.

I served them a cocktail and then began to polish the furniture, although it did not need it. They paid no attention to me, but talked loudly and excitedly.

"As you see, Karl," the younger and dark-haired one went on, "the lieutenant colonel ordered a fresh attack although it was completely hopeless. I had difficulty in rousing my men. Some of them had frozen hands, feet, and faces. They were unable to use their arms or to get up.

The sergeants threatened them with their pistols and some of the sons of bitches still didn't or couldn't get up." He sighed and continued, "You can imagine what happened after that. The three tanks were destroyed one after the other and we crouched behind the burning skeletons in that wood. I'll be damned if I know how I got out of there in one piece."

The other one, a round-faced blond fellow, listened quietly and sipped his drink.

"Yes, it was pretty rough where we were, too." He spoke slowly and with a Bavarian accent. "But what did you think, that they would give up their capital so easily? They have damned good soldiers now, not like the ones we fought two or three months ago. And their equipment is much better, too. Listen, my antitank crews shot a series of shells at their heavy tanks, but I'm not sure they even scratched the armor. After all, who can fight in such bitter cold? I'm surprised I wasn't frozen to death." And he gulped his third glass.

The first one came over to me. "You are listening?"

"Nix verstehen ('I don't understand')," I said and grinned. The German went back to his chair.

My heart was pounding with happiness. So it had happened at last. Their first defeat. I was so happy I got out a bottle of French cognac and poured some into their glasses.

When I returned to the room, both of them were dozing. I accidently made a scraping noise with a chair.

The older of the two woke up and reached for his gun, shouting, "Take up positions, it's the Russians!"

It took him a moment to realize where he was. Then he was angry. "Get out of here, you're a nuisance." Then he went to sleep again.

I was shaking with happy laughter.

In the evening Cilly arrived with a girl friend, Erika, a medium-sized, blonde, lively young creature. Soon Erika was sitting on the lap of the dark-haired fellow. She was not afraid of the dirty uniform, of the lice that he could have brought.

Cilly came into the kitchen and complained about men in wartime, what a bother they were. But she did not mind accepting a big ham that the blond fellow took out of his bag.

That night I remained in the apartment of the Schultzes. It was late, and I was eager to look into the officers' bags, which I did after Cilly disappeared into the bedroom with the blond fellow and Erika took over the couch in the living room with the dark-haired one.

The bags contained Russian booty: clothes, mostly feminine, old silver, an antique clock. No use to a spy.

The Russian front was far away, and the two officers could still enjoy being alive with these German girls. . .

One day the older Schultze sister, Grete, appeared. She was in her forties, a heavy, unattractive female with a round face, well dressed and made up. She told stories about her business trip with her "friend." After hearing about Cilly's love adventures, Grete said contemptuously, "You are as stupid as ever. What makes you so happy and proud that you had in your bed two dozen front line lieutenants? They come and go. They can easily give you their venereal disease and lice. They don't care if you're pregnant. They live today and die like flies tomorrow."

Grete was holding forth, walking about in the living room. Cilly was sitting in front of the stove with a guilty face.

"Look at the difference. You sit here with your vases, stockings, and hams. Look." And she pointed to her fur coat. "Do you see this? And this?" She displayed a diamond ring and a gold wristwatch. "Do you see this? This is from my bank manager. But that is not all. . ."

I could hear all this while waxing the floor.

"Have you ever seen anything like this?" She exhibited something she took from her purse.

Cilly cried out in admiration.

"The colonel got this from a Jewish woman. She asked for the life of her husband, but the man was already dead. And later all the Jews were wiped out. Only these wonderful earrings now belong to me." Grete laughed.

"But the bank manager is old and ugly. And I bet your colonel looks like an ape."

Grete did not even get angry. "Don't be stupid. They might be old apes, but what have you got from your young, handsome gods? I've got something tucked away."

Grete's laughter sounded a little hysterical. Then she smashed a glass on the floor and turned to me. "Come here," she said in her harsh voice.

I got up from the floor with the waxing rag in my hand.

"Do you speak German?" she asked, hiccuping.

"Not much," I answered.

"Well, I don't mind—you're a Jew. Once, years ago, my best friend, in high school, Renate was her name—she left for England with her parents, with her whole family. Now I am here, I am the boss of this place. Come into the kitchen."

Grete made an inspection and seemed satisfied. Then she closed the door.

"Look, I want you to tell me everything my sister does. She is young and stupid. And I have to watch her. Has she had many men?"

At first I didn't know how to behave and pretended not to understand. Then Grete tried again and at last had an idea.

"Look, when I am away, Cilly—much?" And she performed with her hands the most obscene gesture denoting sexual intercourse.

I pretended to be bashful, but finally decided to be straightforward and satisfied Grete's curiosity.

"Always tell me what Cilly does, but don't tell her anything about me, and I'll give you butter and sugar and meat."

Then Grete began talking about preparations for Christmas, about cakes, food, and drinks.

About a week before Christmas, one very cold afternoon, there was a short buzz at the door. When I opened it I saw a tall, broad-shouldered, handsome man in an air force uniform. His coat and cap were covered with a thick layer of snow.

"Good afternoon," he said politely. "Is *Fräulein* Cilly at home?"

"Not yet, but she will be soon."

"Then I will take the liberty of waiting here, if you don't mind." He smiled, shook off the snow, cleaned his boots, and came in.

He hung up his overcoat and cap, but kept his briefcase and installed himself in the living room. He wore a major's insignia.

"Mein Herr, do you care for a drink?" I asked, but my mind was on his briefcase, in the armchair close to his side.

"Yes, and a strong one. By the way, what is your name?"

"That doesn't matter," I replied. "I'm just a Jewish maid."

"I don't understand you, *Fräulein."* And he stretched out in the armchair. I brought him a full glass.

"It is so cold in Lemberg," he said, "but there in Russia it was colder."

"Where do you come from now?" I asked.

"From Kiev and Zhitomir." He took out a package of Moeve, the opium cigarettes. He lit one and offered it to me.

"Thank you, I don't smoke."

"How is my friend Cilly?" he asked. "Has she been faithful to me?"

"I am not the Gestapo of this apartment, and I am here only during the day." I started to leave.

"Wait a minute. That means nothing. My uncle used to say that there are women who can spend the night very well during the day."

"I don't like to listen to indecent jokes about such matters. I'd better go."

"I didn't mean anything offensive."

A new kind of German—polite and talking pleasantly. He must be from a good family, well educated, I thought.

After a while I had to come into the room again with some coal. The major was smoking. The ashtray was full.

"Are you a pilot?" I asked.

"No. I am only an air force inspector."

"An inspector? Once I knew an inspector, but he was from the Department of Education and was inspecting schools."

The German laughed heartily. "Yes, I'm inspecting, too, but neither schools nor teaching nor students."

"What's so funny? Last summer I saw an air force outfit stationed in a school—a former girls' high school."

An air force inspector, I thought. I had never heard of anything like that and wanted very badly to look into his briefcase. But luck was against me that evening. After supper with Cilly—Grete was away—the major took his briefcase into the bedroom and closed the door.

There was nothing more for me to do. I washed the dishes and ran downstairs, where Peter was waiting for me.

Peter was in a good mood and talked about the situation at the front. "They did not get Moscow, but that will not stop them from an early spring offensive. Who knows how long this will last, but it is clear that the Germans will be defeated."

Then Peter explained to me about a specific job he wanted me to do when the sisters were out. There were messages to be transposed into code for our wireless operator. I could understand the key easily. The base of the code was two pages of Tolstoi's *War and Peace* with the letters replaced by two numbers, one number referring to the line and the second to the letter in the line.

"I think it's a very good code, Peter," I said. "I mean, unbreakable so long as the enemy does not know the key. He can break his head trying to discover the secret of the numbers."

"Yes," Peter agreed, "but there are other difficulties. We've heard that the Germans have set up a net of direction finders for illegal messages. So we'll have to move the wireless. It was so much easier to work from a well-established and concealed place, but unfortunately our own messages have betrayed us."

It was not difficult for me to prepare the messages. I would begin shortly after the sisters left for work, or late in the evening after they had gone to bed. My bedroom was a narrow recess in the kitchen wall, where my employers had placed a little field bed and I had arranged a reading lamp for myself.

During the few days before Christmas there were good hunting possibilities, with military personnel going back to Germany on furlough. I was especially glad to bring in two drunken officers from the Adolf Hitler Division. My count increased to twenty-one. After sobering up, they furnished precious information about reinforcements, the supply situation, and routes, about the lost battle of Moscow and the subsequent morale of the troops.

Later the two heroes humiliated themselves begging for mercy. One of them, after he realized that there was no escape, burst out, "But before I die I will tell you something. Yes, kill me, because I killed, too. I gave an order to burn a village not far from Smolensk and to shoot down everyone who escaped the fire. I hanged two partisans, a young fellow and a girl—the girl with her head down. You want to see the photograph? It is with my souvenirs in the wallet you've taken." Then he broke into hysterical laughter. "Well, I will die today, but all of them will follow me. What difference does it make, sooner or later? The Führer and fat Göring and the field marshals—they are stupid if they think we can overrun Russia." He turned to Alex. "Well, make it quick. I don't want to wait too long to be dead."

The other German howled like a trapped animal, screamed and cried and begged for his life.

I knew it was important to increase my score of dead Germans, but there was something I wanted much more. I wanted to get hold of some big, strategic secret, or help in the execution of an important Nazi.

Christmas was prepared for way ahead of time in the Schultze apartment. I heard of two important guests, a colonel and the air force inspector. Then the plans changed. The colonel had to leave and was replaced by the bank manager.

Supplies began to arrive. A Pole brought a big goose, a cake, and liquor.

"It makes me mad," the Pole said, "the damned Germans guzzling all this food—*our* food in *our* country. I hope it is the first and last time they insult God with their presence here, and I hope they choke on the food."

He spat angrily on the kitchen floor. I gave him a glass of vodka. "For the defeat of the Antichrist, and for freedom, ours and yours."

Later another man brought the Christmas tree and a big box of decorations. An old woman brought two live pike. I put them into the washbasin and filled it with water.

It was late evening before everything was ready. The sisters decorated the tree and we set the table. We laid out the silver on a snow-white damask tablecloth embroidered with the initials of a Jewish family.

The air force inspector arrived first, with a bag wrapped in fancy paper that he took to the kitchen. It contained a bottle of French champagne, several yards of black lace, a pair of silver candlesticks, cigarettes, candy, chocolates, and coffee. Cilly was happy and proud.

The major disappeared into the bathroom. A moment later we heard a shout. "Come and help me!" the major screamed.

I ran quickly to the half-open door, where a comic scene greeted my eyes. Two of the major's fingers were trapped in the mouth of the pike. Blood dripped slowly down into the water. He tried to free his hand but couldn't.

Shaking with laughter, I forced open the pike's mouth and freed the major's hand. The sisters stood in the door exchanging words of sympathy and concern. Cilly took care of the bleeding fingers. I said to myself, "Even the local fishes don't like Germans."

The bank manager arrived, smelling of perfume and wearing a very elegant black suit, a snow-white heavily starched shirt, and a Nazi party emblem in his buttonhole. His present was a diamond ring and a basket of fruit. Grete's look disdainfully measured Cilly and her cavalier with his gifts.

As usual, the major kept his briefcase close by him.

By midnight, the mood was "high" and the feasting couples were digesting their food lying in the armchairs and on the couches. Later they were more or less tipsy. There was a buzzing at the door. Erika came in followed by an SS lieutenant. They were drunk, too.

After a while I came in to clear the table. The living room was full of smoke, the smell of perfume, alcohol, and sweat and loud radio music.

Erika jumped up on the table and began to dance in her high-heeled shoes. It was more a series of lascivious movements than dancing. Then she began stripping off her clothes, first her dress, then her petticoat, until only shoes and stockings remained. Her companions were enjoying it and applauding.

Erika had a well-built body, young and fresh. She wriggled about, lifted her legs and arms, and tossed her blonde hair like a mane. Then she kicked the crystal ashtray to the floor.

The sound of broken glass must have roused her, because she jumped down, pulled off the tablecloth, spilling everything onto the floor, covered herself with it, and ran over to her companion, who was dead drunk on the couch. She tried to take him in her arms and then to shake him.

He sat up hiccuping. "You whore, get out of here! I think I got that gonorrhea from you."

"Shut up, you bandit," Erika yelled. "I bet it was from that blonde wireless operator." The major intervened.

"Stop it. Gonorrhea is hardly the kind of subject to discuss at a Christmas party." He pushed Cilly away. "You fat cow, maybe you think I don't know how faithful you've been while I was away."

"That isn't fair at all, Otto," Grete said from the manager's lap. "After all, you are not Cilly's husband."

"I'll be damned if I'd marry her." Otto burst into laughter, lit a cigarette, and walked out on the porch. "Long live victory and the Führer," he shouted, and six pistol shots followed.

"Completely crazy," said the bank manager to Grete, who was resting her head on his shoulder. "This young generation, what do they know? We'd better drink to the good old times and to holidays in good old Berlin."

They drank again.

I was glad when Erika left with her companion. She was wearing her evening dress inside out, but nobody noticed it.

At last it was quiet. Cilly was in the bedroom and Grete in the living room. Now my whole mind was concentrated on one purpose. I knew that the major's briefcase was in the living room, as he had not taken it to the bedroom. But in the living room Grete and the bank manager were sleeping. I listened at both doors. In the living room there was silence. I could hear them breathing quietly and snoring a little. In the bedroom the bed creaked and I could hear whispers.

Well, I thought, he who risks—wins. Soundlessly I opened the door to the living room. Clothes were thrown over the chairs. I removed them slowly and easily. Under the black evening suit I discovered the briefcase.

Then I returned to the kitchen in my stocking feet. Nobody and nothing moved in the house. Where should I open and inspect the major's briefcase?

I decided to do it in the niche where I had my bed and little lamp. I left the door of the kitchen open, in case anyone stirred. To my surprise, I was not excited but very calm.

I opened the briefcase. On top were several packs of Moeve cigarettes with their blue labels. Then carefully folded maps of several districts of the Ukraine, for the most part of Zhitomir. To my disappointment the maps were new and seemed unused. I put them aside carefully, in reverse order.

Then a package of letters and photographs, all of them of a personal character. The next items were binoculars in a brand-new leather case and a Leica camera. Then, a medium-sized file. I opened it. Inside were filed, chronologically, the daily orders of the military commander of Zhitomir District. The most recent was for December 18, 1941. There was nothing of special interest. It contained the standard warnings to military personnel in occupied enemy territory. It referred to sabotage carried out by "bandits"—blown-up trains, mines, and roads, elimination of a patrol, and the murder of some high-ranking SS officers.

I was surprised that an air force inspector had to carry with him this worthless printed material instead of something more specific about his work.

I smiled when I took out two bottles of the Russian perfume "Red Moscow." And then a piece of carefully wrapped sweet-smelling toilet soap. A sewing box, Yugoslav cigarettes, handkerchiefs. I was getting impatient. A compass, a plastic ruler, and at last a file and two bulky envelopes, one sealed with red wax. I looked at the file first. On the first page, typewriting: "ABSOLUTELY SECRET" and "FILE OF THE NN-TH DEFENSE DISTRICT—ZHITOMIR, UKRAINE." As I read it I was sure that every word would remain in my memory. I was startled by the sight of a scale map of the district giving the distribution of garrisons and other troops in the area, the location of bases, ammunition dumps, reserve arsenals, repair workshops for tanks, vehicles, and weapons.

The next overlay, in tracing paper, indicated airfields and airstrips, bases supplying the air force, air force workshops and repair centers, gasoline stores.

The third overlay indicated all the regular airlines connecting the Ukraine with other occupied territories, the rear, and Germany itself. Familiar as I was with the geography of the Ukraine and especially the Zhitomir District, which adjoined the Rovno District, it was not difficult to keep all this information in my mind.

After the maps, printed explanations of the topography of the district, and operational and intelligence evaluations of the territory for purposes of defense and occupation. Here I tried to remember only the main facts.

In the unsealed envelope there was a notebook listing materials required for the air force workshops and troops. Thanks to the methodical German order of Major Otto's notes, the overall picture was clear. The bases required additional winter equipment. The workshops required several kinds of spare parts for engines and the bodies of bombers, fighters, and transports.

The troops wanted additional garrison weapons, especially automatic small arms, light machine guns, and trained war dogs. All of them clamored for warm clothes, gloves, socks, scarves, ear protectors, and alcohol.

The conclusion was clear and easy to reach, even for such a young and inexperienced spy. Spy? That was the name I gave myself! Before the war, the word had had a sinister sound for me. Now it meant something else. Here I was, stealing German secrets, here in the kitchen of a former Jewish apartment, while the major lay in Cilly's arms. Tomorrow I would serve them breakfast and wish them a Christmas good-morning. In the evening the information would be in Peter's hands and at night wired to our Allies.

I covered the material with my bedspread and went on a reconnaissance. There was darkness and silence in the house.

I traced the maps on thin paper napkins. I did it as accurately as possible, folded the napkins, and put them outside in a little tin can. I hid the can in the snow on the kitchen balcony. Then I carefully put back the contents of the briefcase. How sorry I was to be unable to open the big sealed envelope, but I did not know how to handle seals, and I could not go out now to find Peter and ask him, though he would probably know. It would be too dangerous to steal it. I made my way back to the living room and put the briefcase under the clothes on the armchair.

Everything was quiet. Before going to bed I stepped out onto the kitchen balcony. The night was very cold. The stars were pale. The air was clear and frosty.

The major left early in the morning. The sisters slept till noon. I hurried to finish my work and felt happy when it began to get dark. I decided my material was more important than "hunting" and, after all, I could do that later, so I hurried to the house under the pines.

We sat in the little room in the basement while Peter and Alex examined my maps. I was writing down from memory all the other information I had gotten from the major's briefcase.

"This is terrific." Peter jumped to his feet. "You know what we've got here, don't you?"

"I think I know," I answered, not too sure.

"We've got a map of operational planning and even more precious information. Let's prepare it at once to be wired. Here is the code for tonight. But how will we wire the map?"

We were silent for a while and then I had a sudden idea.

"Listen, when you contact them and get to the map, just insert, 'Map follows. Stop.' Trace a map to scale, one square for every so many miles. Give numbers from left to right for the squares, and then we list the information according to squares and numbers. Everyone can understand that."

"That's wonderful," Peter said. "It should be clear to anyone. Let's number the squares and write down the message. As soon as I get to the text we will check it piece by piece and then you'll put it into code for Alex. That way it will go quickly."

We worked a long time.

"There hasn't been a message as long as this since we began," Peter said.

"Who'll radio it tonight?" Alex asked.

"Numbers nine and ten. They will have to do it while driving around in a German air force truck, the personal gift of Göring."

We all laughed. Peter left to take the message to the radio operators. It was about midnight. I decided to sleep there, as I couldn't get home so late. I fell asleep instantly on the narrow couch upstairs.

I awoke when I felt somebody near me. Peter was sitting on the couch.

"You've done a good job, my dear," he said, gently stroking my hair. "I didn't know you could be such a good spy, I mean getting important information so easily."

"I didn't know it myself, Peter. I didn't know I could be a spy at all. I was lucky, that's all."

"Luck is one of the most important qualities a spy can have, if I can call it a quality. I hope you will always be lucky."

"I believe I am."

"Did you notice I mentioned in the message who furnished the information?"

"No, I just worked automatically at the end."

"Yes, it was at the end. 'Information was furnished by 321.' That is your number."

"There were too many numbers. I didn't pay attention, Peter."

We talked till morning. Then we drank boiling hot tea without sugar and planned the next day's work. I had to go back to the Schultze apartment.

Two blocks from their house a German policeman put me to work shoveling snow. My card with the swastika and the eagle didn't make any impression on him but, when my captor walked away, I dropped the shovel and ran away through a narrow passage between two houses. I reached my employers' on time.

That winter broke all records for cold, snow, and ice. The German army was freezing to death on the Eastern Front. In this, the third war year for us, the second of the invasion of the Soviet Union, life was cruel and dangerous.

The police no longer maintained entire control. After several months the population had learned thoroughly how to hide, escape, disobey orders, smuggle, and bluff.

One of the most strict underground rules was never to carry on you anything that could identify you as a member of a group, neither written material—information, records, addresses—nor any objects connected with illegal activities. Your memory had to carry everything. Your eyes and ears had to be sharp, and reactions quick, cold, astute.

The night was very cold, the moonlight pale and clear. Clear as our orders. The big house was dark and silent when we arrived. Ivan and Stephan went in. They wore Ukrainian uniforms. They returned quickly with a man in a long coat, a hat pulled over his face.

Peter drove the car. Nobody talked.

On the outskirts we were stopped by a German patrol. Short sentences were exchanged, papers presented and given a quick glance. The uniforms, the car, and the papers, false as they were, satisfied the bored and frozen guards.

We stopped beside a little grove. The frozen snow crackled under our boots. Only the steps of the unknown man were not so firm and hard as ours. We were certain of his guilt. He had betrayed us for a little money and a little food. And a traitor's reward is death, with only a few minutes to explain the crime and the punishment.

The man did not know who we were nor why we had brought him to this grove. When he was told he broke down completely. He pleaded hunger. He denied, and confessed. We were unmoved.

"In the name of justice, this underground court-martial sentences you to death by hanging as a traitor to your suffering people." Ivan's clear and harsh voice pronounced judgment in the frozen darkness.

Several hours later the dead traitor's body was brought back to the city, with a rope round his neck, and hung on a telegraph post in the darkness of the blackout. To his chest was pinned a placard, in German and Ukrainian, giving the facts. No claim for damages, it added.

Not yet out of our teens, we had learned to be direct, cruel, and sarcastic.

Many other German families lived in the same house where the sisters Schultze resided. On the top floor was a girl named Christine. I met her many times on the stairs. She was of medium height, a round-faced reddish blonde, neither ugly nor attractive. Just another girl.

One evening the sisters were visited by a German woman who also lived in the house, and I heard her talking about Christine.

"Can you imagine? This complete nothing, this local German, the mistress of *Obersturmbannführer* Nagel! And he from the Criminal Police. And not only a mistress—he has a wife still, in Germany. He did not care to bring her here—but now she is pregnant. God in Heaven, to have something like that in our house."

Cilly and Grete exchanged sarcastic looks.

"Don't you see what's going on? She had nothing. He found her in the street with a naked backside and then he got her a job and an apartment—and what furniture, clothes, furs. When one is a high-ranking officer in the police. . ."

Chief of the Criminal Police Nagel's mistress in this house! And he probably spent nights and weekends here. It might be an opportunity to get him into our hands, at least for a couple of hours.

One day I met one of our commanders. I expected to see a heroic-looking man, but the man nicknamed Willy was only of medium height with an average face. Yet his eyes were sharp and deep, and could dig into your very soul. You could not escape the penetrating look of those blue gray eyes.

He wore civilian clothes of German cut, a soft hat, and a Nazi party emblem in his buttonhole. He spoke perfect German with a Berlin accent, and perfect Muscovite Russian. I did not know his true name, his mission and rank, or what our service relation was. It was enough that this man was our commander, and we were not supposed to ask questions.

Willy had a quiet but abrupt and commanding manner of speaking.

He measured me up and down, and squeezed my hand so hard that I almost screamed.

"I like the reports about you," he said. "I appreciate your work. If we had printed orders, like a regular military unit, you would see your own citation. What I want from you now is more information on the Criminal Police *Oberstrumbannführer*."

When I told him I admired his perfect German and Russian, he smiled. "It is not difficult, when one was raised in Moscow and has lived ten years in Berlin."

5

Nineteen forty-two was a bad year. The winter, without coal, wood, food was very hard on us. Though the overcrowded rooms in the Jewish sectors of the city did retain some warmth, men, women, and children collapsed every day from cold and hunger. Typhoid and other diseases increased. Work was unpaid. And how long could people keep themselves by selling their belongings?

The skull of the SS seemed to grin broadly and sarcastically. One day I saw a German policeman put a forage cap in the middle of the street and force passersby to bow before it, and the Jews to crawl before it.

There were rumors of another "action." Nobody knew exactly what it would be until the SS, helped by Ukrainian and Jewish police, started a roundup of old people and cripples. One of the old women from our apartment never came back. I was glad grandmother did not leave the house. She spent her days and nights reading the Bible and prayer book. We hid the situation from her.

One evening I was sitting in our crowded room when, looking toward grandma's bed, I noticed that the book had fallen onto her chest. I thought she was asleep.

After a while, when I looked again, she was still in the same position. As it seemed unnatural, I ran toward her. When I felt her hands they were cold. She was smiling quietly. The Bible was open at the "Song of Songs."

Grandmother's body was placed on a mattress on the floor, according to the Jewish custom. Candles were lit and men prayed. She had to stay there several days, because the Germans were destroying the old Jewish cemetery and removing the rich marble tombstones.

The evening after she died, there were heavy steps on the staircase and then a pounding at the door. I opened it for an officer and two men. The skull and crossbones shone from their uniforms.

"What do you want?" I asked angrily.

"Get out of the way," the officer said, laughing drunkenly. He started going from room to room.

"Are there any old people or cripples here?"

"No."

"What is in there?" The officer indicated our room.

"Take a look."

He took a look, then came out hurriedly, his face pale.

"What's that inside?"

I had heard that the Germans were afraid of the sick and the dead. Now I could see it for myself.

"My grandmother died yesterday but we can't bury her till they've finished destroying the cemetery."

The officer's face had a queer expression, a blend of fear, disgust, and frustration.

"Come here, I'll tell you something."

"I do not talk with Germans."

"Don't be afraid of me. I just want to tell you something. And you," he turned to the soldiers, "instead of looking stupid, get out of here and wait for me on the stairs." They closed the door and disappeared.

"Listen, she was a lucky woman, your grandmother."

"Why?" I became interested, though still fighting back hate and disgust.

"Because she died in her home and not there, where they torture them to death. Do you know what I have seen there? White hair covered with blood, crushed faces, broken bones, torn-out eyes. I know I shouldn't talk about it, but I'm drunk and can't stand it. I am a soldier and a man, not a torturer of old people and cripples." He began to sob.

"You probably are one yourself, *Untersturmführer,* and now you are drunk and have just lost your nerve. Fine heroes your Führer has in his ranks!"

"No, don't say it. I never was, but I probably will be. This regime turns decent men into tigers."

"Please go away. I don't like hysterical scenes and crying men." I very much wanted to give him a kick, but his soldiers might have seen.

In the doorway he bowed politely and said, *"Auf wiedersehen."*

Two days later we buried grandmother in a frozen grave. A little mangy horse was hardly able to pull the carriage to the cemetery.

It may be better for her, I thought as the frozen soil covered the grave. Under her head we placed a little sack filled with earth from the Holy Land. She had obtained it many years ago, had always carried it with her, and had asked me to place it under her head when she died.

She sleeps with the earth of the Holy Land under her head.

We found out that Chief of the Criminal Police Nagel sometimes visited Christine's apartment. She had a telephone. Peter sent a man in the uniform of the German signal corps to connect that phone with the one in the Schultze apartment, so I could listen to Christine's calls. I could cut off the connection when anyone was at home.

One evening, when everybody was out, I heard a man's voice on the phone. He was discussing a trip to Krakow that weekend with Christine. The man was to pick her up after work, in front of the office. What a chance! We knew which cars *Obersturmbannführer* Nagel used privately and on duty. What could be more opportune than to intercept him with his sweetheart on the road from Lvov to Krakow? There were woods and swamps at many points along the road.

All the details were worked out, the place of the ambush and the time. Our agent in Christine's office was to let us know when they left. Nagel was to be kidnapped and taken away in a car, as we were not interested in simple elimination. His knowledge and information, which we could probably squeeze out of him, were more precious and important to us than his body.

At first everything went perfectly. Christine left for work as usual, all dressed up. I saw her get into a waiting police car.

Then, at noon, came the call from our man. The message reached the ambushers immediately. Later he called me—he knew that my employers hadn't yet left the house—to let me know that "my sister left with a civilian in a fancy Opel." I began to worry—a civilian and a fancy Opel? After all, I had never talked to Hans Nagel and didn't know his voice. Maybe it had been somebody else? And a fancy Opel? This must be a terrible mistake. Terrible, because it could not possibly be the much wanted Hans Nagel.

I was worried but had to concentrate on other problems, since we were planning another operation the next day.

It turned out that the man driving Christine to Krakow was an important Gestapo interpreter. Our men stopped the car, checked the papers, and saw the man was not Hans Nagel. He told them everything they knew: that Nagel was on a trip to the capital of the Polish government. He was only the driver and escort for Nagel's *Fräulein*. He tried to speak German but the boys recognized him as a local resident.

I felt stupid and ashamed.

But it's good to miss the target once in a while. The next time you aim more carefully.

The next day I was sitting in a Ukrainian police car next to Peter. We drove to the East Road.

Soon we reached the woods—our dear, familiar Ukrainian woods. The woods. Terror to the Germans. Refuge of the partisans and the persecuted.

We used to love to stretch out on the thick, soft layer of old leaves and pine needles in those happy prewar days. But now we didn't pay attention even to the squirrels dropping nuts from the tall trees.

We thought, each to himself, about the same thing. Peter wore the uniform of a policeman, representative of law and order. And I wore the uniform of a nurse.

The idea made me laugh. Peter questioned me with his glance. I told him. And then we both laughed long and loud. Funny: peace and order! Help and mercy! We are killers. No mercy. No forgiveness.

For a moment we fell into each other's arms. Then we got back into the car.

On both sides of the railroad were tall, dense walls of pine. In the distance the dark gray outline of the bridge.

We took up our position on the dirt road over three hundred yards away from the bridge, eastward. Heavy explosives were being planted under the bridge. Michael and Ivan were there. Michael, a short, stocky miner, our demolition expert. He wouldn't tell where and how he got the ugly scar on his forehead or lost the two fingers on his left hand. He was an escapee from a Gestapo prison.

At two in the morning a patrol would pass on a trolley, checking the line for convoys of trains heading east. The information was accurate. The bridge was not guarded.

Eastward, less than a mile away, two ambushes had been prepared. The ambushers would attack the convoys after the first train blew up.

Peter and I were to play the part of accidental motorists. We had to protect our people, save them if they were caught, and do what we could to increase the damage and casualties. Our papers were in order. We belonged to the auxiliary police force. We were armed. We had pistols and grenades and even a German submachine gun.

The trolley was approaching. And then the noise of the train. It had many wagons crammed with munitions to be used against our Allies.

The first two sections were allowed through. The third was blown up so quickly that we realized it only when the force of the explosion blew the bridge into the air along with the next section of the train. The fourth section had no chance to stop and ran into the demolished third.

At the same time we heard automatic fire and several explosions. Soon the screaming of wounded Germans filled the air. We couldn't hear any more firing.

We jumped into the car and drove up to the track. We had to take cover when another explosion shook the whole area. It was an ammo car. When it was quiet again, we got up and hurried toward the wrecked train.

Peter ran up to a tall Wehrmacht captain with a bleeding face. *"Herr Hauptmann,"* Peter saluted, "can I do anything for you? I am from the Ukrainian police and this is one of our nurses."

"Help me with the wounded, and you" he grabbed Peter's arm, "help us find the bandits."

Peter saluted again. "Let's pick up a couple of men and go."

I had two first-aid kits and started looking for the wounded. The first body was that of a young soldier. His right arm was missing and he was lying facedown. I tried to lift him but then I saw he had no face.

Then I bandaged somebody's leg. I worked automatically, my mind on the untouched cars of the train. What did they contain?

After a while, in the general confusion of the explosions as the ammo slowly blew up, I made my way round to the other side of the train. Nobody followed me. I climbed up on one of the cars and looked through a little window. It was full of wooden and metal cases. More ammunition, I thought, more shells for cannons and mortars. Maybe bombs and mines. I looked around. Nobody there. And who would be interested in what a girl was doing? Without thinking I pulled the safety pin from a grenade, dropped it through the window, and jumped into the ditch beside the rails.

Another terrible explosion shook the area. I didn't lift my head until the last shell had exploded. I was very cold. I got up and went back. Again nobody paid any attention to me. There was some shooting on the other side of the line. That was where Peter had guided the Germans.

Some of the survivors had set up a little camp at the edge of the wood. They had carried the wounded there, and cases and supplies from the wreck.

I joined this group. They sat with grim faces. I bandaged somebody's shoulder. They improvised stretchers and put their wounded on them. There was another long burst of automatic fire from the woods.

Soon the "expeditionary corps" returned. They hadn't found anyone. We stayed with the group and didn't move. Probably Peter had something in mind. I had, too. But how? I gave Peter a questioning look. Peter understood. Let's wait, his eyes said.

I was wondering about the first two cars that had gotten away. Hadn't they guessed what had happened? They hadn't stopped, but it couldn't be that they hadn't heard the explosion. Time passed and they didn't return. Then the officers left with a platoon, probably for the closest railroad station. They left the wounded dying. A major shook Peter's hand and mine and mumbled something about helping the wounded and Peter's looking for bandits—in the name of the German army!

We also expressed our gratitude, but differently.

Before leaving we threw grenades at the little improvised camp and shot it up.

Then we drove off. For about two minutes we were silent. We felt young, strong, happy, and nobody could take that away from us. The Ukrainian woods covered us with their tall trees, and the squirrels leaped about in the branches.

It was the middle of May, but what beauty can flowers have for people immured in the Jewish quarter?

The Jewish population of Lvov was frightened. They knew that in many places Jews were deported, herded into ghettos and concentration camps, eliminated. There were still about one hundred thousand Jews in the city. Rumors spread about the establishment of a ghetto, new deportations, and "actions"— actually journeys to death. Nobody knew who would be next.

Then I came to a decision. I spoke to my mother. "We can't go on like this. We must go. We can't wait here until they take us in the next 'action.' "

"But how can we go? Father might come back one day. How will he find us?"

"Yes, I know," I said, almost sure that father was no longer alive, "but we must go. Get false documents. Change our identities. You and Arthur and I. Let's not wait until it's too late."

"Yes, perhaps we should, but it is not easy. I am not suited to play the role of a Christian."

"But you will have to. Because you must live for us, for father and Misha, when they come back." At that moment I believed it in spite of all terrible doubts. "I'll get all the papers. Would you like to choose a name?"

I looked at my mother's face and my heart ached. How many silver hairs there were in her dark curls. And how many wrinkles around her mouth and eyes. She, the tall, handsome, proud Rachel. How often her hands trembled and how many tears she wiped away, hiding them from us.

Arthur, my fifteen-year-old brother, said that he thought it a good idea. "There is no reason to wait for extermination. The risk is great, but it's better than waiting.

"How can I get the false papers?" my mother asked.

"I have connections. I am going to see Yadwiga, Mrs. Katherina's niece. I was talking to her a couple of days ago. She might agree to take you both to her farm. They live several miles from Rudki. That's about ten miles from Lvov. And when I go over to the Christian side, I'll get a real job. And, by the way, I won't stay with you. It's not good, too many illegals in one house."

"So the three of us will have to separate?" said my mother.

"It will be safer, mother, and a farm like Yadwiga's is not a good place for me. Too far away from events and traffic."

"As far as I'm concerned, I wouldn't mind hiding in a hole in the ground and seeing no human face," mother said.

"I can understand you very well, mother, but that isn't my way. I'll probably go to Krakow or some other big city. Anyway, I won't stay here in Lvov. Too many people know me here. And I don't feel like dyeing my hair, wearing glasses, or using any kind of stupid disguise. It is best to go where you have never been before."

After a meeting with Yadwiga and Mrs. Katherina, I spoke to Peter.

"She agrees to take mother and Arthur until the Germans are gone."

"How much will it cost?" Peter's question was sarcastic.

"Why, they don't want any money now. They are ready to put us up along with all our belongings. All she wants now is the fur coat and the string of pearls. She says the final accounting will be made at the end of the war. Of course, I agreed."

"How in hell did they know about the fur coat and the pearls?" Peter asked angrily.

"Don't forget we lived a couple of months in Katherina's apartment in 1939 and 1940. They know what we owned then and what we own now. And why should we care about a fur coat or pearls? We are trying to save two lives."

"Well, my dear, I suppose we'll have to do it. But remember one thing—I don't like people who perform acts of mercy but ask for a reward. If you want to help, do it with clean hands."

I smiled and pressed Peter's arm. He wouldn't take money for saving human lives. Peter smiled back. "You'll turn into a perfect illegal. I am glad and sorry at the same time. Glad for you and sorry for myself, because you'll be leaving.

"I'll leave as soon as the papers are ready and my people are on Yadwiga's farm."

"You'll be going to Krakow," Peter went on. "It is a nice city, full of historical places. Plenty of Gestapo and all kinds of police. Plenty of Germans. A bad place for our kind. Plenty of rats and traitors. Difficult and dangerous to work there. You'll have to be very careful. Do you understand? Promise . . ."

I had already promised so many times to be careful. And wise. And quiet.

I was holding a handful of papers. Identification cards. Birth certificates. Baptismal certificates. Some typewritten, some written by hand. With seals. Pictures. Old and new.

I read them again and again. Because everything that was written here was tied to a personality and must not be forgotten. It must be perfectly sewn into the memory.

My mother and brother were Catholics. I was Ukrainian, Greek Orthodox. I did not know too clearly the difference between the two churches, but I must remember that the Greek Orthodox do not recognize the pope. I would not pretend to be the religious type. I wouldn't even wear a cross. I preferred to be quiet, simple, reserved. Only I'd use lipstick and perfume and dress stylishly, as I had saved most of my clothes. This was important, because Jewish women's clothes were plain and drab and the girls tried to hide their charms.

I was worried about my mother. She seemed to have lost a lot of her strength, and even the will to survive. Maybe in that peaceful place near fields and woods, she would recover. She wouldn't see many Germans there. And Arthur? I hoped he would help her.

In three weeks everything was arranged. Yadwiga left by train, accompanied by my mother and brother. They had become Mrs. Romana Apolonia Skowronska and Adam Skowronski, born in eastern Galicia. Their story was that their husband and father, a former district court official, had been deported by the Soviets. I persuaded my mother to have her hair done and to use makeup.

When she took off her Star of David, I saw her hesitate as if it were hard for her to part with that symbol. At last she left, looking back at the Jewish quarter, which was soon to be evacuated and the population moved into a ghetto.

Arthur and I walked away quickly without looking back. There was no sentiment binding us to that part of the city. On the contrary, we were happy to get rid of the armbands, of those overcrowded rooms, of that permanent feeling of menace, of the helplessness and fear of the decimated Jewish population.

Before leaving for Krakow I stopped at Yadwiga's farm. In the country you could easily forget about the war. There was a fine harvest. I liked the house with its tiled roof standing on a hill surrounded by trees. I would so much have liked to stay there.

My mother walked with me to the railroad station. We parted at the edge of the fields near a young pine grove. Arthur had gone to the fields with Yadwiga's husband. I looked back as mother walked slowly toward the house on the hill, the big colored bandanna around her head worn in the style of a countrywoman. I got into the train with an almost easy mind.

6

It was a sunny afternoon when I arrived in Krakow. The railway station was full of military police. I could hardly find an exit for non-Germans. In the train there had been two cars for non-Germans. They were naturally overcrowded, but there was a kind of general solidarity and helpfulness. Men gave their seats to women and old people. As a rule, Jews were not allowed to travel by train.

In Jaroslaw the train had stopped. All the civilians had to get out while many military convoys went by. The civilians watched silently. Several hours later a hospital train from the east came by. Through the windows we could see the overcrowded hanging beds, and the nurses and doctors in their white coats. Again the civilians watched silently. They had learned to hide their feelings. Nobody complained. Nobody talked much, and when they did it was only about problems that had nothing to do with the occupation or the war.

I walked with my suitcase and handbag through Krakow. The city was intact. The Germans had conquered it so swiftly that there had been no time to destroy it.

The houses were mostly old-fashioned, and there were many churches and gardens, as Peter had told me, big squares and buildings, cafés and restaurants, most of them for Germans only. Many German stores and business offices, and in the streets uniformed Germans as well as civilians. The German language was to be heard everywhere.

And yet the city was Polish. I walked through Old Market Square. There were the two tall, proud towers of St. Mary's Church, but I missed the Grunwald monument. The Germans had taken it down, because it was a reminder of the battle they had lost in the fifteenth century.

There were many Poles about, not so well dressed as the Germans but with their heads still high. There was even a group of Jews walking to work with guards. They walked in fours, their clothes ragged, each one carrying a sack or basket. I had heard that only a couple of thousand Jews remained in Krakow.

The first few days I stayed at Richard's home. Richard knew only that I was from the underground, and he accepted without question my being a half-Polish, half-Ukrainian girl from eastern Poland.

In the meantime I was looking for a job, naturally with the Germans. According to my instructions, I had to give up the idea of getting a very important job. For that, one would be thoroughly investigated by the Germans.

I bought a German paper, the *Krakauer Zeitung,* and looked at the advertisements. There were many for cooks and maids.

Following up one of the advertisements, I went to an apartment in a narrow, old street. There was a name on the door, "Karl Paul, Police Lieutenant, & Family." On the other doors, all German names, mostly officers. Somewhere a radio blared military music. I smelled sauerkraut and German cooking. I rang the bell. A man in police uniform and house slippers opened the door.

"What do you want?" He spoke in German.

"The advertisement." I pointed to the folded newspaper.

"Come in. Do you speak German?"

"*Nix viel,*" I answered.

And then came the usual questions. He was tall, but not too sturdy, and a little bowlegged. He was polite and smiling, and measured me up and down with obvious interest. After a while, a tall, dark blonde woman came in. She was gentle and spoke German with a foreign accent. I could not identify it. At once the man changed his attitude and walked off, completely uninterested.

They offered me good pay and free evenings, except when they were out. They had one child. I cannot say why, but I decided to stay. The next day I moved into this house.

In the meantime Richard had introduced me to the work in Krakow. Here I had to secure information about the German authorities and the whereabouts of prominent Nazis rather than getting information about reinforcements and supplies for the Russian front, and doing anti-Nazi propaganda and liaison with the partisans and the western underground.

I wasn't too pleased with this type of activity, but to my satisfaction I learned that the legendary Willy was actually in Krakow and in charge of the district.

Life went on peacefully in the family I worked for. After a short time the woman, who was a friendly person, told me that I shouldn't consider her German, as she was English born and had come to Germany with her parents shortly before she met and married Karl. She told me this after a bulletin about the sinking of Allied ships.

"How many English boys must have been drowned," she said in English and sighed deeply.

My knowledge of English was very slight, but I understood the sense of her words, and she felt it somehow.

"Could you understand me?" Her voice trembled.

"No," I answered in German, "I have never learned English."

"Then how did you know what language it was?" she asked nervously.

"Why, I always went to the films a lot. You know, I admired Gary Cooper, Errol Flynn—I know the *sound* of English at least."

"Listen, Danuta, never mention to my husband that I said something in English. You see, I am English and he is German. There is a war between our countries, but he is my husband and the father of my child. What can I do? No German woman will associate with me, as soon as she finds out who I am. You can understand my situation, can't you?"

"Yes, I can, but you should be careful. Don't talk about it to anybody. And now I won't dislike you any more. At first I felt about you as about any German officer's wife, but now you are like an ally."

Louise shook my hand warmly and we felt good after this short talk. But Karl was a German, a Nazi, and a nasty, cocky one at that.

His friends were like himself and spent hours drinking with him. Often he went out alone.

Louise spent her time knitting, embroidering, and reading books. Karl had a car and used to go "shopping" once a week in the country, so there was an abundance of chickens and geese, eggs and butter, brandy and potatoes, fruit and vegetables. This "shopping" did not affect his purse too much.

I was satisfied. This house, with its convenient way of life, with not too much work, free evenings and Sundays, was a perfect background for my activities. I did my best to keep this job. I cooked well and kept the house clean. I tried to be pleasant to Karl and his friends, and was friendly with Louise.

And now I was given an assignment: to check on the Italian troops in the city. There probably was no easier job than to gain the confidence of these unhappy allies of the Germans. It was not difficult to get an introduction, and soon Captain Emilio was one of my best friends.

The young, handsome officer from general headquarters was from Rome. He was a peaceful man in uniform. I was not even sure he could use the little pistol he carried in his belt. But he loved music, songs, flowers, and gardens. He was homesick and did not enjoy being a soldier and part of the war machine.

We laughed, played music, but did not talk much, as we scarcely understood each other's language. Carlo Emilio liked to talk about love and read poetry, especially when we walked in the big gardens and on the shores of the Vistula.

I was next instructed to watch the Gestapo building for two evenings, to see what civilians were brought there after six.

It was quite clear that the building on Pomorska Street was just the place to be avoided, especially by our kind. While peeling potatoes for supper I decided to wear my best clothes and try to look like a girl waiting for a date. So I left the house in a rush, telling my bosses I had a very important date with a sergeant from the air force.

I knew the tall, five-story building, formerly the college students' dormitory. There were lights in the windows. I could see two men in civilian clothes coming out the gate. They attracted my attention because one of them was very tall and fat, had the face of a benevolent uncle, three chins at least, and wore gold spectacles. The second man was rather short, stocky, with an ugly scar on his right cheek. He walked in a military way, stiff and straight. They came out of the building and moved toward a small car, a light green Skoda across the street. Before they drove away, I could see the short one reloading a big automatic pistol. The fat one drove the car. There was somebody else in the car, but I could not see his face.

Then my attention was drawn to an elegant black limousine that stopped at the entrance. In the back seat were three men. Another man, in uniform, was sitting next to the driver, smoking.

The door opened. A civilian jumped out. He wore civilian clothes but German army boots. The man yelled something into the car. Two men got out. Their clothes were wrinkled. They looked like Polish city people. They walked into the building followed by the man in the boots. They must be prisoners, I thought, and now they were going to be investigated. One was of middle age, the other might be twenty years old. Maybe a father and son? Who were they? What did they do? And what would happen to them?

I walked back and forth on the other side of the street. While I was watching, another car stopped in front of the building. Somebody touched my arm. I turned quickly. It was a policeman with a broad, friendly face.

"What are you doing here?" he asked in a rather fatherly way, "looking for trouble?"

"No, *Oberfeldwebel*," I said, "I am waiting for my boyfriend."

"It's a hell of a place to wait. I advise you to move on. That garden over there, for instance." He pointed to Krakow Park.

"Yes, maybe I should, but Fritz mentioned this corner, right here," I said, very sure of myself.

"Get out of here quickly, before you get into trouble with the Gestapo—in case you don't know what this building is," he said angrily and pushed me away.

I was forced to walk slowly to Krakow Park. The benches were empty. The big garden was empty. The ice cream kiosk was closed. The flowers looked dull and only birds hopped about on the sandy paths. I felt lonely and frustrated.

Across the street I could see the tall building with its blinking windows. My wait was fruitless.

One day there was a sharp ring at the door. I ran to open it and there stood Peter, smiling broadly, in a green summer uniform with plenty of red insignia.

Louise's head appeared in the living room door. "Who is there?" she asked.

"My fiancé."

"I didn't know I was," Peter whispered.

"Let's see him." Louise came out and I introduced Peter.

We went to a little eating place on a side street. We walked in the gardens. We talked about "business" in the car. Peter wanted to know if I could accompany him on an important trip to Warsaw and Lublin.

"I can do anything we have to," I said. "After all, if I get fired here I can always find another job of this kind."

"Anything of interest in this police officer's home?"

"No, I've decided that the thief shouldn't steal anything from his own nest. I am pretty careful now."

"You must be getting important. Only important people look after themselves."

Louise allowed herself to be persuaded easily. Peter explained that he was on leave and wanted me to go with him to his parents' farm not far from Warsaw. Louise said I could go.

We took the train and traveled in the civilian section, as Peter had taken off his uniform. "I'm happy to be a decent civilian," he said. "That uniform is beginning to get on my nerves."

Peter had news from Lvov. There had been another "action" against the Jewish population in which about fifty thousand Jews had been deported to labor and concentration camps.

"Where are these concentration camps? Are there any outside Germany?" I asked.

"Yes," Peter said, "quite a few. The most terrible is Auschwitz, on this side of the border. We already have some reports about this place. At first it was a Russian POW camp. Afterward it was turned into a civilian concentration camp, and I hear it's pretty gruesome. Then there are plenty of others. Like Maidenek, near Lublin. The Germans work at double speed, especially Himmler's department."

The train to Warsaw passed through good Polish land, ripe with crops and fruit to be eaten by the German locust. At Radom station there was a change of passengers. An hour later the train was stopped. We could see through the window all kinds of police uniforms. The police boarded the train and checked everybody's papers, accompanying their examinations with curses, yells, and kicks. Those who argued or asked questions were thrown off the train.

"This mess started after the Skarzysko Kamienna ammunition factories were blown up," someone said.

The train stopped at the main railroad station. Destroyed in the bombardment of 1939, the station had been repaired with rough timber, but only the part reserved for Germans. For the natives, no waiting room, no facilities.

We were busy for three days in Warsaw. We met fellow partisans. Konrad, the tall one with a proud face, was the merciless killer and executioner, and at the same time a great violinist. He played for us one evening in a little half-bombed-out apartment while discussing the kidnapping of a Gestapo chief. He interrupted his performance to comment on ways of questioning a captured Nazi.

And Yanek. Darkskinned. With an aquiline nose. Very Semitic looking. Too much so for these times. But, although nervous, twisting his face all the time, he was an expert saboteur and a perfect signals man.

And Irena the nightclub dancer, who extracted secrets from German officers.

"I don't like her type," Peter said to me later.

"I don't either," I answered. "She tries to play the role of a 'Blue Angel.' Doesn't fit too well with us."

"You are right. I would never trust a nightclub dancer. That kind is not far from a prostitute. They wanted to send her into some office in the city, but she feels too damned happy in the arms of German officers, and loves their laces and silks, their champagne and lobsters."

"But she is supposed to be Stanislaw's friend and, you know, he is quite a man."

"Yes, but she is not the woman to be a man's friend. She might be his mistress. But how can he take it?"

"I learned quite a lot about such things," I said importantly, "you know, at the Schultze sisters' home. But I have never been anybody's lover. Only a friend, a true friend. Tell me, does being a lover mean much more than a friend?"

"Sometimes it does, but I would say it has no importance at all. I would like to make the girl I love my wife. That means a lot more than a lover and a friend put together."

"Is there a girl you love? And want to marry?" All the blood must have left my face.

"Yes, there is, only one, the best one, tough and soft, cruel and merciful. She has blue green eyes and dark blonde hair. Unfortunately we are married to a fight and to an ideal. Today we are here and to-morrow somewhere else. Today she is near me, but who knows where she will be tomorrow. We have to be hard with ourselves."

I felt happy.

I didn't answer. I said nothing. And my lips closed very gently on his.

The next evening found us in Lublin. Again several meetings. New faces. With peaceful backgrounds and professions but hard fighters. Here we heard bad news. One of the forest units had been caught in a big German operation. The unit had been annihilated, and there was a rumor that the Germans had captured some prisoners who were being kept under extremely heavy guard. It wasn't yet possible to find out who they were or where they were being held.

On the way back we took the long way, through Warsaw, where we were to part. I was to return to Krakow and Peter to Lvov. We said good-bye after midnight in the crowded railway station.

In spite of everything, this trip had been interesting, even exciting. I came back refreshed to my kitchen, my mops and brooms and dirty pots.

Louise asked me how the trip had been.

"Just fine. We worked in the fields, rode horses, ate good food! And we'll be married when the war is over."

"Do you believe it will be over soon? My husband said only yester-day it would be a long business, there in Russia. And they're beaten in Africa, did you hear about it?"

"I don't care for war and politics," I replied flatly. "That's a man's business." Louise gave me a surprised look as if to say how narrow-minded I was. I changed the subject.

"What shall I get at the market?"

I took a walk that evening with Carlo Emilio. He was feeling unhappy.

"We are going east," he said. "Every time the crazy corporal gets his backside kicked we get a Russian posting. Have you heard the story about the angel who comes down to earth? He sees a little man with a black moustache standing up to his ankles in water and yelling for help. 'Who are you?' asks the angel. 'I am Hitler. I'm drowning!' 'But you are only in shallow water no deeper than your ankles.' 'Oh, that's because I am standing on Mussolini's head.'"

I was becoming an "educated" partisan after several meetings with Willy.

He told me about the disaster at Warsaw. One night the Gestapo had raided two places at once, Red Cross Street, where they caught Konrad and Gustav, and the little side street across the river, where they caught Stanislaw and Yanek with their wireless station. Yanek had time to reach for his pistol and kill or injure three or four Gestapo men, saving the last bullet for himself.

The prisoners brought in for questioning had been confronted by Irena, the nightclub dancer. After falling out with Stanislaw, she had run to the Gestapo and betrayed everything she knew. Names. Addresses. The wireless. The organization. Meetings. Dates. Places.

The Gestapo was triumphant. Until then it had trapped very few members of the underground. Irena's treason was an unusual triumph.

Willy was discussing Irena. "You see what a grave mistake it is to depend on undependable characters. We could have done without her mostly useless information."

"Do you mean undependable because she is a girl?"

"No, I mean that the organization has to be clean. It doesn't mean that we shouldn't use the base elements, but they shouldn't know important people and details. Now we must try to rescue Konrad, Gustav, and maybe Stanislaw. They've arrested some more of our people. They almost got the Major himself. He escaped disguised as an old woman."

"Well, do you think they told what they knew, or did everything come from Irena?"

"It's difficult to know, especially so soon. We have connections but it takes time. And now, after such a disaster, so many things have to be done immediately. All the meetings, dates, places, pseudonyms, addresses, codes have to be canceled or changed. Other partisans still have their work to do. And how can we be sure? Do you think the Gestapo pets them? Even the strongest prisoner can break down and reveal something, if not everything . . .

"A partisan is supposed not to break down under any circumstances, but if they break your ribs one after another, if they choke you with chloroform, if they hang you upside down, if they burn your nails . . . not everybody is able to endure."

I listened with rapt attention. Then I felt a nasty cold shiver creeping up my back.

"We are planning a rescue operation," Willy continued after a while. "We must try to get them out. All of them. For some reason they were transported to Krakow and put into Montelupich Prison. It's almost impossible to break in there. But we will. I want a survey map of the place, gates, walls, guards, and surroundings.

"And if it's impossible to get them out of there, then we'll try to rescue them in transit between the prison and the Gestapo. We'll have to know how and when they will be moved. Well, that's up to me and my friend. I want you and your people to reconnoiter the place as soon as possible."

At that time I had five people working for me, four men and a girl. I was the commander of a "fifth." The whole organization was built on this "fifths" system.

Montelupich Prison was a big red brick corner building, surrounded by a high wall with barbed wire and broken glass on top. My report to Willy was pessimistic. Definitely a bad place. Not merely bad, but hopeless.

Willy's information was even more discouraging than mine. "Konrad was executed two days ago. Stanislaw and Gustav are to be transferred back to Warsaw. Who knows why they are dragging them back and forth? They caught one of the Major's girls, the little blonde Wanda, and her mother. They are being held by the IV-E-I of the Gestapo (that's the department that deals with spies and the underground). They are supposed to be experts, but the only things they know are torture and betrayal."

"Building and operating an underground organization is like hardening steel." Willy looked me up and down. "How hard are you now? What are you able to stand? Pain, broken ribs? I hope you have learned something from your former commander. Have you? He is a young man, but made of hardened steel."

Willy smiled when I blushed.

"You don't have to blush, Danuta. Some day the war will end."

Three days later, on a Tuesday evening, there was a ring at the door. A little girl, maybe thirteen or fourteen, with long thin tresses, said, "Good evening, Miss Danuta. Get dressed and come with me. Richard is waiting for you. I'll wait downstairs."

A green police car was parked at the corner. The little girl pointed to it and ran away. I thought immediately of a possible trap, but Richard called out, "Get in. No time to wait." He spoke in pure, rough German.

I recognized him at once, although he was dressed in police uniform. Next to him sat a silent driver, also in uniform.

Richard explained. "The Gestapo are taking our people back to Warsaw tonight. The convoy will not be very strong, as they are sure no one knows about it. We will ambush them on a deserted section of the road about twenty miles from here. We have to take vehicles." I was to observe the convoy and signal with a red rocket for more than four vehicles, a green rocket for less than four.

"And if it's an open truck?"

"Quite impossible," Richard answered, "because they never use this type of truck for convoying prisoners. Do your job, and then hide or get rid of the rocket pistol and find your way back. We won't be able to take you home. I hope you will excuse us."

I thought it was very nice of Richard to say that. "I'll get a ride or just walk back."

Richard handed me a rocket pistol and a cardboard box.

They drove away without saying where they were to locate their ambush. The convoy was supposed to leave the prison at ten-thirty. It was about nine o'clock now. I found a good place in the shadow of some trees, not too far from the road. I still thought the Germans might be in open cars or trucks and would therefore see the rockets, but they couldn't know where they were coming from, especially while the cars were in motion.

Then I forgot about trucks and Germans. My mind was swarming with all kinds of thoughts. But my ears waited for the cars. There wasn't much traffic. The Germans didn't like to travel at night on the roads of an occupied country.

It was a quarter to eleven, but I didn't look at my watch until the cars approached. In front was a low, open car with four armed men and a driver. In back there was a similar car. I saw what looked like a mounted machine-gun. The convoy passed at medium speed.

I inserted a green rocket in the gun and squeezed the trigger. A green snake twisted in the air. I threw myself to the ground and hid the pistol and the rockets under leaves and branches. Then I waited.

After a few minutes, which seemed endless, I heard automatic fire and several explosions. Without thinking, I ran toward the ambush, keeping well away from the road. Suddenly I came on two burning cars. Firing continued, and several harsh voices shouting commands. Then another hand grenade burst and the voices stopped. I crawled closer. I saw a couple of men running toward dark forms sprawled out on the road.

"Quick, quick," I heard a voice in Polish, "the first car broke through and ran away. They will get help."

After a moment two police cars sped away toward Krakow. I heard somebody screaming near the burning car. There was a German lying on his back. I couldn't see his legs. But I saw a loaded submachine gun next to him. The German screamed again and tried to turn over. I reached for the weapon and before I knew it I had pulled the trigger. There was a burst and the screaming stopped. I ran with the submachine gun into the grove and hung the weapon in the branches of a big oak.

I entered the outskirts of Krakow at sunrise. I caught the first bus and reached my apartment by seven.

Nobody asked me about being out all night, except that the boss winked at me in a familiar, understanding way.

I met Richard the next day in the garden in front of St. Anna's Church. There was a blue mark under his left eye and he limped a little.

"I almost had my skull crushed by a rifle butt, but the fellows are safe. How did you get home?"

I told Richard my adventures. He wasn't too eager about returning for the submachine gun.

"The police have an axiom," he explained, "that the criminal returns to the scene of his crime. It is wiser to avoid visiting that place for quite a while. And they have probably searched the surroundings, anyway." He added, "I have a letter for you," and gave me an envelope.

It was from my mother. Everything was fine.

I replied: "Dear Mother and Brother, Everything is fine with me. The work is good. I live very quietly. Once in a while I go to the movies. I like Krakow with its gardens, old buildings, and the river. Keep well and take good care of your health . . ."

In front of the Grand Hotel I was to meet Willy. He emerged from the ornate entrance of this hotel "for Germans only." There was another man with him. They both wore civilian clothes, Willy's a well-made light gray suit, a white shirt and blue tie, the Nazi party emblem in his lapel. The second man wore tan trousers, a yellow shirt, and a suede jacket. Willy was blond and the other darkskinned and suntanned.

Willy introduced his companion as Bruno. He looked Italian.

We walked to the German Casino, a swank restaurant and café "for Germans only." We sat at a table next to the orchestra. The nightclub was full of uniforms and civilians and very noisy. The dance floor was crowded. The tables around us were empty; we could talk.

Bruno was a German civilian from Berlin, an employee of the Hermann Göring Werke aircraft plant, on a business trip to the Polish government.

Willy said, "We must increase our activities, especially in getting equipment and weapons from the Germans. We cannot depend on the parachuted supplies. We have to supply ourselves, be independent. If we are able to free our prisoners, to infiltrate into German organizations and outfits, then why shouldn't we take from them whatever we need?"

"It shouldn't be too difficult," I said, "since we have weapons, cars, uniforms, and all the necessary documents. Naturally there must be good preliminary intelligence work."

"Let's dance," Bruno suggested.

We mixed with the crowd. Bruno danced elegantly, though a little stiffly.

"One hand grenade!" I whispered into Bruno's ear in Russian. He did not answer and paid no attention to me. His eyes were somewhere else. I followed his glance to a couple of dancers, a tall, dark-haired, handsome officer in SS uniform with a plump German girl.

The music stopped. We returned to the table. Bruno pointed out to Willy the couple he had been observing: "That's him, Franz von Berg. He is the main executioner in the local Gestapo. They need an officer, even a *von* for that dirty job."

Willy said, "He does it for fun, so far as I know. His real job is paper work in the prison administration. Let's get back to work. The command would like to see a series of weapons operations. Bring me your suggestions for three operations in your district, with detailed plans. And now I want to dance. Just a romantic tango."

Willy danced smoothly and no less elegantly than Bruno. When I looked back at our table I saw a fat officer standing and talking to Bruno. But I did not ask Willy anything. That's the courtesy of the underground.

We had a big meal on our German ration cards and then went to the films.

First, the news. The film was run off so rapidly we could not see clearly what was happening. Battle scenes, the Atlantic lapped dead bodies on the beach. The camera focused on the body of one young soldier. The waves played with his hair. His face was very young, frozen by some superhuman effort and pain. He was Canadian. I had to control myself not to burst into tears. I was not ashamed. This young Canadian had come across the ocean to fight the German invaders. He was our friend. And he lay here dead.

"Is everything clear?" I said to Antek, a young blond boy. "I want you to get that information from the airfield. I want you to bring back a plan of it in your skull. You have three days."

I gave his hand a friendly squeeze and walked in the direction of the Planty garden. I sat down on a bench next to a girl knitting a pullover and took out embroidery from my bag.

"Well, Helena, got any news?"

"Yes." The girl went on with her knitting and whispered close to my ear everything she knew about the *Schutzpolizei* base—gates, guards, stores, ammunition, offices, and location of buildings. Her sister worked in the kitchen and she had replaced her for a couple of days.

I looked at Helena. She was only seventeen. She looked innocent while talking about guardhouses.

I left her sitting on the bench and went to a little café on the other side of the river. While drinking cheap ersatz coffee, I listened to Valentin. His report was precise. He was a mathematician; he could probably have given the dimensions of the guardroom and the size of the trees in feet and inches.

"The camp of the *Todt* organization is located eleven miles away. The gate is twenty feet wide. The guardroom is located sixty-five feet northeast of the gate. Headquarters . . . explosives . . ."

I did not listen any longer. Valentin would be the commander of the operation. But afterward he would become an illegal. He was single and had nobody to support. Just right for the woods.

All my notes were written down in my mind; in all this time my memory had never betrayed me.

In the evening I listened to two other reports and drew up in my mind a plan of synchronized actions in four or five German camps.

I had a date with Bruno. Temporarily he was the chief of staff, while Willy was away in Warsaw.

As usual Bruno was well dressed and clean-shaven. I did not know who he was. His German was pure *Hochdeutsch*. I had never heard him utter a word in any other language. Sometimes I thought he might be German, and yet it did not seem possible.

We sat in another café for Germans, this time the Esplanada. Bruno caressed me from time to time. We did not pay any attention to attentive civilians at the nearby table. We exchanged information behind the caresses. To my surprise Bruno gave the two unpleasant-looking strangers a friendly greeting.

"Who are those two?" I asked Bruno, defying regulations.

"Just two little rats from the Gestapo, quite stupid, but very useful once in a while."

We sorted out the details for Operation Arms.

Suddenly in the entrance appeared two tall officers in air force uniforms. I began to tremble when I recognized one of them, the air force inspector from Lvov.

"Is anything wrong?" Bruno asked.

"I have met one of those officers before, and I would not like to meet him again."

"Do you look the same now as then?" Bruno danced in such a way that his back concealed me from the gaze of the two officers.

"Not at all." I calmed down when I realized how different I was now from the Jewish maid in the Schultze apartment.

"Would he be jealous?" Bruno asked a little quizzically.

"Oh, no," I said. "There is a more serious reason, nothing like being jealous."

"Well, don't pay any attention to him. You're occupied with me."

In a little while we left and walked into the cool evening. The sky was overcast and fall was in the air.

The operation, or rather a whole series of operations, had been well planned.

I was disappointed because there was no place for a girl. Bruno refused to let me disguise myself as a German nurse or wireless operator. It could cause trouble.

"Isn't planning enough for you, or are you so arrogant you must take part in every operation? We might need you for more important things."

Several days later, Operation Arms was carried out without losses and with gains of considerable booty.

My life in Krakow was divided between underground activities and daily work. I seemed to forget for long stretches of time my true identity. Ghettos and labor camps, the cattle trucks, the Star of David on the left arm—these became something very distant, nothing to do with me. I was the Christian girl, Danuta. I was a partisan. Even the fact that I was a maid in a German family meant nothing. It was just something temporarily attached to me.

Once, on the streetcar going along the west bank of the river, I noticed a high wall with barbed wire. I asked a woman what it was. She gave me a peculiar look, as if I had come from some other planet, and explained curtly, "That's the ghetto. For Jews, you know."

Oh, yes, I knew! Then, for the first time since I had left the Jewish restricted area, which was only the prelude to a ghetto, I asked myself the question: How come you escaped from your people and their fate? How can you enjoy a certain degree of freedom while they are condemned to death? But what would I prove by being another victim of the Nazi regime? What would I accomplish by waiting helplessly for the day of my extermination? No, I preferred to be a partisan and fight back.

Several days later, traveling to a village on the Krakow-Lvov line, I reread a letter from Peter, something very unusual, as we seldom wrote to each other. The letter was a song called "Friendship." It was a Russian love song:

> We are so close that no words are needed
> To tell one another again
> That our affection and friendship
> Are stronger than passion and more powerful than love.

What does he mean—I thought—affection and friendship, passion and love, and what is each in itself, and what are they all together?

I had been so busy with my thoughts that I missed the beginning of the general conversation. My attention was caught by a young girl. "Naturally in our district there are no more Jews. All of them were deported. There are rumors that they have been sent to ghettos, concentration camps, and heaven knows where else."

"Well," a fat man said, "that is one good job the Germans did. They rid Poland of the Jewish pest."

"You'd better be careful what you say," a young man interjected.

"What do you mean?" The fat man became excited.

"I mean that in different times they get rid of different people."

"You can think whatever you want," said the old woman next to me, "but our Catholic religion does not teach us to excuse murder. Even if they are unbelievers. The best way for the Jews would have been to get converted centuries ago. That way they would be sure of salvation, but like this God punishes them through his Antichrist." She stopped when kicked by her neighbor, who whispered so loud that everyone in the compartment could hear, "Your stupid tongue will destroy you one of these days."

Another girl took over. "I don't like Jews myself, but there are other ways of solving their problem. I shiver every time I hear what the Germans do to them. I wonder how many Jews they have left. And when it will be our turn."

"Ghettos. Deportations. Labor camps. They're nothing. I can tell you of something worse. Where I come from there were a couple of thousands Jews. Somehow the German didn't touch them until lately. Oh, they took over their businesses and properties, and some of them disappeared, but the rest got along without much trouble. You see, there weren't too many Germans around. But last week a big SS unit arrived. At night they surrounded the Jewish quarters, and before sunrise they had them marching in fives toward the woods. After a while we heard shooting. It lasted for about half an hour. Everybody in town preferred to go home and mind his own business. Then we saw the SS men going off in a convoy, eastward. Everyone went back to work and there was quite a crowd in the market square, where I was selling apples.

"Suddenly we heard a piercing voice, 'Help me, help me!' A young boy, maybe thirteen or fourteen was running through the market with a bloody face, his left arm hanging helpless and bleeding. Somebody recognized him as David, the pharmacist's son.

"Women tried to bandage him, but he freed himself and started yelling, 'Let me go. I want to go back to my parents. They are lying over there, in the big trench in the pinewoods. Mother was all bloody, but she screamed, and father's head was almost shot off. But maybe they were alive when the Germans started to throw earth and sand on us, because the soil moved even after all of them were covered up.'

"He began to howl like a puppy. After a while he jumped up and ran toward the woods, still yelling. 'There, people, the soil is moving. There are people dead and half-dead. Help! Help!' "

The girl's voice broke. The two old women crossed themselves. The fat man stopped eating his sandwich. The two young men exchanged an indignant look.

There was a long silence. Nobody tried to break it. Then a man spoke up. "Tell me, was it true what the boy said?"

"Do you have any doubt?" the girl answered. "Don't you know them? Certainly it was true. When some of the braver townspeople went out, they found a fresh trench covered with earth and sand. Arms were sticking out of the freshly piled soil." The girl wiped off a tear.

The two old women started praying. They repeated again and again some endless litany, responding after every line, "God have mercy on us." The fat man started eating his sandwich again and said, his mouth full, "This can only be done to Jews. They wouldn't dare do it to us."

"And why not?" someone said. "Just because we are Poles and Christians? Who do you think they will bury half-alive after they are finished with the Jews? How many of our people die every day in prisoner-of-war camps and concentration camps?"

After a while the fat man turned to me. "And what about you, young lady? Don't you have an opinion about such important events?"

"No, my dear sir," I answered in Ukrainian. "What do I care what happens to your ex-Poland?"

"I didn't understand."

"So you'll have to learn Ukrainian," I answered and turned away.

My destination wasn't too distant. But it seemed to me that all the time the wheels of the train were whispering . . . They bury them half-alive . . . or half-dead . . . and the soil was moving . . . the soil was moving . . . they bury them half-alive . . . and the soil was moving . . .

My employers were going on holiday. I noticed that Karl left in civilian clothes. That meant that for two weeks there would be three complete police lieutenant's uniforms here in the house. We'd find good use for them!

I ironed one of Karl's uniforms carefully and handed it to Richard.

"Well," he said, "it's the highest-ranking uniform we have. We'll be able to make use of some papers that have been lying idle a long time."

The liaison girl brought me a message from Peter. I met him in a milk bar. He was dressed in civilian clothes—leather jacket, breeches, boots.

"Have you been discharged from the police service?"

"Worse than that. I never expected an honorable discharge from that organization, but I got away just before being fired, and I don't mean merely losing my job."

"So what are you going to do?"

"I'm leaving for the woods."

"Take me with you," I pleaded.

"I want to very much, but it is impossible."

"Why?"

"Your commanders won't let you go. They say you are very good at intelligence work. All we can do now is spend an hour together."

We walked to the river and looked at the Vistula.

"What are you thinking about?"

"Not much," Peter answered absently. "I'm just thinking about that princess Wanda in the legend who did not want to marry a German and drowned herself in this very river."

"Well," Peter continued, "times change. But we don't change. If you changed, I would kill you."

I realized how deep Peter's feelings for me were.

"I'd rather die." I answered clearly.

"I'd rather die, too," he said.

An hour later Peter left. I wondered when I would see him again.

The next day I was on the move again. A trip to several places in the country and in the Carpathian Mountains. I met a lot of rain and fog, but the worse the weather was, the fewer the Germans.

I came back on the ninth day after the departure of Karl and his wife. There were lights in the dining room and bed room, and Karl sprang to the door with a catlike jump.

"So here you are," he said mockingly and looked me up and down. "Come in, my child."

I did not like the sound of his voice. What had brought him back so soon? And why hadn't I considered the possibility that he might get back early? It was too late for such questions.

Karl's face expressed mixed feelings, part triumph and part uncertainty. He was standing near the door to the hall, so I walked into the living room. Karl got out his pistol and pointed it at me. I don't know why, but the whole situation seemed so ridiculous that I burst out laughing.

"You couldn't be serious, lieutenant," I said, but stopped at once because I saw the answer in his eyes. He was serious and really meant it.

"Do you want me to put my hands up?"

"Yes."

I did not move.

"I hope you are not armed," Karl continued and came up to me. Then he began searching me.

"You shouldn't laugh," he said. "It is not a joke."

"I thought it was," I answered.

"Well, sit down and tell me where my uniform is. But no fooling around."

"The uniform? Which one?" I asked. I realized now what was wrong.

"Not the new one, the other one."

"But it is in the clothes cabinet. What are you talking about?"

"I am talking about the uniform because it is not there. And," reaching for the telephone, "I do not like to waste time. The Gestapo will know what to do. Criminal investigation is not my profession." He dialed a number.

What should I do? Attack him? The uniform would not be returned until I saw Helena. There was nothing on me that could prove anything. And if I attacked him and failed. . . . I had no weapon, and he was armed.

While waiting for the Gestapo we faced one another.

"You are not afraid?"

"God protects the innocent," I pronounced solemnly.

What a stupid situation, I thought, to get caught in such circumstances. I remembered my meeting with Peter before he left for the woods. How angry he would be when he heard.

There were steps on the staircase. Karl put the pistol in his pocket and opened the door. Three men entered, two civilians and one in uniform. To me they all had the same face.

"Heil Hitler!" all three of them said simultaneously.

"Heil Hitler!" Karl answered.

"What has happened here?"

"I got back home," Karl explained, "and this is our maid. I returned a couple of days earlier than I should have."

It seemed to me that Karl was a little afraid of the Gestapo men. Anyway, he didn't sound too self-assured. "And when I got home, the girl was gone, impossible to know how long she had been away. And my old uniform is gone. Disappeared."

"Do you speak German?" the uniformed man asked me.

"Yes, a little," I answered and tried to smile.

"Don't smile, don't smile. You'll probably be crying soon."

"I am innocent," I said.

"They are all innocent. Lieutenant."

One of the civilians shook his fist at me. "Where is the uniform? Tell us where it is. You little Polish swine."

"I am not Polish and not a swine. I happen to be Ukrainian and Greek Orthodox."

"If you carry on talking like this you'll hang fast. Well, where is the uniform?"

"I don't know," I said and began to cross myself, "so help me God and Holy Maria. I was gone for several days and when I come back Mister Lieutenant starts to ask me about a uniform. They know I am honest. Did I ever touch anything here, sir?" I turned to Karl.

"Well, the girl is honest, that's true, but you see, she was supposed to look after the house and everything."

"Where have you been?" the second civilian asked.

"To Lvov, with my boyfriend from the air force."

"Well, she admits having left the place without permission. Take a towel, soap, toothbrush, comb, and a change of clothes. We'll have to take her with us, *Herr Oberleutnant*. I am naturally sorry to leave you without a maid, but I'm sure you'll get another one. But you should be more careful with your choice of girls. This uniform might mean a lot of trouble for some people."

I followed the man in uniform. The civilian walked behind me. Karl was standing in the doorway.

"Good-bye, *Herr Oberleutnant,*" I said quietly. "I hope to be back here soon."

Karl looked a little embarrassed, made a slight bow, and slammed the door.

THE BIG JOKE

7

The black car was making its way through the crowded Reichstrasse. The darkness was a relief. I could not see the faces of my escort.

The car stopped noiselessly before the Gestapo building, across the street from Krakow Park. We crossed a big hall to stop in front of a door inscribed "Duty Officer." The uniformed man knocked on the door and entered. I was left outside with the two silent men.

Soon I stood before a desk behind which sat a uniformed officer. He wanted my papers. I handed him my passport and other papers, all of them false. Would it be better if I didn't have them? But it was too late now. Then he listened to the report of my escort.

"Well, he said, "where is the lieutenant's uniform?"

"I don't know," I answered. "I really don't know. What could I do with such a uniform?"

"She doesn't look as stupid as she tries to appear," the escort observed.

"I am not stupid," I said, "but I was away for several days and I don't know what happened. It must be a mistake."

"I'll show you what a mistake is," the officer said as he got up and came closer. "Will you be reasonable or will I have to squeeze it out of you?"

"You can't get out of me what I don't know," I said.

"You're a stinking Polish tramp—"

"I am a clean and honest girl," I shouted, "and I'm not Polish, I'm Ukrainian."

There was an expression of surprise on the man's face as he walked back to his chair.

"After all, it is not my business to investigate. It is quite enough to be on duty Saturday night. Take her over to Monte, Fritz." He picked up a magazine on his desk.

The car stopped at the gate of Montelupich Prison. This was the notorious prison of the Security Police.

The uniformed man returned with a tall Gestapo man.

"Who told you to stare like that at us?" He grabbed me by the chin. "Don't you dare touch me!"

"What? You dirty whore, you don't talk that way to *Rottenführer* Sopker." Pushing my face to the wall, he kicked me.

"Is this the way you treat prisoners? Are you allowed to kick a girl? I'll complain to your officer."

"Shut up," the German barked and returned to his office.

I saw the stained gray wall. Some of the stains resembled drops, others were long streaks. They looked brown in the pale light. I touched one. It was dry and rough. But a light smear next to it was still wet. And then I knew it was blood. How many before me had faced this gray wall?

I was called into the office. Behind the desk sat a little, round-faced man in glasses.

"Dear God," he complained, "they always make you work, even Saturday nights. What did you do?"

"I don't know," I said. "They accuse me of taking my master's uniform, but I didn't touch it."

"You see I ask the questions, but I never believe anyone's answers. I mean, any prisoner, male or female. Something must be wrong, otherwise you wouldn't be in our sanatorium. Well, tell me your name, date of birth, and so on."

My personal data were written down in a big black book. They took away my watch and bracelet. Then the man called, "Mia, Mia, come over here."

A big, fat woman came in. She was young, with a face like a full moon. Her narrow eyes were almost drowned in fat. She laughed a little stupidly as she came in.

"Search this girl."

The fat girl looked me up and down and opened another door. I had to take off my clothes and she searched them slowly and methodically. She never looked at me. She found a pretty handkerchief edged with lace and said, "Give me this. You won't need it anymore and I can use it."

"Are you German?"

"Of course I am German," Mia answered.

"I won't give it to you."

"Why?"

"I don't want to, isn't that enough?"

Mia turned away, insulted. Then we were through.

When we returned, she said, "Didn't find a damn thing," and left the room.

The man opened my suitcase and searched it. He took away my leather purse, a belt, and photographs.

The little jailer took a bunch of keys and opened the door. "Well, I'll show you to your room, madame."

We walked through the long corridor and stopped outside number seventy-seven. The key turned in the lock. It was a small cell, narrow and long, with a tiny window close to the ceiling. There was next to no furniture, just an uncomfortable-looking mattress and a pail with a tin lid.

"Good night, gracious lady."

Suddenly I felt tired and sat down on the mattress. It was perfectly still all around. I could hear rain outside and the monotonous steps of a guard. I don't know how long I sat exhausted or what I was thinking. Maybe I even fell asleep.

All at once the little cell became crowded. Four men in civilian clothes were staring at me, and *Rottenführer* Sopker was standing in the doorway. I sat on the mattress and looked back at them. Among them was a tall man wearing a leather coat. He had a pale oval face and watery, colorless eyes. A fish face, I thought. And a small man, with a low forehead and a mean look.

For quite a while nobody said a word. The Germans looked at me and looked. I looked at them. Fish face broke the silence.

"She doesn't even find it necessary to get up when we walk in. Don't you understand German?"

I did not move.

"Yes, I understand," I answered in German.

"Where is the uniform?"

"I don't know," I said, but before I had completed the three words a heavy blow shut my mouth. I got so angry I didn't feel the pain. I jumped up.

"You have no right to hit me, whoever you are. Who are you? Take me to an officer."

The other men laughed. "Have you ever been talked to like that, Hansi?" the short one asked.

"Shut up, you bastard," he yelled at his companion. "And you, you little Polish whore, are you out of your mind? You know you're in a Gestapo prison and you'd better tell us the truth or you'll be shot this morning. What did you do with the uniform?"

"It's a mistake, my being here. I left the lieutenant's house for a couple of days, and who knows what might have happened during that time."

"Bullshit," said fish face.

Shorty said, "She just looks a housemaid to me. And stupid."

"You're right, mister," I said. "I am a poor girl from the country. Could I make a suit for myself from a police uniform? If I tried to sell it, there'd be no one to buy. What interest could I have in *Herr* Karl's uniform?"

"I don't believe a word," fish face went on. "Will you talk? Or shall I hit you so hard that all your teeth will march out through your arse-hole?"

All the men laughed at his joke.

I crossed myself and said, "In the name of God and His Holy Mother, I am innocent. I don't know anything about that uniform."

Fish face spat on the floor.

"Let's go," Rudi said. "We still have that bottle of French cognac. We are wasting our time. And as for you," he turned to me, "you'll be shot before sunrise."

Rottenführer Sopker was still standing in the doorway. He had a stupid look in his big eyes. "You're not afraid," he said and shook his head.

"God protects the innocent," I repeated.

The German burst out laughing. He closed the door, whispering,

"Yes, yes, that's something." He turned out the light and his steps died away.

"How wonderful that they are such fools," I said aloud and wondered at the sound of my own voice. I wasn't worried about being shot the next morning. I knew I would never be shot before they'd investigated me thoroughly.

Again I sat on the mattress. I could not tell how long I had been thinking, or maybe half sleeping. What was it? A sharp sound, muffled by distance and the heavy prison walls. A human voice. Then again and again . . . A man screaming. I could hear quite distinctly the words, "Christ, our Lord, Christ, oh . . ."

That voice of utmost misery continued. Then it stopped as if cut off. Is he dead or has he merely fainted, I asked myself and wiped my forehead. My hands trembled. I walked to the door and tried to listen, but there was silence and darkness. How I wished it were day again. This darkness and this solitude. These cold, silent walls hiding so many gruesome things.

I threw myself on the mattress and hid my face in my arms, but the tortured man's voice still sounded in my ears. I did not even think about myself being at the mercy of the Gestapo. I tried to think about something else, to recall past events in my life. It did not help. I kept seeing that tortured man.

When the faint light of a rainy October morning filtered in through the barred window, I felt a little better. There was no reason to feel so, but I did anyway.

There was movement in the corridor. At last the door opened and two men, apparently prisoners, spooned out steaming liquid into a bowl and handed me a piece of heavy, grayish bread.

"Did you come in last night?" one of them asked in Polish.

"Yes," I answered. "Have you been here long?"

"A couple of weeks. Are you Polish?"

"Half-Polish, half-Ukrainian," I said.

"If you're hungry or need anything badly, just let us know." And the young man walked away with the steaming caldron.

I felt comforted. Decent human beings still existed.

As I had nothing to do, I walked back and forth in the little cell. Four yards from the door to the window. Two yards the other way. I was not used to being inactive or unoccupied. Then my eyes caught names, dates, sentences, written on the wall, scratched on the door.

There were several different handwritings. "Joanna Hanausek, arrested June 1, 1942"—carved with a nail on the wall. "Sent to Auschwitz concentration camp"—underneath in pencil, in another hand.

"Paul Mankewizs from Warsaw was in this cell in May 1942"—another inscription. "Even a great nation can fall, but only a base one can perish"—written in block letters. "There is not time to be sorry about roses, when the woods are burning"—the same hand had inscribed this on the window. And right next to it in the same hand: "Christina Makowska, March 1942. Long live free and independent Poland":

> We will not give up the land we were born in,
> We will not let our language be extinguished,
> We are the Polish nation and the Polish people,
> The Piast's royal tribe.
> The Germans will not spit in our faces
> And Germanize our children,
> Every doorway will be a fortress,
> So help us God, so help us God.

I was deeply moved by the words of the unofficial Polish anthem. Naturally, I knew it—we had all learned it in school—but never before had I felt the true, deep meaning of it. Who was this Christina Makowska? Why was she here, and what had happened to her? She was a patriot, of that there was no doubt.

"Marian Walewski, arrested April 8, 1941"—and underneath it, in Christina's handwriting, "Executed by the enemy. Date unknown. God enlighten his soul."

Christina must be well informed.

"Our Father Who art in Heaven"—carved in neat block letters.

Two more days passed uneventfully. I was still alone with my thoughts and doubts. The prisoner Paul would give me an extra piece of bread, but I was not really hungry. I was tired of doing nothing.

On the fourth day, after breakfast, the little jailer in glasses opened the door. He had a large printed sheet of paper and was running over the list with his finger.

"Skowronska, Danuta," he pronounced with difficulty. "Oh, God in heaven, those Slavic names break your tongue. Take all your belongings; you're moving. Hurry up."

"Moving where?" I asked, grabbing my suitcase.

"Somewhere, don't ask me questions I can't answer."

I was taken downstairs with two other young women. They were flashily dressed and heavily made up.

"Shut your dirty mouth." The dark-haired one kicked her companion. "Here is a decent girl, not our kind."

"Where are we going?"

"I see you have never been here before. To the Monastery, naturally."

"Monastery?" I was surprised.

"The Monastery is the women's department. They don't keep women in this building, except for those they isolate. And there it is much better. Clean, warm, with woman jailers. We have been there before."

"And they let you go home?" I asked.

"Well, in our trade we're always having trouble with soldiers and the police. But they usually don't keep us too long."

We were given showers. Our clothes were disinfected and came back wrinkled and steaming. Then a doctor, himself a prisoner, gave us a superficial examination.

After a while all three of us walked escorted through the stony yard. We walked across narrow Montelupich Street. We came to a long building half-hidden behind tall poplar and linden trees.

The escort reported, "Three women from Monte," and handed over some papers.

Two men came into the hall. "Why are you here?" an SS man with two stripes asked.

"I don't know. I am innocent."

He laughed. "Rosa," he shouted to an unpleasant-looking woman returning with a bunch of keys. "We have an innocent among us."

"Don't worry, Sergels, they'll un-innocent her here." She giggled. She ordered me to follow her. We passed along corridors and stopped at cell fourteen.

We entered a large room with two big barred windows. In the middle stood two lines of women. A young woman with blonde braids and

a plain, honest face shouted, "Cell number fourteen. Twenty-six prisoners. Everyone here. Everything in order, *Frau* Inspector."

Rosa looked around contemptuously and without saying a word
walked out, locking the door.

The young woman with the braids came over to me, looking very
friendly.

"Good morning," she said. "You're welcome here. I am Zofia, the
cell commander."

"Hello, I am happy to join you. I am Danuta Skowronska."

Someone asked me, "Are you Polish?"

"Not quite, only my mother was Polish. My father is Ukrainian."

"Why are you here?"

"I don't know. Just a mistake. I was working for a police officer,
one of his uniforms disappeared, and they accused me."

"Oh, I see."

"Maybe you can tell us the latest news." A distinctive and deep voice
came from the mattress next to the left-hand window. "It is quite a
while since we've heard news from the outside."

From a pale face, gray eyes gazed up at me with a sharp, almost
piercing expression. The girl's hair was straight and combed away from
her forehead. She was rather homely, but her eyes had beauty and
strength.

"What would you like to know?" I put my question in the friendliest
manner.

"I am Christina . . . Makowska . . ."

So this was Christina Makowska! I was shocked by her pitiful
condition. I had imagined her strong, erect, and smiling. I didn't know
that she had been mutilated. Though deeply moved, I suppressed my
feelings and merely asked cautiously, "Do you think I am likely to
know the latest news?"

"Yes, you are."

In spite of my sympathy I said, "You are wrong, Miss Christina. I
am a poorly informed girl. I was only the maid of a German officer
and I am not well educated."

"It is up to you, Miss Danuta. I hope later . . . I mean when you
get established here . . ."

I walked away. An inner voice whispered: Don't talk unnecessarily.

Don't get friendly too fast. Be careful. Nobody should know what the Gestapo doesn't know.

Most of the women were from Krakow. Almost all of them received food parcels through the Polish Red Cross. Once a week they filled in forms for food, clothes, medicine. I refused to fill in any.

There was a small circle of girls who kept together: the very tall Vladislava, the tall dyed-blonde Laura, the elderly teacher Zofia. I listened to their talk. They were in jail for the same reason; as government officials they had issued false passports and identity papers to Jews.

Another member of the circle was Wanda, a night club dancer from Warsaw. I saw that she was quite a clever girl, although she tried hard to cover it up with vulgarity and horseplay.

Could she be the Wanda arrested during the August disaster in Warsaw? She never talked about it, nor about her investigation by the Gestapo.

Laura was a university professor's daughter. She used makeup even in prison and her dyed hair began to show dark at the roots. She pretended to be very distinguished, even patriotic. She talked a great deal about her boyfriends and gave us all the gossip of the prison, as this whole group worked in the garden every morning. They would bring back plenty of greens they had picked and distribute them to everybody in the cell.

Christina, who had been educated in a Catholic convent, was the leader of another group. She had around her several girls who worshiped her as a symbol of patriotism. Later I learned more about her. She had been arrested for underground activities, together with her father, her fiancé, and her sister. As the Gestapo, with the help of a traitor, had uncovered their organization, she could have talked freely. Christina had been tortured by the Gestapo. But throughout she had prayed and sung the national anthem and looked proudly into the faces of her torturers. She had not revealed anything about illegal activities. She had unbelievable courage. She remained impassive before threats. For the last two weeks she had been lying on the mattress. She had an infection of the kidneys. She moved with difficulty and had to crawl across the floor to reach the toilet.

It was obvious that everyone respected her, not only the prisoners but the jailers. One of Christina's best friends was a doctor, a kind elderly woman. She was the Monastery doctor, and left the cell every morning and came back in the evening.

Then there were others. Gypsylike Helena, for instance, who was polite, religious, and well liked for her good humor and gay songs.

And Irena. Locked in herself, plainly dressed, with rich brown hair in wild curls. There were rumors that she was a Jew.

Above our floor were the cells of the German prisoners. We could see them while walking in the yard. They had been SS men, policemen; a few were from the Wehrmacht. All of them had been sentenced, or were being investigated, for desertion or serious disciplinary offenses. Some helped the jailers by calling prisoners to investigations, delivering orders from the guardroom, maintaining order.

There was a cell for Jewish women. Once in a while we could see them during our weekly one-hour walk in the yard. We had to walk in couples. No talking was allowed. All the windows would be full of faces: the Germans on the second floor, the other women on the first floor, the Jewish women at the cellar windows.

The Germans yelled, whistled, threw candy and sometimes cigarettes. We never paid any attention to them. All the noise was neutralized by the bawling of the guard.

The faces of the Jewish women were pale and indifferent. They were waiting for extermination or, at the least, for transport to a labor or concentration camp. One day we saw three Jewish girls, chained together, being chased by a Gestapo man around the yard. They got twisted and caught helplessly in the long chain between their arms and legs. Some Germans giggled and whistled through the windows, but the Poles maintained a cold and disapproving silence.

In addition to German prisoners, there were a small number of French prisoners of war. One day the girls who worked in the garden came back earlier than usual, all terrified. A French officer had tried to escape by climbing through the fence of the nuns' wing. Grot, the cook, a tall, bull-like, heavy brute, saw the man trying to get out and caught him. There was a short fight between the handsome, slim Frenchman and the big German. The prisoner fought as best he could, but finally Grot beat and tortured him right there in the yard, until there remained only a bloody mess that could not be called a man.

The spots in the yard turned brown, dried out, and disappeared under dust and mud. We hadn't even known his name.

The third week of my stay in the Monastery was coming to a close, and I was surprised and worried that the Gestapo had waited so long to investigate me. It was impossible to judge whether this was good or bad. Could they have forgotten my case? That could hardly be. Then what did it mean? At any rate, I was fortunate to have all this time for building up a story. A Gestapo prisoner about to be investigated must learn how to talk with other prisoners, with jailers and investigators. But most of all he must learn to talk with himself, think things through, and memorize his story. What was I to say?

ı was aware of my youth. I knew I had a fresh country look and, though small, was athletic and might even be considered pretty. I decided that I must combine youthful charm with a splash of arrogance, to give them the impression of a belligerent yet intelligent out-of-place adolescent. They must hate, love, and respect me at the same time. I must arouse enough interest and confusion to prolong the investigation. My weapons would be my youth and impertinence.

8

A big black Buick carried me toward Pomorska Street. Next to me sat a man in civilian clothes. I went over my story in my head. There was a big door inscribed "IV-E-I." I was frightened when I saw where I was being taken. What did they know about me in this notorious department of the State Police?

We stopped at Room 410 and my escort left me. A uniformed man came out and stared at me. He had sharp features but a soft chin and mouth. He was young, in his thirties.

"Good morning," he said politely but coldly. "So you are Miss Danuta Skowronska." He had obvious difficulty pronouncing the name. "Do you speak German?"

"Yes, I do."

"Then I hope we'll understand one another."

"So far as language is concerned we will, but I make no promises."

"Are you scared?"

"Not at all. What an idea!"

"Well, you'll have to wait. I'll be busy for a while."

"Don't disturb yourself, Mr.—er—I'm not in a rush. Don't worry."

The German smiled broadly. "I am Criminal Secretary Walter Betz." He turned toward his room.

Once I was seated with Betz, he dismissed the interpreter and also the plump girl secretary. He took out a pack of cigarettes and put them in front of me. I took one.

"I want only one thing from you. Who are you?"

"You have my papers."

"Don't be silly. I'll admit some of them are well made, but . . ."

"You see, Mr. Betz, it is not easy for me to tell you the whole truth at once. Things are complicated. I am in such a difficult situation. Alone, among strangers."

"But that's the only way for you, to tell me the whole truth." He tried to be fatherly. And then, "I hope you realize you are facing the highest German State Police and I warn you, if you lie just once you won't be trusted again."

"I realize that, but I am afraid I'll be in a bigger mess than ever if I talk freely."

I fooled around for another quarter of an hour or so and then said, "Well, I see I'll have to tell the truth. You want to know who I am? My true name is Marie-Josephine Menard and I am French."

"Unbelievable!"

"But I am and I can prove it.

"I was born in Dunkirk." I had chosen this place because it was so heavily damaged. "My father was a naval captain. My mother died years ago. My two older brothers went to Africa with General de Gaulle. I was married to an engineer from Calais who is now a prisoner of war somewhere in Poland. I got news about Robert from his army commanders who returned to unoccupied France, where I had been living since the defeat."

I added five years to my age to make it believable that I had studied languages at the Sorbonne. I admitted knowing French, German, Latin, Russian, some Polish, Italian, ancient Greek. I said I had been educated by a White Russian after my mother's death and explained that I had come to look for my husband, to help him escape.

I admitted having spent perhaps eight or nine months in the territory of the Polish general government looking for various French POW camps. Disappointed by my vain search, I had given up. I was looking for a way of getting home, but meantime had to find a job and earn enough money for my return trip.

Betz didn't interrupt. He was listening and observing me all the time.

Once in a while he shook his head in amusement or surprise. I didn't know if there was anything wrong with my details.

He said finally, "Very interesting, very unusual, but almost unbelievable."

"Well, you can check. I am ready to give you any particulars you want."

"Tell me, Marie, did anybody send you over here on a mission? It would clarify the story quite a bit . . . Don't be afraid of us. Then everything would be less complicated . . . Maybe you were sent by some political party?"

"Oh, no! Do you think I'm crazy, to go off on a mission so far away from home? Only my love for Robert could give me the courage to go through all this. In a way, I feel better now I have told you the truth and I'm in your hands. After all, we are both Europeans, isn't that so?"

"Of course, dear Marie." Walter was delighted. "Naturally there is a difference between us western Europeans and the inferior Slavonic races. We would never hurt a Frenchwoman. But remember one thing. We will write down your whole story and check it. If it turns out that you have tried to fool us, naturally you will have only yourself to blame for the consequences."

"Of course, I understand. After all, I am an intelligent girl from a decent family, Monsieur Betz."

"Marie, do you realize that the German nation is the master of all Europe at the present time? We can find out anything."

"Certainly, monsieur."

It was lunchtime. Betz lifted the telephone. "Gustav? Well, come up here and bring a meal for my guest. Yes, Marie, you'll have to stay here." And he left the room, explaining that regulations wouldn't allow him to take a prisoner being investigated into the Gestapo mess hall.

As I ate I tried to remember everything I knew about France. And if they should try to check my French—well, I had studied the language for many years. It was lucky I had been a good student. And Betz himself seemed not too clever an adversary.

And then he was back. He had a self-satisfied smile.

"Did you enjoy your food, madame?"

"Yes, but I am afraid the French cuisine suits my palate better."

"Well, let's go back to work." Betz sat down. "Now I'll call in the typist and we'll write down your whole story. You'll have to retell everything and answer several questions."

Betz paid no attention when I gave names, addresses, and circumstances that differed a little from my first account. I was worried, but realized with relief that his memory was inferior. I changed several questionable details of my story.

Betz was suspicious of the fact that I knew many languages. Especially German, Russian, Polish. I had some difficulty convincing him I had had a nurse, a White Russian aristocrat, who had developed in me an interest in the Russian language. It was a mistake to have admited knowing Russian.

Then I had to explain how I got the documents found on me when I was arrested. I spun a web of cities starting on the German border and extending to Poland and the Ukraine. I gave the names of so many men, German, French, and Polish, Russian and Ukrainian, that Walter was lost.

"Hell, you've been around too many men," he shouted.

"You see, for a woman it is always safer to be helped by men. And believe me, I never got into trouble by accepting their help. I got what I wanted. When I was a young girl it was predicted by Madame Ida— you know, that great fortune-teller in Clichy, in Paris . . . Never heard of her? Oh, what do you know about France? Yes, she told me I'd be in trouble during the war, but I'd be helped and saved by men, uniformed men especially . . . And, you see, everything is turning out true . . . And, after all, how do you expect me to keep in my memory all those Slavonic names, names of towns and streets? My tongue still twists when I have to pronounce *psh* and *bsch*."

"Yes, but I've heard you speak it not so badly, even though with a foreign accent."

"I have a flair for languages. What do you think of my German? Not bad? I swear I could learn even Chinese and Arabic if I had to."

I gave my tongue plenty of freedom and chatted away, apparently perfectly at ease. As I noticed that this pose was working well, I became calmer and more relaxed. When I was about to sing some French songs, Betz stopped me.

"It's a pleasure to listen to you, Madame Marie," he said politely, "but we still have a lot of work to do and I am afraid we are slipping away from the main subject."

"Excuse me, monsieur," I said, "you are perfectly right, but it is so nice to meet a true European. You do understand me?"

Beltz melted into a delighted smile and forgot he had to ask me more about that man in Berlin from the Herman Göring Werke who had helped me get a pass to Poland.

When I left Betz's office both of us were smiling brightly. Walter gave me a pack of cigarettes, which I hid in my brassiere, and walked me down the stairs, assuring me that everything would be all right and I'd be sent back to France if what I had told him turned out to be true.

The unbelievable had been accomplished. Betz had swallowed the Marie-Josephine Menard story, swallowed it whole. But how long would it take them to digest it, or reject it as indigestible?

Antonina was a woman in her thirties, tall, lean, with a sharp face. She spoke with a harsh country accent. She had been appointed to help the doctor, since she claimed to be a graduate nurse. She was well liked.

One day at the end of November we heard loud screams in the corridor and then downstairs. We could hear two voices. The angry voice of a German, yelling and cursing. And a woman's voice.

We ran to the window and saw one of the guards driving Antonina before him in the yard. Her hands were chained, her long hair disheveled and hanging loose, her clothes ripped. The German was kicking and pushing her toward the gate. The woman was screaming.

"What a shame," Zofia, the teacher, cried.

A couple of women came to the window and started shouting and cursing. Soon Rosa rushed into the cell, enraged.

"What is going on here?" she yelled. "Shut up!"

"It's a rotten shame what they are doing to that woman out there," I said.

"You dare say that, Polish trash!"

"I am a Frenchwoman!" I cried.

Rosa raised her keys to hit me, but I caught her hand and twisted it.

The Polish women laughed. I pushed Rosa away and released her arm. She took me to the prison commander.

The *Obersturmführer* sat at his desk. His face was lost in fat.

"Who are you?" he asked in a shrill voice that recalled for me the gossip I had heard about him.

"I am French, Marie Menard. A colonel's daughter."

"How nice. I didn't know it, madame." He seemed delighted. "Why did you behave—how shall I put it—against the regulations of this establishment?"

"Well, major," I said, "I won't take any insults from this little jailer. She dared to call me Polish trash. And I couldn't stand the way the policeman was treating that woman in the yard. In France, ladies are not treated like that."

"I'll tell you what happened. You see, that woman is a Jew. She was calling in her sleep for her children by Jewish names."

"What!" I was stupefied.

"A Polish woman reported it to the guard this morning," the commander explained.

"But I don't like to see brutality, especially toward women. It makes no difference who they are. You know, in our country we are raised democratically."

"Yes, yes, we are all democratic, and socialist, too. That is why I respect your opinions. You are lucky you are not Polish. You are a western European and we don't want to hurt you. But I ask you to control yourself. I don't know whether I can be as gallant again."

I walked away, wishing I knew who the informer was. And I was amazed by the commander's behavior. Do they really care about my opinions? What would they say if they knew who I was?

I told the story in the cell. Most of the women remained indifferent. Christina prayed and some joined her.

Many women and girls passed through our cell, number fourteen. Prison for me was a useful school of human nature.

When Sylvia entered our cell everyone followed her with an admiring look. She was a true Slavonic beauty.

All she would tell us was that she came from the Carpathian Mountains, was an artist's wife, and expected her child in three months. When asked why she had been arrested, she just waved her hand as if driving away a nasty fly. At night we heard her sighing and weeping to herself.

Sylvia was taken out to investigation the next afternoon. She did not come back at suppertime, nor at lights-out. We were worried.

It must have been after midnight when steps from the corridor approached our door and the key squeaked. We sat up.

The light was not turned on, but in the strip of blue light from the corridor we saw a woman who seemed clumsy and unnaturally motionless. After the door was slammed, the woman collapsed on the floor like a big bundle and lay still.

Several of us jumped up and ran toward her. Somebody lit a match. Yes, it was Sylvia. Her beautiful hair hung in tangled strands. We saw bloodstains and blue welts.

"Bring a mattress, quickly," ordered the doctor. "Lift her up!"

In the meantime somebody began hammering on the door. After a while Rosa came.

"What happened?" she yelled through the closed door.

"Open the door and turn on the light, please. Something is wrong with one of our women."

Rosa turned on the light and walked in. Sylvia screamed like a hurt animal and grabbed her swollen belly.

"I am afraid she is going to have an early birth," the doctor said in Polish.

"So what?" said Rosa insolently.

"I have to take her to the hospital," the doctor said.

"There is no hospital for Polish prisoners. Hurry up, I want to go to sleep."

Pelagia approached Rosa. "Go and tell whoever has to be told that the woman must be sent to a hospital. Otherwise she may die. Hurry, for God's sake!"

"She can die for all it matters to me. What do you think she is? Just another Polish pig."

I jumped after her. "You German pig! You German whore," I yelled, as she ran out and slammed the door.

Before morning Sylvia gave birth to a dead child. The doctor's arms and clothes, the mattress and the floor were spattered with blood. We didn't have enough water to wash it away, and the dead little bundle was wrapped in a rag. Sylvia was very weak. She could only whisper to the doctor that she had been kicked in the belly.

In the morning two Ukrainian policemen took Sylvia away on a stretcher, and we scrubbed the cell.

Rosa did not show up for about ten days.

In prison you had to learn whom to trust and what to believe. You had to cope with types you had never known before, that you had only heard of vaguely or read about in books. Many women appeared, lived among us, disappeared.

One day I was taken again to Betz's office. He smiled pleasantly and again assumed his western European role.

"We have just one little thing to clarify, Marie-Josephine. I have started a search of POW camps all over Europe. I told you, all Europe is ours. Have you heard the latest news? Concerning your fatherland?"

I knew what Betz meant, but I couldn't admit I had been listening to the radio.

"I am sorry to inform you we have been compelled to occupy all of your country. We have entered the unoccupied zone of France."

"So you did it," I said in a choked voice and covered my face with my hands.

"You should be happy. Now that your country is under our Führer's protection, you'll have the privilege of joining the New Order in Europe."

"Are you sure you are not joking?"

"Joking?"

"Let's talk business, if there is any."

"As you wish, Marie," Betz replied and opened a green file numbered 3002/42.

"Look, in one of the camps in Poland we discovered a man by the name of Robert Renard. He admits being married but doesn't know you."

"The man is right. I do not know a Renard. My name is Menard."

"Well, I thought there might be a very small mistake. Just one letter."

"I am a very exact person, monsieur."

Betz took out a picture and showed it to me. It was of a young man in uniform, with a sympathetic face.

"A handsome fellow," I said, "but, sorry, not my husband."

Leaving Betz's office, I asked myself: How long will it take them to uncover my impossible lie? How long will I have to play the role of a French lady? I knew that time was passing mercilessly and that probably soon I'd have to face Walter Betz's anger. So I had to work out an alternative plan. And to remember Goebbel's rule: The bigger the lie—the easier it catches on.

It was December. Our cell was poorly heated and we froze at night.

For Christmas the Polish Red Cross sent us food, Christmas trees, and presents. Most of the Polish women received big holiday packages. On Christmas Eve the atmosphere was solemn and full of longing for home. Many women and girls wept.

We opened the window and heard German singing, and shooting in the air. Then the Polish women sang their Christmas songs, some naïve and childish, others serious and thoughtful. We missed Christina, who had been transferred to the hospital.

I had even forgotten that I had had a birthday on November 5. A year had passed since the Christmas Eve in the Schultze sisters' apartment, and I was now nineteen. It was eighteen months since the Germans had come.

Two days after Christmas I was escorted by Gustav to the Gestapo.

This time Walter Betz had no smile for me. He immediately went on the attack. "So that's the way you fooled me!"

"What do you mean? I don't understand," I said.

"What do you mean?" Betz repeated several times, sarcastically. "You fed us insolent lies and dare ask what I mean?"

"There must be some mistake."

"Yes, a hell of a mistake. I should have beaten the hell out of your French stories."

"What in the world makes you use such ungentlemanly language?"

"Gentleman! *Donnerwetter noch ein Mal.* Does my masculine speech really hurt your delicate French ear? I don't give a damn. That was a stupid story. A little thing like you fooling the old police fox, Walter Betz."

I could not control myself and burst out laughing.

"Stop laughing or you'll cry," he warned.

"Don't ever hope to see me crying. And why get so angry? An old police fox should know better than that. Everybody tries to protect himself. So why shouldn't I be allowed some minor inaccuracies in my story? You should understand that a young woman can get a little mixed up. War, so many men, foreign countries, people, investigations . . ."

"Little inaccuracies! That's really something. I felt right away that you were too clever. I never believed you were more than seventeen. And claiming to be twenty-four and married. Tell me one thing, were you a teacher before the war, or were your parents? Tell me the truth."

"No," I decided finally, refusing to go in deeper, "neither my parents nor I were teachers."

"What about your husband? But now it's clear your whole story is a lie. The most barefaced lie I've heard in my whole career."

"What's this about being a teacher? At least you could tell me how you discovered my story isn't true."

"Here it is," Betz yelled. He took out a page from the file and threw it at me. I read it.

It contained a report from Dunkirk stating that there had been a school at 6 Republic Street before the war and that the only people who lived there were unmarried teachers. The whole street had been destroyed and there was no means of establishing any names or further information.

"And this little paper is enough to wipe out my whole confession? But it is not exact at all. Behind the school there was another house with a big garden and it carried the same number."

"Stop this lying or I'll have to try other methods on you."

"I am ready to talk reasonably," I said quietly.

"All right, all right. You can't cling to your story any longer. It wasn't only the business with the school. The whole story is breaking down in many other places. Be sensible."

At this point it was my turn to get angry. "What do you mean, Walter Betz? I am your prisoner, but I think my position is better than yours."

"What!"

"Yes, you are dying to know my true story. You have wasted almost three months investigating the fantasy I offered you in a tasty French sauce. But that happens to be just what I wanted. I never believed I could delay my investigation this long. Never believed I'd win almost three months. After all, I am pretty lucky, aren't I?"

He digested my little speech. Then he frowned and said angrily, "That's a hell of a thing to say to me, Marie, or whatever your real name is."

"Maybe it is, but you were asking for it. Look, I am arrested by the Gestapo. Brought to Pomorska Street. Then I am thrown into the notorious Monte Prison. The first night, four idiots come to yell at me, ask idiotic questions, and threaten to have me shot in the morning. Then the Gestapo leaves me alone for three weeks. After that you bring me straight to the IV-E-I. And you swallow my impossible story about a Frenchwoman from Dunkirk running around over half of Europe looking for her husband. What should I feel about all this? You have completely disappointed me, all of you. I have had no experience with the police in my whole life until now, but I venture to say your work is very poor."

"How dare you! Who do you think you are?"

"I am only a prisoner, your prisoner, Mr. Betz."

"Marie, you have a completely wrong idea about us. We have a bad reputation but it is exaggerated. You see, we gave you a fair chance to tell us the truth. You used it to fool us with your sensational story, but we didn't lose anything. You are in our hands, and one day you'll tell us the whole truth. We are so strong that we needn't hurry. We'll get the whole truth out of you even if you rot in our prison till you're a grandmother."

"Then we are in the same position. I too have plenty of time, but I sincerely hope I'll be a grandmother in a more pleasant place. And if you don't mind, give me a cigarette."

Walter pushed a pack of cigarettes toward me.

"I can understand how you feel and why you talk the way you do. But you must understand that you've reached a dead end. You must tell me everything about yourself. And again I assure you nothing will happen to you. We are even ready to forget little details like the uniform and the French story."

I smoked and pretended to be thinking seriously. "No," I said after a while, "I cannot agree with you. There are different true stories.

But mine happens to be the kind that cannot be confessed—to the Gestapo."

"Well, don't worry, you won't lose by telling the truth, no matter what, so long as you're not a Jew in disguise."

"No," I said again, "I can't. Did you ever hear of anyone asking for a death sentence for herself? I feel like living a while yet."

"Marie, don't think your story is so terrible. Believe me, we have already had partisans here, spies, paratroopers. But they don't necessarily get death sentences. Your verdict is in your own hands, and I swear to you, on my honor, no woman was ever sentenced to death here. Well, make up your mind. Look how gentle I am. I could twist your little head off for that impossible lie of yours if it weren't so amusing. Listen to me; I am your friend now. Only I can save you. I decide what to do with you. You're young, good-looking, intelligent. Don't waste your time rotting in a prison. You deserve better than that."

He went on with his talk, like a glass of tea with too much saccharin. I did not listen any longer. The sound of his voice buzzed around my ears like a wild bee caught in a window.

"What are you thinking about?" Betz stroked my shoulder. I moved away. "Yes, yes," he went on in the same tone, "that's how things end up when nice girls get mixed up in wars. Couldn't you stay at home with your mother?"

I reached for another cigarette.

"I'll give you till tomorrow morning. Do you appreciate how generous I am? Think it over, but tomorrow I want the whole truth."

Curious and friendly faces in the afternoon. Facing plenty of questions, not giving too many answers. The noise of supper being given out. Evening roll call. Preparing mattresses for the night. They didn't let you think quietly. Lying awake on the mattress. At every hour of the day and night, there were women around you, and there was no escape.

The guards measured the big yard with their heavy tread. I repeated my new story like a lesson. Names, places, events. I was not myself anymore. I was somebody I did not know too well as yet . . .

Before falling asleep I remembered the mocking laughter of the "old police fox." In the morning he did not forget to send for me.

Betz was cleanly shaven and smelled of German perfume. He wore civilian clothes and looked like a butcher from a little Prussian town, but he appeared satisfied with himself.

We measured each other. I could feel his anxiety under the mask, and he searched my face for traces of a sleepless night. I tried to look open and honest.

"Well," he began, "I hope you had enough time to think things over and you slept well."

"Yes, I slept like a rock."

"Remember, your fate is in your hands. Don't forget that there is no other way for you than to confess the whole truth. You tried to fool us, but let's forget about the past now and think of the future. I am listening and waiting." He leaned back in his chair.

"I don't know how to begin it. I am still not too sure whether I should tell the truth."

"I am ready to help you. Look, there are three explanations for a person caught living with a false identity. The first is, you might be a spy. The second, you might be a member of an underground or resistance organization. The third, you might be a Jew in hiding. Well, since the third possibility is eliminated—by the theory of human races you are a pure Slavonic-Baltic type—then, you see, Marie, there are only two left. Either you're a spy or a member of the underground. And now you've got to tell me who you are."

"You are getting really clever," I answered, more or less relaxed after being absolved of the worst "crime." "Now I can see that you can think. Almost a reincarnation of Sherlock Holmes. But I think my story is perhaps just a little more than you have been expecting, Walter Betz."

"I am ready to listen to anything you have to say."

"Well, you have convinced me," I said slowly.

"Go on, go on, I feel we are getting somewhere."

"Then listen to me. You want to know who I am. Well, I am Russian."

Betz's face showed such deep surprise that it could not have been faked. But he said, "Yes, yes, I have been sure of it, since I saw you the first time."

"Aren't you joking?"

"I am not joking. It is perfectly true. Ever since I've known you I've had a feeling you were Russian."

"And it was that prophetic feeling that made you swallow my French story?"

"Well, that's not important. Now maybe you'll tell me your true name?"

"My name is still Maria, but not Marie. My family name is Arsenyeva. Maria Alexandrovna Arsenyeva."

Walter had some difficulty pronouncing it. "Anyway," he said, "you remain Maria for me."

He grabbed the phone and dialed several numbers, inviting the persons at the other end to come to his room. I heard him using the word *commander.*

"You're phoning for witnesses? But remember one thing—the show is mine and not yours."

"What do you mean?"

"I mean that you can have this show only because I am willing to give it."

"Certainly," superman smiled.

"I start when I want, I stop when I feel like it, and I say what I wish. Is that clear?"

Betz did not have time to answer as the door flew open after a quick knock and three men filled the small room. One of them, with the insignia of *Hauptsturmführer,* had an ugly scar on his right cheek. I knew him at once. I had seen him before my arrest, outside the prison, climbing into a fancy green Skoda. Then I remembered his companion —a tall, fat man in gold-rimmed spectacles.

The second man was a tall, blond, handsome young civilian. The third was an *Obersturmführer* with a brutal face and a slight limp.

All of them exchanged greetings with Walter Betz.

"This is your Russian girl?" asked the highest rank.

"Yes, Commissar Lux."

The three of them stared at me.

"I did not know you had commissars in the Gestapo and, by the way, I am sure I have seen you before, *Herr* Commissar."

"Seen me before?" The German was surprised. "Where?"

"Who cares where?" I answered. "Naturally, here in Krakow. And your companion was a tall, very fat fellow with two or three chins. In gold spectacles, if I am not mistaken."

The men exchanged a quick glance. Then the blond one laughed.

"Right, she means that fat swine Brotesser."

"That's for certain," Betz and the clumsy captain agreed.

"I saw you in a fancy green Skoda, made in Czechoslovakia—excuse me, in the temporary Protectorate of Bohemia and Moravia. Isn't that so?"

"Well, it makes no difference. Where are you from?"

"Born in Leningrad, lived in different parts of the Soviet Union. Before the war in Alma-Ata, and in Moscow."

"How did you get here?" the clumsy one asked.

"Parachuted."

"When?" Betz broke in.

"After your defeat in the Moscow battle," I replied.

"That's no way to talk!" The commissar didn't like that.

"Must understand it—Bolshevik education," the clumsy officer explained.

"How old are you?"

"Twenty-four."

"Civilian or military?"

Another delicate question. Must be careful about this. "Well, half-civilian, half-military," I answered, but the Germans didn't pay any attention.

"How many were parachuted with you?"

"Where did you jump?"

"Who sent you over here?"

"What were your tasks?"

The Germans fired the questions one after another, apparently not paying much attention to my answers. I decided to get angry.

"Do you think this is the way to investigate me? I am not used to such methods."

"She is right," the commissar smiled, "and I must say she has guts."

"She certainly has," Betz agreed flatteringly.

"Thank you, gentlemen," I said. "I am only afraid that you wouldn't have the guts to jump down somewhere in Russia."

To my surprise all four Germans began to laugh as if I had told a splendid joke.

"Damned right," the clumsy captain managed to say, "especially you, Betz, and you, Gerhard," he turned to the blond civilian, "have you ever been in an airplane? And to jump—I wouldn't guarantee the contents of your pants."

They left shaking Betz's hand. He looked very important and proud.

He sent for a good lunch for me and gave me a pack of cigarettes. Then he left for the mess.

9

After lunch, Betz resumed the investigation.

I began. "I was born in Leningrad, in November, 1918. It was a good time to be born. You know, children of the revolution. I know nothing of my parents and family. All of them disappeared in the revolution. I was raised in an orphanage, at the government's expense. All I remember are the teachers. They tried to give us what we had never had—a home and love.

"Well, this is neither the place nor the time to get sentimental." I smiled sadly. "I stayed in the children's home until high school age. Then we moved to a boarding school. In the meantime the country developed under the new regime. Living at government expense, we were to serve our country.

"After graduation from high school each of us was brought before a special commission of teachers and government administrators to discuss our future. Naturally the commission made it clear that we were duty bound to volunteer for patriotic service. An NKVD, a secret policeman, was a member of the commission and he painted for us the fascinating life of a foreign agent."

"Agent?" Betz smiled contemptuously. "Why do you use such grand words? Why don't you say spy?"

"Spy?" It was my turn to smile. "Let's use that expression for those despicable individuals who spy for money. By foreign agents I mean those who carry out tasks in enemy territory out of idealism, whose only reward is the respect and gratitude of their fatherland."

"It doesn't make too much difference to me, a spy is a spy."

"What would you call a convinced Nazi who carried out such work, who entered Russia illegally, maybe parachuted, with no diplomatic privileges? How would you describe such a man?"

"A hero, of course."

"But when I do the same for my country, you call me a spy."

"Don't you see the difference?" Betz did not give up. "You seem to be an honest girl, but you don't realize what a mistake you have made. You are serving a gang of international criminals, Communists, anarchists, Jews, and other scum."

"Whom do you think you serve? A gang of murderers and torturers. Don't you think I know what the Nazis are?"

"You have a lot to learn about us."

"Well, there is a Russian proverb, 'Learn, learn all your life, and you'll die a fool.' "

"I don't understand proverbs."

At this point the argument expired.

"Please go on with your story. We'll have plenty of time later for political discussions."

I picked up my story where I had left off. "I liked the idea of becoming a foreign agent. After a summer spent in the Crimea, I left for the NKVD school. Before leaving we went through Moscow."

"What do you mean, 'we'?"

"We were a little group from our high school. There were four boys and two girls."

"Give me their names and describe them for me. It might be useful."

"We stopped three days in Moscow. We were lucky to get opera and ballet tickets. We saw Ulanova in *Swan Lake,* Tchaikovsky's. You know it?"

"Never had an ear for classical music. I am not even sure I could sing the 'Horst Wessel.' "

"I am not surprised. Then we visited many places of interest. The trip from Moscow to Alma-Ata took three days by train."

"Where is Alma-Ata, or however you pronounce it?"

"You don't know? You should at least know the capitals of the Soviet republics. It is the capital of Kazakhstan, Central Asia."

"You can see I am doing well enough with the knowledge I have."

"Yes, here in the Gestapo. In the NKVD you wouldn't even be a corporal."

"That's enough, Maria! Don't you think you are a little fresh?"

"What do you want of me, Walter? You have to realize I have my own views and I don't intend to change them just to please you. I'm myself!"

"All right, all right," Walter interjected, and I returned to my story.

"After three days of traveling we arrived at Alma-Ata. When we alighted from the train the air was sticky and heavy. The city was quite big, with plenty of semitropical trees, mostly white houses with flat roofs and balconies. As it was early afternoon and the heat was oppressive, the streets were deserted. There we became acquainted with the Oriental siesta."

"You are a very good storyteller. But I'm afraid we're digressing."

"We had to take examinations before beginning the course, in Marxist-Leninist science, the organization of the Soviet Union, the history of our country, and so on.

"In the NKVD school the discipline was very strict. We studied hard. After study hours we had everything at our disposal, swimming pools, sports facilities, music, folk dancing and singing, libraries, a dramatic circle."

"Is it true that the NKVD is hated and feared by the population?" Betz asked.

I feigned surprised. "Can *you* ask such a question? Well, I could ask the same of the German people vis-à-vis the Gestapo—are they scared of it? The decent people in Russia don't feel it exists. The ones who get caught feel sorry for themselves. Is that clear enough?"

"Yes. Anyway, it's a good joke."

"If you are looking for good jokes, here's one. In Berlin, a Gestapo man got into a streetcar. Everybody shut up. Suddenly an old man sneezed. The Gestapo man looked all around the streetcar and asked in a menacing voice, 'Who sneezed?' Everybody started shaking and people pushed the old man forward and told him to own up. Finally, in a trembling voice, the poor old fellow said, 'It was me.' Then the Gestapo man smiled, said '*Gesundheit,*' and jumped out at the next station."

"Very good." Walter laughed till the tears came to his eyes. "Do you know any more like that?"

"Of course, but not all at once. You'll hear them, one at a time. I feel like talking about my school." Then I began going through the curriculum. Betz interrupted me.

"It sounds like what we already know about this type of school in the Soviet Union."

"But you have the luck to hear it from a genuine pupil." I laughed because it was amusing to me to talk so freely about things of which I had no firsthand knowledge.

Betz seemed to be satisfied. "Later on you will give us more particulars about the teachers and professors, the other students, and the studies themselves. When did you graduate?"

"Our class graduated on June 15, 1939. About 60 percent with excellent reports. But even during the summer, from the second year on, we were already being sent on little trips abroad. As I spoke good Polish and Ukrainian, I went to the western Ukraine. I visited the eastern part of Poland, contacted the illegal Communist party, and easily obtained information about the Polish army. My Polish was good and I hadn't the slightest trouble. I also made several trips to Finland."

I noticed that Betz had made some notes. "What are you writing?" I asked.

"I am marking down questions for later," he replied.

"Then came other activities, like intelligence, radio work. And traveling again. Intelligence work on the German-Soviet border in Poland." By the time we reached the outbreak of the German invasion on the twenty-second of June, 1941, it was already evening.

Betz turned on the radio. The narrow investigation room became filled with soft jazz music. I relaxed in my chair. Then he sent me back to Montelupich with a "see you tomorrow."

I picked up my story where I had ended the day before. "I joined the 114th Special Battalion of the NKVD troops. We took a long combat detour from the Ukraine and landed in the southernmost area of the Moscow front. My principal job was combat intelligence and investigation of Nazi prisoners. It would take a month to relate everything about this work."

"I am not very interested in it. You will talk to someone else about that later. Go on."

"What do you want to know?"

"What happened later?" Walter asked.

"Well, in November, 1941, I was taken from my unit and flown to Moscow. I reported to a certain apartment in Mayakovsky Street and was received by an officer who informed me that I had the honor of being given a job behind the front lines, in Nazi-occupied territory. I spent about ten days getting ready for the trip and securing information and instructions. I was instructed to contact the Moscow-led spy net, to assist them and to head several groups under the command of local chiefs."

"Wait a minute," Betz interrupted, "what kind of office was it at that place in Moscow?"

"Now, don't be naïve. You know that secret services use private apartments, for greater security."

"Who was the officer who gave you the assignment?"

"I am sorry, but I do not know his name; he didn't introduce himself. Anyway, it was clear that he belonged to the department of foreign agents working in occupied territories."

"Who were the others in the group? How many? Men or women?"

"We were seven. Two girls and five men. But they wouldn't interest you much. I was the only one sent to Poland."

"When, how, and where were you parachuted?" he asked.

"Are you familiar with the geography of western White Russia?" I said.

"We can look at a map. But now I want the general information. The particulars we'll go into later."

"I was dropped near Siedlce." I was acquainted with this part of Poland, as I had spent a summer there once in a Scout camp. "Not far from this town there is a village called Jelnica, surrounded by big woods. There I was to land. Two peasants were to meet me there."

"Where did you go from there?"

"I took the train to Warsaw as soon as possible. I gave all my equipment to the men who met me, kept only papers, money, cigarettes. They gave me a woman's suitcase and some hints on train travel. After I'd carefully checked the Warsaw connections and people, I established my relations, meetings, and a way of life."

"But I want to know who was the first one you got in touch with."

Here I had prepared a story of persons already dead and clandestine apartments discovered long ago, but all this was for the long term. I wasn't ready yet to give any definite names or places.

I avoided a direct answer. "You have to know that one of my first jobs was to inspect the work of the net over almost all the territory of the general government of Poland. I had plenty of work traveling around the Lvov, Warsaw, and Lublin districts. At that time I did not have any regular residence. I traveled with a list of appointments. Well . . . have you any idea what a secret agent's schedule looks like?"

"No," Betz admitted.

"For example, with person A, I met on the first, eleventh, and twenty-first of every month in a definite place. If there is no meeting for security reasons, there is always an alternate place and the dates move on one, two, or three days ahead, as agreed. This way we never lose one another. In addition to the schedule of meetings, I also had to meet my commanding officer."

"I would like to know as much about him as possible." Betz sounded eager.

"It would not mean much, as this man worked with me between October, 1941, and January, 1942, and after that we lost contact."

"That makes no difference. Tell me about him."

"Well, he is a quiet man, and not at the very top of our service. He has lived in Germany since 1930. Maybe you'll explode—but he happens to be a member of the Nazi party, and even wears some Nazi medals. I could not tell you exactly who he is, as I met him once as an air force lieutenant colonel, another time as a civilian driving a swanky Opel-Kapitan. The third time he was an SS *Hauptsturmführer* with plenty of combat medals and even an Iron Cross. The last time I saw him before he went back to Germany, he appeared in the Nazi party uniform. Hans was his nickname."

"What does he look like?"

"It's quite difficult to describe him," I went on. "He is tall, well built, and good-looking. Very good-looking. About thirty-five. I have seen him with and without a moustache, blond, medium, and dark-haired. With dark and with light skin. Once he wore glasses and a a monocle. Even with and without a wedding ring. Once he wore the skull and bones *SS* ring."

"Fantastic," Betz exclaimed. "But where did he live?"

"Don't ask silly questions," I said, smiling. "My main task was to improve the work of the net. The Russian command wanted more and better information and at the same time more and bolder action. Then later came the preparatory work for big operations."

"How did you work, and tell me, what was your position in the net? Quite important, I understand." Betz looked at me with undisguised admiration.

"Oh, don't overestimate me, please," I said reproachfully. "It should be clear to you that I was only a very little cog in our machine."

"Maybe not such a little one," he said, "parachuted by a special plane, as I understood, especially recruited by some mysterious personality from Moscow, sent with a task to improve the activities of the net and information service. Well, it sounds quite important."

"Maybe, but there were so many persons doing no less than I did."

"Where did you get the money?" Walter demanded.

"Don't be a fool. From the party, of course."

"I must admit you are a hard nut. We talk for hours, but I don't get any definite information. You must give me names, addresses, descriptions of underground people and their foreign leaders and helpers. Otherwise we won't make any headway." His voice was insistent.

I tried to explain. "But you must understand one fact, Walter. Even if I gave you the most detailed information, including addresses, descriptions, would you consider it of any value?"

"Naturally, provided you were not lying."

"But even if I am not lying, it is too late now. I was arrested on October 3, 1942, and we are now approaching the New Year. What do you think our people did after my disappearance? They changed all names, addresses, meetings, codes, and identities. They destroyed all the valuable information I had. That is the usual procedure when one of us gets caught."

"Of course, we know that. But you'll have to tell me all you know anyway."

"If you are ready to waste time on old, useless stuff, then I don't mind. The time is yours."

After this, we spent another two days dictating my "confession." The way it began made me laugh.

"I, Maria Alexandrovna Arsenyeva, an investigated prisoner, born November 5, 1918, in Leningrad, Russia, no religion, member of the Young Communist League, citizen of the USSR, am making the following declarations of my own free will, without being coerced by any physical or mental violence or threat, before Criminal Secretary Walter Betz, on December 29, 1942, in Krakow."

I felt a kind of relief when it was finished and I signed it.

It was New Year's Day and I hoped to rest, at least for a few days.

Back in prison, I did not reveal a word about the unusually long investigation. Though back from the Gestapo safe and sound, I felt uneasy, and my uneasiness increased when I noticed how several of my close friends seemed now to avoid me.

One of those unpleasant days we had a newcomer, a typical country girl from the Ukraine. She spoke a songlike Ukrainian, but also knew Russian, some German, and a little Polish. Her name was Galina, and she had escaped during her enforced stay on a German farm.

Her coming gave me the opportunity to clear myself. I addressed Galina in Russian and then in Ukrainian. Before long we were in the midst of a conversation that nobody could understand, though they knew what language we were speaking. After a while Galina said to me, "I am homesick. Let's sing."

And we sang Russian folk songs, beautiful and sad Ukrainian songs, several patriotic marching songs. Then Galina went into a dancing song. She jumped up and down, shaking her shoulders, beat out the rhythm with the heavy soles of her clumsy work shoes. A handkerchief fluttered in her right hand. When she stopped in front of me and stamped her feet impatiently, it was my turn.

"A true Ukrainian gopak, huh, Maria?" the girl shouted happily.

Galina left after a couple of days. On her departure the attitude of my companions changed for the better, but they still did not ask about the investigation.

I was called again to investigation. There was a knock at the door. Two SS men, Gerhard and a fat man, entered the room, bringing with them a Russian soldier in a greatcoat and boots. His insignia had been removed. A prisoner of war, I thought.

"You can talk in your own language," the fat man proposed, and then I understood it might be a test. Well, it didn't matter to me, even if any of them knew the language.

"Hello, *landsman*." I used the popular Russian greeting. "It's wonderful to meet here, with all the Nazi scum."

He was a simple young fellow. He looked around. The German faces hadn't changed their expressions, so he answered, "A hell of a place to meet. Where do you come from?"

We had a vivid conversation. The soldier told me about his capture, about the terrible prisoner-of-war camps, until he had arrived at a more or less decent place not far from Krakow. After a half hour the fat one gave a sign and the guards took the prisoner away.

"Did you enjoy meeting a *landsman*?"

"Now you are trying to be clever, trying to test my language. Well, your counterespionage experts are progressing."

The fat man walked out without answering.

"Who is he?" I asked the other.

"Another fat swine," he giggled.

"An expert?" I asked.

"An expert! That's some joke. Him—an expert. Maybe at buying chickens and pig fat."

"You have some outstanding personnel."

"Well, you still don't seem to realize that in this organization jobs aren't given on the basis of knowledge."

Then the telephone rang and Gerhard took me to Betz's office. Betz was again clean-shaven and smartly dressed. "You are now going to meet a very important personality," he announced solemnly.

I smiled. "I am going to be greatly honored."

"I hope you won't disappoint me," he added, and then there was a knock on the door and Betz ran to open it on a rather plump man, in glasses, wearing a green army uniform. The first impression was of plenty of silver. The plump man was a major.

"Major, this is my friend Maria from Moscow." Betz was fawning.

The major gave me the look of an old counterintelligence fox.

"Good morning, Maria," he said.

"Good morning, Mister X."

The major bowed. "Excuse me, I am Major von Korab. From army counter intelligence, my dear lady."

"I must have a good look. It is the first time I have had the honor of meeting an aristocratic human being. A live one. What are you, a count or a prince?"

The major and Betz exchanged a glance and laughed. I noticed that Betz laughed only after the major.

"That's wonderful. What a joke."

"I am already used to Maria's wit," Betz said.

He kept modestly to one side while the major started working on me. I understood at once that here was an experienced dangerous enemy, well equipped for his job and not a fool like Betz.

First he attacked my Finland story. He asked for place-names and information about the territory. I was very precise in my replies.

Then he unrolled a series of maps. He selected about half a dozen of them and put them before me.

"Take the maps and show me the places where you were dropped and where you operated." He watched me carefully while I bent over the maps. I was given the map of Viipuri, then another to the northeast of it. To my joy, I discovered places I knew on it.

"Here you are, major," I said, "we were dropped on this big clearing. Here is the edge of a big wood. Here you see some lonely trees and houses. One of them signaled to the plane. And here is the place with that funny name, as I said, two words both starting with an *s*. Then here, behind these hills, were field batteries."

"Why behind the hills?" the major asked suddenly.

I didn't know much but I heard something about it from artillerymen.

"Well, to hide the flash."

The major looked at me with surprise. "Where did you hear that?"

"I told you about having spent a good while at the front. We happened to see some gunners and we talked to them. It surprises you that Russian gunners should know why they put guns behind hills?" I asked with false surprise.

Then I was sure that I had passed my test on Finland, and I was even more sure when I saw the major put down the pile of maps.

"What time is it?" he said to Betz. "I feel like having a little snack."

"It's about noon." Betz excused himself and left the room.

The major took off his cap and his belt with the sword, and opened the window.

"It is too hot in here." He dropped into an armchair. "I feel much better when the Gestapo man is out," he said, and frowned.

I smiled. "Don't like them? I don't either."

"They don't know a damned thing about intelligence work. They mess up the best cases, like yours, for example." He sighed again.

"I never believed I would be able to fool around with my French story, if you heard about it."

"Well, I am not so sure you are not doing the same thing again," said the major and looked at me sharply.

I smiled, but felt a sharp tug at my heart.

"No answer?"

"No, because it is your job to find out. I didn't expect you to ask questions like the Gestapo."

"You are very clever," the major laughed, "a girl with plenty of guts. They must go crazy here with your stories. I laughed till I cried when Betz told me your impossible story. The French one . . . And they swallowed it. What idiots." The major laughed again until he had to wipe away his tears.

"You can try anything you want on me. I just love to listen to young girls. Anything they say is charming. Even the wildest hoax . . ."

Then he switched over to the Russian secret service. And he knew a lot more than I ever would. But still I had the upper hand. I drowned him in a sea of Russian names. I was grateful for having read *The Records of Major Pronin*. He had been connected with government security and had written about many old spy stories.

Betz came back with a soldier in white apron and cap. The desk was cleared and set for a sumptuous lunch. Ham and sausage, potato salad, herring, pickles, bread and butter, and three bottles.

Betz filled the glasses. I covered mine. "I do not drink," I declared.

"Why not?" the major asked.

"I refuse to drink with Germans."

"But you'll eat, Maria?"

"Yes, because I am hungry."

After the meal the major attacked another problem. I had mentioned border intelligence on the Soviet-German demarcation line, between September, 1939, and June, 1941. Here I had to be extremely careful, as the major was familiar with this problem.

When I mentioned the sector along the San River, von Korab smiled broadly. He was obviously more familiar with this area than I had thought him to be.

"You naturally met Colonel Mamonov?"

"Personally, never, but it seems to me I have heard the name," I answered, though I had never heard it before.

The major looked surprised and began asking about my activities.

The only things I could bluff about were alleged trips over the border to several places I had known before the war, about intercepting German agents, and watching for any signs of possible invasion. This part of the investigation did not satisfy the major.

"I do not know what to think," he said finally. "It could be that you don't know a damned thing about border intelligence, but I rather believe you don't want to be honest with me. Could that be so?"

As I did not answer, he changed the subject. I became a little confused, because for the second time in several hours the old fox had come close to the truth. I really didn't know a thing about border intelligence except some vague stories heard long ago; the rest was imagination. But somehow I felt confident. First, because nobody would confess to the most dangerous charge in wartime for the sake of covering up underground activities. Second, I was sure there were very few things the Gestapo could check in my story. Third, Betz would never give up the claim that he had uncovered a serious and sensational espionage case.

Naturally I was aware of the possibility of facing a court-martial with only one verdict possible. Yet I was convinced they would take no such action so long as they believed I could give them valuable information. Instinctively I pushed away the idea of an end to my story and became so involved in it that I actually lived it and even believed myself to be a Russian girl, a paratrooper and a foreign agent.

I caught myself making speeches in the customary Russian manner. I even began thinking from the point of view of the young Russian generation. After all, I had learned enough about it during the occupation from 1939 to 1941.

Next the major asked with whom I had been connected and with whom I had collaborated since my arrival in Poland. I tried the same tactics as with Betz—talking a lot but avoiding definite names and places. This tactic didn't work with the major. After listening patiently to my fabrications, he frowned, shook his head, and melted into a smile.

"Dear little baby, you must remember one thing. You just can't feed old Major von Korab milk and strained children's food. Do you understand me?"

"No."

"You don't want to understand, I know. I hate to use violence or call for sharp measures. But you must understand that the moment the IV-E-I department and army counterintelligence lose their interest in you, you'll find yourself before a firing squad."

"So what? Whatever I did, I did with full consciousness of the consequences. Are you trying to scare me with a firing squad?"

"We know you are a heroine, but still I am asking you to be reasonable." The major's voice was oversweet again.

"You can go to blazes, all of you!" Suddenly I didn't care about anything.

To my surprise the major began to laugh as if he were enjoying himself immensely. Anyway, he changed the subject and started discussing the aims of the Russian spy net in Poland. I surprised him when I mentioned a fictitious operation, Stop. Its aim had been to cut all communications to the Eastern Front—by blowing up roads, bridges, main railroad stations, at the same time attacking supply and communication centers. I went into minute detail.

"Unbelievable!" the major cried.

"Fantastic!" Betz almost screamed.

"Get the chief," the major ordered Betz, who left the room. "I hope you're not bluffing. To tell the truth, I had heard something similar recently. But I hardly believe you would be telling us the truth about such an operation when you don't want to disclose even the tiniest details."

While waiting for his chief's arrival, he took out a fountain pen, played with it for a while, then, bringing it to the level of his eye, pointed it at me, and I heard a click.

"Thank you, Maria," the major smiled. "I just wanted to have your picture."

"Is that your most modern and secret camera?" I smiled. "I used to have one in the button of a jacket. Somebody else had one in an earring."

"Indeed?" the major said sarcastically. "I could see it in a button, but in an earring? How in the hell would they take their pictures?"

"I don't know. I am not a photographic expert."

"And where is your button?" he asked suddenly.

"I gave it to Hansi," I said carelessly.

"Uhum." And the major couldn't control his laughter. "Isn't that that fantastic superspy you drilled into Betz's tough brains? Maybe he is an *Obersturmbannführer,* too? And a submarine admiral? And maybe a tank field marshal?" He shook so hard with laughter that his armchair started creaking. "I bet Betz didn't sleep for a week!"

"You shouldn't either. You won't admit that we have such expert foreign agents?"

"I admit only what I have seen myself." The major stopped laughing. "Do you understand me? I don't give a damn for birds flying in trees or in the sky. I care only for plucked and roasted ones. And with cranberry sauce and white wine."

"You're a materialist."

"Remember, old von Korab isn't as stupid as he looks to you. I am an old counterintelligence bird. And I come from Vienna, not from Berlin," he added.

"But, being an Austrian, doesn't it disturb you to serve the Prussians and Nazis?"

"Makes no difference, Maria, no difference. I prefer Hitler's Great Germany to Stalin's paradise," he replied.

"You're a disgusting Nazi lackey," I said.

Betz came in, following a rather lean, blond man wearing pince-nez, with four stars on the black collar of his SS uniform. He measured me with his sharp blue eyes.

I smoked my cigarette and relaxed. He sat down in Betz's armchair and said, "I want to hear about Operation Stop." I repeated my big bluff and drowned it in endless names of towns, rivers, villages, and even drew a sketch without using any maps, to the surprise of all three of them.

The new arrival listened in frozen indifference. Betz was fascinated. Von Korab smiled sarcastically now and then. When I finished, their chief didn't ask any questions, but made a sign to the major and Betz, and they all left the room.

Betz came back, apparently satisfied. "We are making progress. Not bad at all. And the major liked you a lot, although he said you are a big swindler. And my chief was very interested. Now we'll give you a little break and then I'll see you again."

He offered me a pack of cigarettes and I returned to the prison. I knew everything was going well—at least I wanted to believe so.

Life went on in prison. But that sixth sense of prisoners smelled something in the air. There were rumors that something was going wrong at the front. Especially in Russia, in the Stalingrad area.

About the middle of January the cells of the German prisoners began to fill up. They were housed on the floors above us. We could hear stamping, yelling, cursing.

One day we heard from Emil, a half-German, half-Polish SS deserter, that the soldiers upstairs had organized a revolt. They had complained it was too crowded, that the food was vile and there was no entertainment. They had cut up their mattresses and scattered the straw around.

Next afternoon we were ordered to pack our belongings and evacuate the cell. There were hundreds of arrested soldiers in the yard and corridors. Later we heard there was a big transport leaving for a concentration camp because the prison was overcrowded. We moved to the first floor. The sickroom was evacuated and Christina was sent back to our cell. She had been operated on. The big swelling around the kidneys had been drained, and now she felt better and was able to sit up and to walk. She had regained a lot of her energy and wit. We gave her a warm welcome.

Then we had newcomers. Three young girls. They introduced themselves as Emma, Tosia, and Jadzia. Very Polish names.

But the women in the cell began whispering that they were Jewish. And one of them even asked Jadzia, "Do you really want to act the part of a Polish girl? Your nose is too Jewish."

It was Pelagia who defended the girl. "You'd better mind your own business. She is a prisoner, just like you."

The dark-haired Tosia asked for paper and pencil and spent her time writing. One day she sang a song full of despair and anger:

It burns, brothers, it burns.
Our little house is on fire,

And you are standing with folded arms
While it burns.

When she was asked where it came from, she lifted her head proudly
and replied, "It is a new song. It was written by a man calling on his
brothers to rebel." Nobody said a word, because the tune was Jewish.

Tosia and Emma were called together to investigation. When they
returned several hours later their faces were calm but desperate. In
the evening Tosia called Pelagia, Helena, and me to one side.

"There is something I wish to confess to the three of you. Our fate
is decided. Everything is finished for us. But we want our story to
survive us."

"Why did you choose us?" Helena asked.

"Because you seem to be the most decent anti-Nazi people here. I
want you to guard our story till the end of the war. Well, tell me
whether you are willing to accept my," she corrected herself, "*our*
last will."

We made it clear that we were willing to do so.

"On these pages I have written the story of our struggle against the
Nazis. We organized the youth in the ghetto. We called the organization the Fighting Pioneer. We had connections with the Polish patriots.
We smuggled weapons into the ghetto. We had several trained fighting
units, some of them in the woods. We dreamed of a rebellion. We
wanted every Jew to fight. If they had to die—then with weapons,
while trying to kill the killer. But we were exposed, maybe betrayed.
Many of our members are dead, in prisons, awaiting death. Tell the
world, after the war is over, that not all Jews surrendered. Tell them
about Fighting Pioneer." She stopped. Her face was hard, the dark
eyes flashed angry sparks. I shall never forget that face.

Pelagia broke the silence. "I thank you for the story. I'll keep it
with me and never forget it."

"I, too," Helena said and crossed herself.

"So will I," I said.

Then she began to read the story of a hopeless life in a closed
ghetto. About actions and privations. About the resistance of the young.

I felt comforted. There were young Jewish fighters who were resist-
ing the Nazis! I shook Tosia's hand long and warmly. That was all I
could do.

Several days later Tosia, Emma, and several young girls from other cells were taken away. We could see them being escorted by SS guards as far as the Monastery gate.

Next, Christina, Laura, Zofia, and many others were sent to the concentration camp.

Soon after that, my "holiday" was interrupted.

10

At the end of January I was called to an investigation in the late after-noon. Why this time of day? I asked myself on the way to Betz.

He was friendly and almost familiar. "I have some plans for us," he announced.

"Do you mean for yourself and me?"

"Yes, my dear." Betz melted into a smile. "We are going to visit some of those fancy places you mentioned, here in Krakow. While enjoying ourselves, we might meet some of your former—shall we say acquaintances."

A faint hope awoke in me. Maybe there would be a chance to escape.

"Do you have any clothes to change into?" Betz asked.

"None."

"Well, I'll take care of that. What do you need? Let's see, a fur coat, a shawl, a dress, shoes. Or do you prefer boots?"

"Makes no difference," I replied, feeling uneasy.

We went to a nightclub, the Roma.

"I'd like to ask you something," I began.

"Then do so."

"Doesn't your conscience worry you, Betz?"

"No, why?" His surprise was quite sincere.

"Aren't you sorry for Wanda?" I asked.

"To be truthful, I am," he replied. "Such a nice young girl and mixed up in such a mess."

"But you found her guilty enough to execute her."

"Who told you such nonsense?" Betz's surprise was genuine.

"There was a rumor in the prison," I said.

"Nonsense, I can tell you where she is. She was only sent to a concentration camp, at my suggestion, for an indefinite period."

"Can I believe you?"

"Yes, on my honor." Betz gulped down another glass of brandy. "But why do you care about Wanda?"

"I care about myself."

"About yourself?" He was puzzled.

"If Wanda was only a little member of a local resistance group, as you told me, and she was sent to a concentration camp, then what will happen to me when you decide the affair is closed?"

"There is no comparison between Wanda and you, Maria. Wanda's boyfriend got her involved in something bigger than she. But we consider you an important personality of the Russian intelligence in Poland. Can't you see the difference?"

"I was working with the local organization."

"You never mentioned that before, Maria." Betz became interested. "To prove it, tell me whom you know in the local organization. And where you met them."

"Well, Red Cross Street in Warsaw. Does that mean anything to you?"

"Of course, now I begin to understand where you belong, at least at the local level. But give me names."

"I'll tell you one name."

"Good."

"I used to work with Konrad."

"I'm very glad you're telling me all this."

"I'll be glad to see you promoted." Betz seldom understood sarcasm, and this time was no exception, since he looked pleased. He said, "You once mentioned a friend of yours, Anna, an agent working in a police casino in Lvov. We have decided to take you there for a little trip. Maybe we'll be luckier there than here in Krakow."

He walked me from the car to the prison gate. He stopped and looked at me intently. "Maria, you are giving me real hopes. You won't deceive me anymore? You promise?" He asked me in a strange, soft way and pressed my hands.

"I promise," I whispered.

Betz believed me, or at least seemed to. "I admire you so much, Maria," he said and tried to pat my shoulder, but I couldn't control myself and jerked away.

"I'll do everything—help you, protect you, only don't deceive me, remember." His voice sounded at once reassuring and menacing.

My companions on the trip to Lvov were Betz and Franz. We occupied three places in the compartment of a train "reserved for Germans."

A trip of about two hundred miles lay ahead of us. I looked out the window. The Polish landscape was familiar. Big flat spaces covered with snow. Villages and little towns. Everything looked grayish, frozen, asleep.

It was after midnight when we arrived in Lvov. The Gestapo prison was a depressing-looking gray building with a big yard in the back. We entered the prison guardroom.

Betz insisted on a clean place for me, and decent treatment. Then he left, saying he would be back next morning.

The cell was small but clean and white. There was a barred window, a bed, a water closet, and a sink. Quite luxurious.

I lay awake a long time, dreaming of running away. Going to the house surrounded by those tall pine trees. Meeting my friends Ivan and Stephan. And maybe Peter. Where might they be? Somewhere in the woods? Memories and longing assailed me.

In my dreams, I climbed stairs, jumped through fences and walls. But when I thought I was free there was Betz's grinning face. From that night on, this dream, with variations, recurred.

Betz and Franz were waiting in the guardroom the next morning, both clean-shaven, well dressed, and in good spirits.

The first place we went to was a *Schutzpolizei* casino.

"I am here about a very serious espionage case," Betz whispered into the officer's ear.

"What can I do for you?"

"I want to see all the women working here. Call them in for a talking-to."

"But what should I tell them?"

"Just use a little initiative, lieutenant. For example, you can talk to them about venereal disease."

"That's a good idea, but the women don't understand much German."

"Don't you have a translator?"

"They're all busy right now. Last night we had a big action. There is plenty of work."

"Well, Maria will help us."

"Does she speak Polish and Ukrainian?"

"Of course."

A dozen young women filled the office. The officer began an idiotic lecture about venereal disease. The women listened shyly. When he stopped, one girl asked, "What was that? I didn't understand."

"Neither did I—or I," other voices chimed in. "Maria, please," Betz turned to me. He watched us as I repeated the instruction on venereal disease. The women did not change their expressions. They listened indifferently.

"Thank you," the officer said, and the women walked out.

"Then, according to your description, the mysterious Anna is not here," Betz said.

"No," I said, and we left.

Betz seemed worried and finally said, "I think you are bluffing again."

"Don't get discouraged. Do you expect to find the mysterious Anna the first place we try? After all, it was a long time ago."

"Well, we'll try some other places."

Almost the same scene occurred in the police and Gestapo casinos. I was bored and annoyed and glad to get back to the cell. There I knew I was locked in and safe, more or less. In the street, with the Gestapo men, it was neither freedom nor prison.

The next day we returned to Krakow. It was clear Betz's patience was wearing thin and his hopes were dwindling. The trip was long and monotonous for both of us. I was happy when Krakow finally came into sight.

Days crawled by. I had no possibility of knowing what the Gestapo had decided about me. They gave no sign. The most terrible thing is to live without the knowledge of what is to happen to you. Anything is better—a trial, a court-martial, or at least a date.

In the middle of February a guard called my name. In the guard-room Major von Korab was waiting.

"Can we have a separate room for a private talk?" the major asked.

"Certainly, sir." The sergeant major led the way to a room, bare except for a table and chairs. The window was barred.

"Not too luxurious," the major smiled, "but you could have a better-furnished room."

"I don't know what you mean, von Korab," I replied.

"Did it ever occur to you that you needn't waste your life in prison? The solution is in your own hands."

I concentrated on listening and being prudent, like a dog hearing a suspicious noise.

"Don't you see, Maria, that you could very easily, let's say, improve your accommodation in the prison. I mean—better food, a separate room, books and newspapers, visitors . . ."

"What are you getting at, von Korab?"

"I mean that we admire you and your knowledge. But most of all your courage, Maria."

"So what do you want?"

"Maria, don't get excited." Von Korab's voice became warmer and his smile sweeter. "Instead of wasting your time in the cell you could work with us. Not much in the beginning. For example, if you could help us find out how the black-eyed Christina, well known to you, maintains her connections with her family, who smuggles her letters out, and how she gets her replies. It is not too much to ask, is it, Maria?"

"Stop talking nonsense, major. Aren't you ashamed of yourself? You, a man, an officer, proposing to a woman prisoner such a low deed. And did you really think you'd succeed?"

"Be reasonable. I only want to give you a chance. You know what you'll face otherwise."

"You mean a firing squad? The gallows? I knew what I was facing when I went abroad. I won't collaborate."

"But look, Maria, I never proposed to you to betray your own colleagues. But those Poles, what do they mean to you? You know as well as I do how much they hate the Soviets. What are they to you? Another capitalist bunch." Von Korab didn't lose his smile.

"Don't you have any dignity, major?"

"Well, Maria, after all, that's your own business. If you prefer to stay in prison and take the consequences—it's up to you. Let's talk about something else, Maria. You mentioned to Betz that you contacted the famous house on Red Cross Street in Warsaw and that you knew Konrad. Is that true?"

"Yes."

"Tell me something more about your work with the people from Red Cross Street."

"There is nothing to tell. Look, don't make yourself ridiculous asking me about last year's stories. You most likely know more than I do."

"But they didn't stop working? Did they?"

"Some of them did. Because they are dead."

"How do you know? Who is dead?"

"I read some obituaries in the underground newspaper."

"Sometimes I do not know what to think of you, Maria. One day it seems to me that you know a lot. Another day—I would swear you don't know anything. But you're a real Bolshevik snake. Oh, yes, a real snake."

He did not know how close to the truth he was. For answer I smiled insolently. "That's just what I wanted. That you should never know who I am and what I am and why. You're not even sure you know who I am. Isn't that true?"

"Yes, it is true," the major suddenly admitted, "but," and he stopped, "it is not very good for you."

"That's none of your business. Now that I am in a foreign country and in an enemy prison, I am my own boss."

"I am sorry not to have been successful with you. As long as we can part with a smile, it isn't too bad, Maria," the major said and stretched out his hand to me.

I did not take it.

"Won't you shake hands with me, Maria?" He sounded a little offended.

"No."

"Well, it's up to you. I hope to see you again soon. Maria, you have a lot of character."

We parted. I did not know what the outcome would be, but I wasn't worried or sorry. And I realized that in some strange way I no longer cared about anything. Had I reached the border of indifference?

Rosa opened the door.

"Danuta Skowronska," she called, "take your kit and come with me."

I put together my belongings.

Rosa closed the door after I had said good-bye to my cell mates.

"Where are you taking me?"

"The chief guard from Monte will tell you. I don't know," she answered.

He was standing there outside the office. "Is this the bird?" he asked.

"Yes," Rosa answered.

"Come with me. My building is better."

They handed him some papers and we walked toward the gate. I looked back, but it was too dark and I couldn't see anything but the outline of the Monastery where I had spent four months.

The guard brought me to the office of the main Monte building.

"Here she is, Karl."

Karl looked me up and down. "So this is the dangerous Russian spy? The girl with the sixteen passports?"

"Sixteen passports? What's that?" I asked, startled.

"You should know, Miss Maria. Anyway, that's what they say. But I want peace here in my building."

"I'm a very good prisoner."

"Yes, we know, we know. But you'd better behave yourself here."

My cell was number sixty-six—a single one. The window looked out on a part of the yard next to the police building. I could reach the window by standing on the table near the wall.

The cell contained the usual equipment. It was cold and unpleasant.

"Any blankets?" I asked the guard.

"Of course. I'll send some, and if you're cold send for me."

I turned away. Here I'm going to be alone, I thought, exposed to the insolence of the guards.

"Don't worry, Karl, I don't go near Germans."

Soon he returned with some blankets.

"Tell me, why am I here? On the way to a concentration camp—or for a court-martial?"

"No, no, Pomorska just ordered you to be isolated, that's all. Have you been nasty with them?"

"I don't think so."

"Don't worry. Here among so many men you'll have it much better. Good night."

On a painted brown tile were scratched the words, "Tell me why people are worse than beasts." It was signed Tosia. It recalled her to me.

I don't remember how I fell asleep, but I was awakened again and again by bedbugs.

In this way I began my life as a prisoner in isolation. At first I did not mind being alone, but after a while the days became unbearably long and the nights brought no relief. Occasionally the guards took me out in the yard for an hour. But nobody would talk to me. The guards must have been warned, and the policemen in the yard kept away from all prisoners. Slowly I got used to the regime of Monte and the prison guards.

Evald Juergen, short, ashen faced, with deep shadows under his eyes, walked a little crookedly. When he couldn't get drugs he went berserk, beating prisoners. Known as an executioner and torturer.

Yemelsky, short, monkeylike, a *Volksdeutscher* from Silesia. Always drunk. Mistreating prisoners.

Sopker, a big man with bovine eyes, vulgar and noisy.

Gebhard, a quiet, smiling, middle-aged fellow, more indifferent than friendly.

And last of all the Austrian Franz, the best of them. Calm, serious, never raising his voice.

Naturally, as an old experienced prisoner, I had a pencil and a couple of nails, cigarettes, tobacco, and paper, and even a homemade lighter composed of a shoe polish can filled with a burnt rag, a nail, and a piece of glass. By scratching the nail on the glass, sparks would catch on the burnt rag and it was possible to light a cigarette. And I drew a calendar on the wall.

The days went by slowly. Winter was still reluctant to turn into spring. The nights were bitter cold. Several times there were air-raid alarms, but I never had the luck to hear Allied bombs.

After a time I was able to get some magazines—love and detective stories—and even newspapers from the more docile guards.

From my window I could see a section of the yard, the outer wall, and heaped-up coal. One morning I noticed several bundles lying between the wall and the coal. Somehow I did not like the look of them. A little later I saw an ambulance near the coal. The mystery was solved.

These were dead bodies. Two prisoners carried them into the ambulance. I counted them—there were five.

Every morning from then on, the first thing I did was to look at that spot near the wall. Then I lost count.

The most miserable prisoners were the Jewish men in the cellar. I saw them while walking in the yard one day. I was attracted by a whisper through a barred window level with the ground.

Inside I could see a small, dark, crowded cellar that gave off a sickening smell. It held about twenty-five unshaven and ragged men. There was a kind of table and on it—I hardly believed my eyes—medium-sized vessels the shape of urinals. I stopped and asked the man who had whispered to me who they were. He laughed bitterly. "We are Jews," he said. "They say we are the lowest form of life."

"Not true," I answered, looking toward the approaching guard, *"they* are," and I walked away.

I imagined my father being treated like this. I could not bear the thought, and for the first time since my arrest my eyes filled with tears.

On the way to the cell I stopped to talk to Franz in the guardroom. A fresh newspaper lay on the desk. The headlines screamed "Stalingrad," "desperate," "heroic defense."

"What's happening at Stalingrad?" I asked Franz.

"Nothing of importance."

"Don't put me off. Just tell me the truth or don't say anything."

"Our armies are encircled. But the important thing is that the Führer gave an order to fight until the last drop of blood, and we'll make it."

"Are you a Nazi, Franz?"

"Naturally, for over ten years."

"But you are Austrian?"

"So what? We believe in sharing one country with our German brothers."

"You disappoint me, Franz."

"Why, Maria?"

"Because you seem to be decent and not cruel. That's rare here."

"Perhaps that's because I have had a taste of prison. There I learned what it means to be a political prisoner. That is why I never raise my voice or my arm. I'm against communism, too, but I wouldn't beat or mistreat you."

"But you would mistreat a Pole or a Jew?"

"I might, just because I don't like them. But I do like you."

"You are stupid. What kind of nonsense is that?"

"Don't get mad, Maria. Don't you see I'm a little drunk today? I want to forget our disgrace at Stalingrad. But I can't."

Betz turned up, escorted by Yemelsky.

"Hello, Maria, how are you?" He was all smiles.

"Very well."

"I thought you might be a little bored over here, without company."

"I am not alone. The spirit of Lenin is with me. And prisoners all around. And giant-size, first-rate bedbugs that I'd be glad to share with you."

"I am glad to see you full of good humor, as usual."

"Well, what brings you here?"

Betz had a package of books.

"Better look at these. I brought you the best National Socialist literature. The essentials of our ideology. The Führer's *Mein Kampf,* our bible. *The Myth of the Twentieth Century* by Alfred Rosenberg, and also his *The Struggle for Power.* And here's a beautiful edition of *Song of the Nibelungs.* It will help you to understand the psychology of the new German generation. How do you like it? Wasn't it nice of me to think of you?"

"Well, I hope my head won't blow off from all these Nazi ideas. So long as I have nothing else to do I'll read them all."

"If you could absorb the Marxist theories without that happening, then there is nothing to worry about."

"Is that all that brought you to my cell, or were you curious to see how a prisoner lives?"

"This place is not new to me. By the way, I might ask if you have anything to tell me. Maybe you have remembered something or changed your mind? Or maybe . . . you regret your refusal to the major."

"It's no use."

"All right, Maria, it's up to you, but let me know if you have something to tell me."

"You'll wait a long time."

"Makes no difference. I won't be in charge of your affair much longer. I am almost finished with it. Good-bye."

The news about the Russian victory in Stalingrad spread through the thick walls and locked doors. Prisoners whispered it while distributing food, in the corridors, in the shower, in the dispensary. We even knew Churchill's words, "It is not even the beginning of the end, but it is perhaps the end of the beginning."

Then followed the news that Rommel's Afrika Korps had been kicked out of North Africa. We were full of hope.

Spring looked into the prison window with a smiling face, with a light wind and golden sunrays, with the smell of flowers and of freedom. We felt it through the barred windows and the gray walls.

One April night the lights went off at 9:00 P.M. as usual, but I measured the cell back and forth until I finally was so tired I fell asleep in my clothes.

Suddenly the sound of the key in the lock woke me. The light went on and I jumped up. The door opened and Yemelsky appeared in the doorway. Behind him in the dark corridor I could see the shadow of a civilian.

"Get dressed, quick," Yemelsky yelled.

"Why?"

"Shut your mouth and get ready. They want you, the hell knows why."

I washed my face, combed my hair, straightened my clothes.

"What time is it?" I asked.

"Late enough, almost midnight. Ready? Let's go."

Near the doorway stood the little civilian, whom I knew from the Gestapo.

"Just a minute," he said. "Show me your hands."

When I did, there was a click of metal and my hands were caught in two steel bracelets connected by a chain. "Isn't it nicer this way, girl?" he grinned.

"Go to the devil, you miserable coward," I replied. To my surprise, they both laughed.

I walked between them through the long corridor, into the yard, to a small car parked in the shadow of the outer wall. I could see the driver and another man next to him. The Gestapo man opened the door and almost pushed me inside. Then he whipped out an automatic pistol, charged the chamber, and sat down next to me, the pistol still in his hand.

"Not one word or I'll shoot," he said, first in German, then in Polish.

"Who would want to talk to you?" I said.

The man next to the driver turned around and I could hear the chains on his wrists clinking.

The driver rode all around the southern part of the city. Then, leaving the outskirts, he took the western road, drove for about twenty-five minutes, and turned again. We might have been riding around for more than an hour. Then we were on the main road again, and to my surprise we re-entered the city through another suburb. Where were we going? To be executed? Was this my last night? And the man—who was he? Were we connected in some way?

The car sped along in the darkness, crossed the entire city, only to stop in front of the Gestapo building.

The Gestapo man said as he opened the door, "Come on, forward, quick," and he was jumping around us.

"How do you like this little monkey?" I said in Polish.

The man with the manacled hands smiled broadly, although his eyes remained cautious. He did not reply.

We walked upstairs and stopped in front of a row of chairs against the wall. Here the Gestapo man locked my arm to a chair and did the same to the man, at the other end of the corridor. Then he left us.

It was quiet and I could not bear the silence. I felt like having some fun. I was relaxed after the car trip and I could smile about my fears of driving "into the unknown." The situation seemed so funny to me that I burst into laughter and then decided to sing.

The door in front of me opened and Commissar Lux looked out. "Is that you disturbing me at night work, Maria?" he smiled.

"Sorry, I didn't know."

"I will see you after a while," and he closed the door.

More time passed. At last the Gestapo man returned, released my arm, and pointed to a door.

As I entered I was blinded by the strong light. In the middle of the room stood a tall, handsome SS major in a fancy green field uniform, his chest full of medals and an icy look in his blue eyes. Behind him sat three civilians.

The officer looked me up and down several times, then a spark of interest appeared in his cold eyes. "Good evening, Maria," he said.

"Good midnight," I answered.

"Well, have a seat."

I sat down near a little typewriter table. The officer walked back and forth, then suddenly stopped in front of me and bent down a little.

"Tell me, Maria, how do you feel in prison?"

"Like on a furlough to hell."

"Is it that bad?" His voice softened.

"Are you sure you can distinguish between good and bad?"

"What do you mean?" He raised his brows.

"I have found that Nazis don't know the difference between good and evil."

"You're a philosopher," he smiled.

"No, only a careful observer."

"How do you feel in prison, anyway?" he repeated.

"I don't pay much attention. I don't care how I spend my time. I care only about the future."

"And what do you expect from the future?"

"With a little imagination you could answer that yourself."

"I can imagine that you don't like it—being limited in freedom, without activity, without adventures, without love." He kept his eyes on me.

"You are very clever, SS man, but you don't happen to understand a foreign agent's psychology."

The officer smiled, offered me a cigarette, put one in his own mouth, and used the lighter.

"You are wrong, Maria. I do understand foreign agents, if you prefer that expression to the word spy." He smiled. "Anyway, I was just passing by here and accidentally got to see you."

"So?" I asked.

"So, I heard about you and read this thick file, and I have an idea it is the most shameless pile of swindle I have ever seen in my life."

"But it is a true confession," I insisted, while I felt cold sweat breaking out on my forehead.

"Is it?" he screamed suddenly in a shrill voice. "I don't believe it! They've just been too soft with you, that's all."

I stood up and came closer to him. "Too soft? Then listen, hero, you can try. Beat me, torture me, and see if you'll get anything out of me."

"Why get excited?" He quickly quieted down. "I'll tell you something. If you insist the story is true, I could parachute you back into the Russian lines, together with your confession."

"Are you drunk, crazy, or an ass?" I asked.

To my surprise the officer burst into loud laughter. The three civilians joined him.

"Naturally, I'm joking," he said.

"But what is it you want?" I asked, annoyed.

"I want only one thing from you, Maria. You are young, attractive, intelligent, courageous. Why should you spend your best years in prison?"

"Because I have been arrested by my enemies."

"Oh, no, forget it. I mean you could be set free on conditions. But—" he hesitated.

"But what? You don't know how to present your proposal? Well, go on, go on, SS man," I urged.

"Look, Maria." He sat on the table in front of me. "Your confession is interesting, thrilling, sensational, but you have never given us anything we could consider valuable information. I mean . . ." he coughed, "we have not been able to find anybody or anything through your information. We cannot trust you. I mean," he coughed again, "about setting you free."

I listened, my interest aroused. It sounded unbelievable, but I waited and did not interrupt him.

"But if you would name one of the most important and two of the lesser members of your spy ring, we would have reason to liberate you and give you an intelligent, interesting job suited to a wonderful girl like you."

"You could indeed liberate me?" I asked seriously.

"Naturally, if you would give us what we want."

"In whose name would you confirm it?" I was deadly serious.

"In the name of *Reichsführer* Himmler." He was very serious, too.

"Do you have it on paper or are you just improvising?"

"Naturally, if we get that far I'll give you a printed and signed guarantee."

"So what do I get? What job? What conditions?"

"I'll give you a general idea. In the beginning you'll have to be under discreet observation. You'll work with us at your choice. I mean, against the Poles, the English, or anybody you wish to. We will not ask you to work against your own people. Well, there'd be good pay, a good apartment, good clothes, plenty of men all around. . . Well, isn't that fair enough?"

"Yes, it is fair enough for some miserable riffraff, but get it through your thick German head that I wouldn't collaborate with the enemy for anything in the world. Me collaborating with the Nazi bunch!" And I laughed loud and long.

The officer looked amazed. The three civilians sat with frozen faces.

"Goddamn," he yelled, "who do you think you are?"

"I am a Russian."

"And you dare talk like that?"

"I do. And, by the way, I am completely fed up with the Gestapo. I acted against the German army and I want to be brought before a court-martial. I am sick and tired of the Gestapo imbeciles. Give me a court-martial!"

"Do you realize what you are asking for?" the officer said, surprised.

"Certainly, but I prefer it to the Gestapo."

"Well, you Russian snake, so you identify yourself with the rotten international bunch, the Communists, the Jewish Uncle Churchill, and the Jew Roosevelt. That's what you are going to die for!"

"A crazy corporal, murder, and oppression, that's what you are dying for."

The German jumped up and slapped my face hard. I was so angry I didn't feel the pain.

"You miserable hero, hitting a woman. Why aren't you at the front? Saving Stalingrad?"

"So you won't change your mind?" the officer tried again.

"I am not crazy yet. And especially after Stalingrad, *you* should change *your* mind."

"Shut up about Stalingrad!" the German yelled.

"Why should I? This is just the beginning. The Red Army is advancing all the time and will come to the walls of Krakow."

"Then we'll evacuate you to Germany."

"But they'll come to Germany, too."

"Then we'll take you with us and if necessary drown you in the Atlantic."

I was enjoying the situation. "I like to hear you say that, but I hope you'll drown there without my company."

"Shut up!" the officer yelled again.

"You could be more gentlemanly."

"Well," the German controlled himself, "I have to make it clear that you are rejecting my proposal. I cannot understand it. You prefer a court-martial to getting out of prison and starting a new life?"

"At the price of becoming a Nazi collaborator? Why don't you understand? Let's put it another way. If you had been sent to Russia on a secret mission, and you were caught by the Russian counter-intelligence, and you could set yourself free by betraying your comrades and working against your own country or Hitler's allies, what would you call it?"

"That would be a vicious, despicable betrayal."

"So you are proposing that I commit that basest betrayal of my country!"

"But I would be betraying the Führer and Germany, while with you it is only that rotten bunch."

"You, a Nazi, have no right to talk about rotten bunches, because yours is the most rotten of all. And I love my country and my people, and all our allies and all the oppressed nations of the world."

The German yelled again, "So, you'll rot to death in the damned prison, for all the oppressed people in the world."

"I'll die with honor, don't worry, but you'll be mounted on the gallows, together with the whole rotten bunch, after you get knocked out."

I was interrupted by another blow on my face.

"You swine!" I lost my control. "Wait, the day will come when you'll dance with Hitler in the air—"

"Shut up, shut up!" the officer screamed. "We have means of breaking you down. We'll show you."

"Don't be an idiot," I said, suddenly quiet. "You can kill me but I won't be a traitor."

He understood it this time and calmed down. "Well, let's get rid of you. I can find a better way to spend this night than bothering with a Russian snake."

The officer lifted the telephone. The three men remained in their frozen silence.

"So goddamned stubborn and tough," the officer said aimlessly.

As I walked out he looked at me with a strange expression, and the shadow of a smile passed over the handsome face. "Think it over in the cell and let me know. I won't be here too long."

"Never," I said and walked out.

While I waited for the other prisoner, Commissar Lux came toward me. "You made a terrific impression on the *Hauptsturmführer*," he said.

"And he made a terrific mistake," I said.

"It's time you stopped playing with us," he suggested.

"It's time you delivered me to the court-martial of the Wehrmacht."

"Oh, Maria, Maria." He seemed stunned. "There you'll get a bullet."

"What else will I get from you?"

"I don't know. We'll have to submit your whole affair to Berlin and ask for a decision. Betz is completely disappointed working with you."

"Send him to the Eastern Front for a while. Maybe he'll learn something about the Russians."

"That's a good idea, damn it!" Lux laughed and walked away.

There were pale stripes in the east when the small car brought us back to the prison.

The other prisoner was hardly able to walk, and my face was swollen and sore. We exchanged a farewell look, as if saying, "It could as well have been our last night. But we'll not surrender."

My cell was cool and immediately I fell into a dreamless sleep.

Every time I climbed to my cell window I could see the pile of coal. One Sunday morning I heard loud voices in the yard, yelling, screaming, whistling, all in one. I climbed to my observation post and saw a crowd of people.

I could distinguish white bands on the arms of some, yellow patches on others. Must be Jews, I thought, and knew that something was about to happen.

I had heard that a Jewish prisoner had escaped a few days before on the way to work in the city. In the evening he had been caught and brought to the prison, beaten and bloody. The Nazis had put him back in the cell for the Jews and notified his cell mates that they must eliminate him before the next morning or else all of them would be executed. In the morning the man was dead. He had strangled himself with a rag while one of his companions pressed a brush over his mouth and nose. The man had died for the sake of the others.

The noise in the yard increased: more screaming and exclamations of pain. I heard the blows. The crowd began to run amid whistles and yelling. The men were coming closer and closer to the pile of coal. "Lie down! On the ground!" the drunken voice of Yemelsky ordered. The men lay down on the stones of the prison yard.

Then Evald Juergens and Yemelsky jumped on them, using sticks and kicking them with their boots.

Juergens struck a white-haired head with his nailed boot. Blood stained the hair.

Yemelsky grabbed another man by his collar and hit his face on the stones again and again. The man screamed and tried to get away, but Sopker knocked him down with his heavy stick. "Damned swine, tried to get away," Sopker laughed. He took a long sip from a bottle, then passed it to Yemelsky, who didn't stop till he had emptied it. Then he broke it on a young boy's head.

Now the men were made to crawl over the coal, under a hail of kicks and blows. Some of them couldn't go on. They lay helplessly on the ground. But Yemelsky was there to lift them up. One of them did not move. Yemelsky grabbed his pistol. A shot, another shot, and another, and another.

The "entertainment" went on for several hours. When it got dark the men had to pick up their dead and put them between the coal and the wall. There was a row of them, nine altogether.

They carried the wounded to the cellar. Every one of them was injured. The drunken laughter of the Nazis followed the sorrowful procession. Now they would return to their cellar, eat from the pots, or maybe get no food at all.

A prisoner has plenty of time. No jobs. No responsibilities. Nothing to prepare for a definite hour. I began to study Betz's books. I wanted to know the gospel of nazism.

Although I did not know how long I was going to live, it seemed important to become familiar with the enemy's ideology. "If you want to win—study your enemy," the proverb says.

I started with *Mein Kampf*. I was surprised by Hitler's bombast. After having my fill of that, I turned to the great theoretician, Alfred Rosenberg. Poor Waltz Betz! Did he really believe that nazism printed so clearly in black letters on white paper could convince a human being?

The two neighbors on my right were very young soldiers. Hans-Jurgen, a lean, blond boy from western Germany. Gustav, black haired, darkskinned, half-German, half-Hungarian. They had both deserted during the Rostov battle, were caught, and court-martialed. The sentence was the customary seven years. But they knew the war was not over for them. Soon they would be sent back to the front, perhaps in a punishment battalion.

"If so we'll run away."

We talked freely through the window. They were like others of their age. They dreamed of studying and learning a good trade. They hated war and did not care for the Nazi plan of conquering the world.

"Let the queer corporal do it himself," Hans-Jurgen answered when I asked him why he had deserted his combat unit.

One day Hans-Jurgen asked me to make him a little bag for his food. I sewed it for him out of cloth he gave me, and inside I embroidered in German, "The world must become better. Millions do not suffer in vain."

When he got the present, he called through the window, "Maria, believe me, when I get back to the front I'll surrender to the first Russian. Not because I am a coward, but I don't want to die for Hitler. The world must become better and we Germans have to help, too."

His friend, a cowboy from the Hungarian plains, said to me one day, "The Germans can find out things about you that you never knew. They found out one of my grandfathers had married a German girl. That was enough to make me a *Volksdeutscher* and land me in the SS division. I don't think it's even true, because there is more gypsy blood in our veins than any other. I am as much German as you are Chinese!"

The two boys smuggled into my cell cigarettes, chocolate, fruit, and pieces of sausage and cake from the packages their mothers sent them. One early morning the guard opened my door. Behind him stood Hans-Jurgens and Gustav. They had come to bid me good-bye, as they were leaving the prison and had persuaded the guard to let them see me.

"Good luck, Maria, we hope you get home to your country safely," Hans-Jurgen said.

"Good-bye, Maria, don't forget us. All the best to you," said Gustav.

"Good-bye, dear boys, be careful and don't be foolish. You have to get back home, remember!"

Betz put some paper into the typewriter and began typing. When he had finished, he handed it to me. It read, "I, Maria Arsenyeva, declare herewith that I have nothing to add to my former investigations, that I identify myself with the international plutocratic-Communist-Jewish-American plot of criminals and that I am ready to accept the verdict of the Security Department of the German Empire."

There was a space left for my signature.

"Will you sign?"

"Are you serious? Do you expect me to sign such nonsense?"

"Will you or won't you?"

"All right, I'll sign it." I reached for a pen and wrote in beautiful letters across the page, "DEATH TO FASCISM AND FREEDOM TO THE NATIONS"—the famous slogan of the Yugoslav resistance.

Betz couldn't read Russian, though he could have seen it wasn't a signature if he had used his brain for a second. "You know, Maria," he said after filing the paper, "you disappoint me bitterly. I hoped to make a success of your case and to create a brilliant career for you. I tried to convert you. You pushed away the outstretched hand of Major von Korab. You do not understand the gospel of nazism. You remain a stubborn, thickheaded Bolshevik, ready to die for that rotten bunch."

"If you knew how you annoy me, Walter," I said. "You're wasting your time, just as you've been doing ever since we first met."

Betz wanted to say something, but changed his mind and called for an escort. I walked out without saying another word. He was looking out the window, his back to me. I slammed the door like a nasty little girl doing something on purpose.

On the way back I saw white, pink, and purple lilacs and blooming acacias, the green trees and the blue sky. But the delights of May were not for me that year.

I was beginning to get used to living alone, difficult as that was. I found many things to occupy my time. I could not complain of lack of writing materials, magazines, books. I amused myself composing crossword puzzles, writing geographical names, trying to compile a dictionary and an encyclopedia. I made designs and carvings on the walls, on the door and the window frame. I learned to weave purses and shopping bags out of colored cord. I made sandals from paper cord, as my shoes were in a deplorable condition. I repeated poems, songs, musical compositions by heart. I made translations from and into all the languages I knew. I improved my knowledge of German, including slang and a rich vocabulary of curses.

It was a strange way to live, in a cell, isolated from all normal life, without knowing how long the situation would last nor how it would end. There was no use trying to imagine what the future would bring. You began to live within the limits given to you. You no longer shivered at every turn of the key in the lock. You just ate, slept, thought, washed, dreamed, listened, observed.

One afternoon while walking in the yard I met the handsome, sympathetic policeman I had talked to before. He always greeted me with a friendly smile and gave me cigarettes, magazines, other little gifts. This time he looked around carefully, then whispered, "You are Danuta Skowronska?"

"Yes," I answered, surprised.

"I have a message for you," he said, coming closer. "They thank you very much for being as you are, but that is all they can do right now. Do you understand?"

"Who sent you to me?" I asked carefully, because it might have been a trap.

"Your friends," he said. "And you do not need to send any message. They know plenty about you. Probably more than you know yourself."

"Well, thank you, friend."

"Don't mention it. By the way, I'm leaving. I won't come here anymore."

"I'll miss you."

"And be careful, girl. Gather your strength. You'll probably need plenty of it in the future."

"Good luck to you," I said. "I'll never forget you, even though I don't know who you are."

"What difference does that make? I am a friend. Isn't that enough?"

"For me it is."

Across from my cell was another isolated prisoner, a young SS officer imprisoned for contracting venereal disease. (In the SS, this was considered tantamount to desertion.) He began talking to me at every opportunity. He knew I was a Russian girl, but this fact seemed rather to attract him. He was tall, handsome, with a scar across his face, and he introduced himself as Sepp. He could sing well and would serenade me with love songs all evening, until the other prisoners shouted at him to stop. Then he began writing me love letters. I found him a nuisance.

One day when Sepp, together with the German deserters, was taking a constitutional in the yard, I heard him under my window. "Maria, Maria, come up to the window."

I didn't want to, but after a while I climbed up and told him to leave me in peace. At that moment Yemelsky came in.

"That's what you're doing, fooling around with German soldiers. I'll show you," he shouted.

"I'm not fooling around, you imbecile," I shouted back. "I just have to drive them away like hungry dogs. That's a fact."

Soon he returned with the chief of guards. "It's impossible to keep her here," Yemelsky said. "She drives the men crazy." "Well, we'll lock her upstairs. Let's check her belongings." And I had to see all my treasures being taken away, the pencil, paper, magazines, cigarettes, matches, and homemade lighter. They left only my clothes and toilet articles, which I wrapped in a blanket.

I was taken three flights up and given Cell 177. It was even smaller than Cell 66 and had a concrete floor.

The new cell was clean and narrow, with a tile stove near the door, a thin mattress on the floor, no blankets, a small crude chair, and a shuttered window that didn't let in much light. I could see a tiny piece of the summer sky and distant outlines of trees and houses only if I climbed up on the chair.

But why should I be sorry at being transferred to the top floor? The guard had mentioned there were anti-Nazi prisoners all around me. Soon I'd get in touch with them. And no Germans would bother me here. It was perfectly quiet and cool.

Again I found names and dates on the walls, door, and stove. After a while I scratched a calendar on the wall with a rusty nail I had found. I began at June 21, 1943.

There was a sudden knocking on the wall. It came at regular intervals from the direction of Cell 175. I didn't know the code. I tried to knock on the wall with my fist, but the wall was too thick. I took off my shoe and used the heel. An answer came—three short knocks several times. Did it mean, I hear you? I felt less alone—there was someone who wanted to get in touch with me. My neighbor, or perhaps neighbors, understanding that I didn't know the code, stopped signaling.

Soon it was time for supper.

Men prisoners took out my bucket and fetched me water in a jug. I got my ersatz coffee, a piece of bread, and cheap liver sausage.

Then it became perfectly still again. But after a while the corner came to life, with voices, noises, knocking, even shouting and whistling.

The first clear voice was that of a young man. "Father, he shouted, "father, good evening. How are you, dad?"

"I am well. Haven't been bothered all day. Aren't you hungry?"

"No. I still have the package. Shall I send you something to eat?"

"No, no, I have one also. Well, good night, and God bless you."

"Roman, Roman," someone called in a harsh voice.

"I am here. What news, Jurek?"

"No news, the sons of bitches have still not realized the mess they're in. It will take them awhile, probably."

"Hello, boys," a deep voice, accustomed to command, shouted above all the rest. "We have a newcomer in our corner. Better be careful until we know who it is."

All this conversation was carried on in Polish. I wasn't sure whether I should break in. I waited.

"Where is the newcomer?"

"Right here, in 177," one of my neighbors answered.

There was an unintelligible sound of voices behind the doors.

"Hello, hello, who is there in 177?" the commanding voice shouted.

"Me," I yelled as loud as I could through the door. I used the word for *me* that is the same in Polish and Russian.

"A girl, a girl, a woman," several surprised voices cried out.

"Who are you?" The commanding voice took over. "We are dying to know who you are. Introduce yourself, please."

"Yes, yes, we're dying to know."

"I am Maria."

My Russian accent worked immediately.

"You are not Polish, are you? What are you, Russian?"

"Yes, I am Russian."

"What did you do to land here?"

"I feel very much honored to be here. They hate my guts."

"They must have good reasons, Maria."

"And who are you? Are you all Polish?" I asked.

"Yes, except for one foreigner. He is isolated. He must be an Englishman or an American, nobody can talk to him."

Then I heard a hoarse voice, quite foreign, but I could understand that much English. "Lawrence, Lawrence, are you here? Are you here?" he repeated again and again.

"He is calling his friend," I said, and then, in my bad English, "Hello, Englishman, who is your friend?"

"At last someone who speaks my language. He is a big fellow, an Irishman, a redhead. Maybe somebody has seen him?"

To the satisfaction of our whole corner I was able to explain to the Royal Air Force flight lieutenant, an expert at escaping from POW camps, that his friend the Irishman had been seen downstairs only two days ago by one of the new Polish prisoners.

The exchange of information, greetings, blessings ended. It began to get dark. Another day was gone and surely everyone did what I did —struck off another day on the calendar.

When I thought the prisoners had gone to bed, there was a fresh knocking on my wall. I answered. Then a voice shouted, "Maria, take out the second tile in the second row above the floor. It moves."

I tried, and to my great surprise the tile moved. Once I'd removed it, I saw a young face with a moustache. Someone spoke in Polish.

"Good evening, Maria. My name is Jozef."

In this way, through the tile stove, began my friendship with my neighbors. There were three prisoners in Cell 175: Jozef, who had escaped from slave labor in Germany; Richard, a severe, middle-aged man, who never gave the exact reasons for his arrest; Thomas, betrayed and caught while operating an underground wireless. As the Gestapo was fully informed about him, he had nothing to hide.

Thomas told me about the prisoner Roman, who had been isolated for months in the next cell. He was a miner and had organized the resistance in many areas of western Poland. He was chained at the wrists and ankles. He could take only tiny steps and had learned to eat without utensils. The Germans opened his chains just once a day, when he went to the toilet or took a shower. He did not answer the Germans and paid no attention to them whatever they did. They could not break his spirit.

After several days I became familiar with the names, fates, and stories of many men. They asked me to tell them my story. They asked me to sing songs. I did all this with great satisfaction. And I was happy, in the only way a prisoner can be while facing an unknown fate.

I was no longer lonely. I was surrounded by friends and comrades. They sent me gifts from their packages. They asked how I was, if I had slept well, if there was anything they could do for me. The corner lived like one big family.

About the end of July there was a big transfer of prisoners. Round about midnight doors were opened and slammed. We could hear names being called, screams, commands. Then it reached the third floor, but our corner remained untouched.

The next day our Englishman left. He shouted as he followed the guard, "Keep well, boys. We'll knock them out, all together."

Several days later the door opened and a handsome blond *Obersturmführer* entered my cell. "Good day," he greeted me and looked me up and down with an arrogant expression. "Hm, hm," he murmured, "so this is how the famous Maria looks."

"Yes, this is how she looks. But who are you, trying to look like the sovereign of this place?"

The handsome German smiled. "I am the commander here."

"You have replaced the fat homosexual?"

"Yes, his job but not his qualifications," he laughed. "Tell me, Maria, how are you doing?"

"Very fine, king of Montelupich, and you, how do you feel as prison boss?"

"Not bad. Good rest after the Eastern Front."

"Got fed up running back?"

"Don't you think you're a little too fresh?"

"That's one thing you cannot take away from me, to talk the way I like."

"You have guts, Maria."

I did not answer, and he went on, "I have heard a lot about your being a dangerous, experienced spy, a paratrooper with sixteen names, giving a lot of trouble to Pomorska Street. Isn't that too much for a little girl like you?"

"If you like sensations, you should read thrillers. I don't like to talk about myself."

"And what do you like to talk about?"

"Tell me about the Kursk battle, about the war in the Mediterranean area, about the invasion plans of the Allies."

"I hate to talk about war and politics." He assumed a bored look. "Especially with a woman."

"But I am no woman to you. I am a prisoner and an enemy."

"I don't believe you feel hostile when you look at me, and don't play innocent. We know all about spies."

"What you know may be from cheap stories. We do our job because we believe in it."

"Are you serious? Perhaps I have made a mistake. You seem to be quite a girl. Tell me, do you have any complaints?"

"Even if I did, I wouldn't cry before a German. This is a prison, not a sanatorium."

"You have a lot of pride, Maria, I must admit."

"We have something to be proud of."

"What about right now?" he smiled.

"For example, the Kursk battle."

"How do you know about it?"

"These walls aren't thick enough, commander, to keep prisoners perfectly isolated. Have you ever been in prison?" I asked suddenly.

"Hell, no. Why?"

"Because only one who has been a prisoner would make an efficient prison boss for Nazis after the war, if I live that long," I laughed.

"You're a cocky one. I'll come to see you again. I don't remember ever meeting such a tough girl."

"Come on, quick," the rough new guard yelled at me, opening the door of my cell.

"Why? Where?"

"Come when I tell you."

I followed him to the guardroom, where he turned me over to a civilian I had never seen before. "Let's go," he said.

This time we walked to Pomorska Street. He did not say a single word. When we reached the Gestapo building, we went up two flights and stopped before a door numbered 251, with the initials II-B-I. I did not know their meaning. He knocked on the door and let me in.

"A hot Bolshevik greeting." I heard a voice speaking Russian, and when I looked up I saw a lean man in a Gestapo uniform. He had a little reddish moustache and a pair of hard gray eyes that looked me up and down with hatred. I couldn't be mistaken. This was not a German speaking Russian, but a Russian speaking his own language.

"A hot greeting from a thousand guns," I said, "right into this building, and a good one personally for you."

"Trying to play the heroine? I hope that after this meeting with me you'll forget about such things."

I was worried. A Russian in a Gestapo uniform might be worse than any German.

"And who are you? A former prince? Ready to collaborate with the devil himself?"

"What difference does it make to you who I am? The important thing is that I am the investigator and you the prisoner."

The gray eyes glittered cruelly.

"All right," I replied, "but you don't even feel an insult. Like a hog —everybody spits on him and he thinks it's raining."

"I don't take insults from your kind. Let's get down to business. After it's over, you won't feel like insulting anyone."

"You're a disgusting collaborator."

"I hate the Reds so much I would collaborate with hell itself against them."

"Well, now I know who you are," I answered and suddenly became very quiet.

"Sit down and have a cigarette."

I sat down but refused the cigarette.

"Now, listen, Maria, or whatever your name might be, I am going to ask you several questions before we get to the main ones. Were you in Berlin before you were arrested in October last year?"

"No."

"Are you sure?"

"Yes."

"Very strange, very strange. What was your job in Kiev before the war?"

I shrugged my shoulders. "What a lot of nonsense. I have never been in Kiev, so naturally I hadn't a job there."

"Don't try to lie to me. I know a lot more about you than you think."

"I have never lived or worked in Kiev."

"I'll expose your bluff. Tell me the truth before I stop being nice to you."

"I am telling the truth. I have never seen Kiev, except in pictures and on maps," I insisted, and as God was my witness it was true.

"You're lying like a tramp. I'll break you to pieces if you go on like this."

"Be careful, ex-prince, if there was a tramp it must have been one of your kind."

He began punching me in the face.

I protected myself as best I could and abused him.

"A big hero beating a girl."

"I'll show you, I'll show you," he repeated, "but it's still not as bad as the NKVD. I'll show you worse than that." Then he took out a photograph. He thrust it under my nose. "Who is this? Quick! The truth!"

A man's face stared at me from the photograph—round, with a low forehead and little eyes, straight hair and big ears, absolutely unknown to me.

"Never saw him before."

"You're lying." He lifted the telephone. "I'll prove it to you in a minute."

After a while the door opened and the same civilian who had escorted me entered with another man. I recognized him immediately, although his face wasn't as round as in the picture and his hair was cut short. But he had the same big ears, low forehead, and little eyes.

"Come closer, Nikolai Ivanovitch. Do you recognize this girl?" he asked in Russian.

He looked at me nervously.

"Hello, Lisa," he said.

"What? I am not Lisa."

"Oh, Lisa, stop it, let's be reasonable," he insisted.

"But I'm seeing you for the first time in my life. It could be a mistake, but you seem to be a big liar."

"You see, sir," he turned to the Gestapo man, "I told you she would never confess. I'll try my best . . ."

"What are you trying to do? You liar. Where have you met me before?"

"Dear Lisa, don't get mad, but it was in Kiev, before the war. We worked together in the NKVD offices in the foreign agents' department."

"It's a lie. I have worked in many places, but never in Kiev—and never met this despicable individual."

"I have no reason to believe you. Nikolai Ivanovitch has given me valuable information and proved his faithfulness; your whole file is full of impossible lies. And so you'd better confess."

"I have nothing to confess. And get rid of this dirty liar."

"Take care of her," the Gestapo man ordered.

The civilian began punching my head and face and kicking me with his boots.

A beating hurts your body, but even more it hurts your human pride. I was so angry I hardly felt the blows. I poured out on them all the insults I had ever heard in my life.

"Stop," the Gestapo man ordered. "Now, Nikolai Ivanovitch, tell me, where did you see this bogus Maria, or Lisa, later, after the war started?"

"Well," he went on, looking insolently at me, "later, at the beginning of 1942, I met her in Berlin. She looked very elegant, lived with some official from the Hermann Göring airplane factory, and acted as a Soviet spy."

"Where did she work?" the Russian asked.

"I don't know, but I don't think she worked at all. Why should a good-looking girl work?"

"On top of everything else, you try to make a whore of me. You're the worst kind of scum."

"Go on."

And the civilian started beating me again. I could see the indifferent face of the Gestapo man and Nikolai's greasy smile.

"Beat me as long as you like, but I won't say a word. Playing dirty tricks with this filth."

A blow closed my mouth. I spat out two teeth and blood. When he began beating me again I fainted.

I woke up wet from the cold water they had thrown over me. I was lying on the floor. When I opened my eyes, the civilian kicked me, all over my body, with his boots. I felt sharp pains in my back, arms, legs, inside my belly, and then I fainted again.

Later the Gestapo man bent over me several times. I remember vaguely trying to hold my ripped dress together and only answering, "No, no," when he spoke to me.

I woke again, fully conscious and lying on the floor of a car. A civilian was sitting in the backseat. He didn't pay any attention to me, and I felt sick because my head was banging against something hard, but I couldn't say anything. My mouth was bloody and swollen. After all, it was all the same to me where we were going. I just didn't care about anything.

I was dozing when the car stopped. Then somebody got me out of the car. When I almost collapsed, he lifted me in his strong arms. I couldn't see in the darkness who it was. "Franz, come and help me." I heard the voice of the big guard.

I didn't know anything more until I was lying on the mattress in my cell. My whole body ached and my mouth burned. My head was big and heavy, and I could hardly see because of my swollen face. Then I felt someone wiping my face with a cloth and covering me with a blanket.

"A drink," I said in Russian.

"What do you want, Maria?" I heard Franz's voice. "Tell me, I'll get it for you."

"Water," I whispered.

Then I felt the edge of a cup. I was thirsty, but the water burned my mouth even more.

"Hell, hell," I heard Franz's voice. "What did they do to you, the sons of bitches?" and he stroked my hand gently.

Later a man in a white jacket came and bent over me. I recognized the prison doctor. After swallowing some pills, I slept. When I awoke the next morning, there was a bowl of coffee and a portion of bread near me.

It took me about ten days to recover. The doctor was a young Pole, friendly and efficient, although he had only limited supplies and medical equipment. I had lost three teeth, and he asked in a whisper, as he dressed my face, "How come you don't complain?"

"It wouldn't be dignified. And I have seen other women who got—"

"Excuse me," the doctor interrupted, "maybe you know what happened to a girl by the name of Christina?"

"Do you mean Christina Makowska?" I asked.

"Yes."

"We spent a long time in the Monastery together last year and this past winter, until she went on transport to a concentration camp—to Auschwitz. That's all I know."

"I imagined that. Her father is gone, too. A whole family destroyed. But she was a heroine. I saw her after that butchery. It was terrible, insane. Worse than a battlefield in war."

"Do you wonder? They are Nazis, isn't that enough?"

"Oh yes, enough, enough, damned enough. Last week we had a young fellow from the woods. With five bullets in his body. They brought him from the hospital half-alive. After a couple of days, a whole bunch of them came to investigate him. Would you believe what they did? They ripped off the bandages and picked in the wounds with pieces of wire." The doctor's face turned pale and I felt a cold shiver creeping up my back. "But the young man did not say a word."

"And what happened to him?" I asked.

"Now he is lying, almost helpless, between life and death, with severe blood poisoning."

"What about talking so much?" The guard put his head in. "Are you ready, doctor?"

When I had recovered sufficiently to eat solid food, my neighbors did something unbelievable; they persuaded the guards to bring me a piece of homemade whole wheat bread, a slice of bacon, and two apples. There were tears in my eyes when I received this exquisite present, a part of their packages from home.

In another week I forgot my injuries. Only the holes between my teeth reminded me of the Nazi system, especially a root with its sharp point that scratched my tongue until the doctor filed it off.

The news sneaking into prison was wonderfully comforting. The Russians were advancing steadily. Mussolini had been overthrown. The American Flying Fortresses had bombed the Ploesti oil fields in Romania.

This information made all of us more confident in the approaching liberation and the defeat of the Axis. We began to think of the Germans around us as future prisoners, accused and executed. The idea of the reversal of roles excited and sustained us. It was only a matter of time. The prisoners looked into the faces of their guards with insolence, answered them arrogantly, and laughed when the guards tried to beat them.

This attitude unnerved the guards. They became less arrogant and cruel and even looked repentant at times.

We sang anti-Naiz songs, laughing and whistling and driving the guards mad.

Once in a while they would come running in, lashing out and cursing, but the prisoners laughed and cursed back.

One day my door opened and the prison commander stood in the doorway.

"Hello, Maria."

"Hello, Wehmayer."

"You're not polite, Maria. When you use a man's name you should give his rank."

"For me you have no rank."

"Why?"

"What does a man's rank mean in the light of eternity?"

"What are you referring to?"

"A dead man doesn't care about his rank."

"You consider me a dead man?"

"All of you are sons of death," I declared in a prophetic manner. "Oh, but you probably don't know that I can tell the future."

"Indeed?"

I knew a few facts about the prison commander so I decided to use them. "Do you want me to try? Just show me your hand, the left one, please."

I took his hesitantly outstretched hand. I pretended to study it, then dropped it and turned aside.

"What is it? Anything wrong?"

"You are a terrible person, and your fate is even more terrible. Do you want to know?"

"Yes."

"As you wish. You are not very well educated, but are very cruel, a sadist, I would say, and there is plenty of blood on your hands. You have lost somebody, an airman, I think."

"How can you know that?"

"I told you I have a gift," I answered, controlling the laughter that rose in my throat. "Don't be a coward. You are divorced and there is a young woman crazy about you. But you are indifferent to her and other women; you have your own kind of pleasure." I stopped because the handsome face had turned ashen and anger glinted in his eyes. But he didn't say a word.

"Well, no use getting angry. You see, I don't care, because I can see everybody's fate but my own."

"Tell me more, Maria."

"Well, if you wish. Later, I mean in a year or so, you'll be one of a big crowd of beaten men. You will smell a little combat before the end, I mean before the Nazis collapse, and then you'll die."

"What a lot of nonsense. Well, let's hear, how am I going to die?"

"You? Naturally not in a bed surrounded by grandchildren. You'll be hanged on a tree or a post, an electric post." I said this in an indifferent but still prophetic tone.

"A nice future. But I swear to God, if it weren't you, Maria, I would—"

"Would what?" I asked briskly.

"I don't know what, but I would make you sorry."

"I don't care. One Gestapo man has already used Nazi methods on me. Ask him how much success he had. It's true I lost a couple of teeth, but that's nothing."

He got angry. "Every time I come here you steer the talk the way you want it."

"Well, I have learned that from experience with the Gestapo investigators. But tell me, now, why did you come this morning?"

"Just to have a look. I heard you have been . . . in a . . . how shall I say, an unpleasant situation . . ."

"Don't try to play a part, say straight out, 'I heard that you were beaten by the Gestapo and I was curious to see whether they broke you down!' That's nearer the truth, isn't it?"

"You're getting on my nerves." He took out a silver box and offered me a smoke. It was Moeve, the opium-spiked cigarette.

"I don't smoke tobacco with dope."

"Then here are some Memphis."

We stood awhile smoking.

"You must have plenty of time," I said.

"Why?"

"Well, if you have so much time to waste here on me."

"Time is not wasted with you. I would like to meet you, not as a prisoner, but privately. I talked with Walter Betz just an hour ago. And I was glad to hear that he doesn't insist any more on your being isolated here in Monte."

"Wehmayer, it doesn't make any difference to me what Walter Betz does to make you glad."

"Don't be nasty, Maria. I just wanted to explain something to you. I don't like your being here. You drive the men prisoners crazy, you sing anti-German songs, you're insolent to the guards. I am going to send you back to the Monastery."

11

Next morning the guard came to my cell and told me to get my things ready.

"You are going back to the Monastery," he whispered, then looked around to see if anyone had caught him in the act of telling something to a dangerous prisoner.

The Monastery guardroom was full of smoke, as usual, and from behind the smoke screen emerged the familiar faces of Rosa and Sergels.

Rosa looked surprised. "You're back at the Monastery?"

"What did you think—that I was hanged or shot? But who knows who will hang first."

Sergels laughed, "She'll never change, the Russian snake."

Rosa picked up the keys and we walked upstairs. I was to be put in the work cell, she said. It was on the second floor. She let me in and slammed the door behind me. I stood with my bundle near the door, looking into the big room, full of light, with about twenty women staring at me.

"Good morning, comrades," I said in Polish.

A tall, blonde young Polish woman came over and greeted me, introducing herself as Anna. "We have it good here and hope you'll like it. We've heard a great deal about you."

"About me? I'm just another prisoner."

"Well, we'll talk later. Now, I'll introduce you to everyone."

Her fellow prisoners were busy sewing, ironing, knitting, and embroidering.

I was introduced to a handsome middle-aged woman. Her name sounded familiar—of course, of course, it was the name of the father and son at Monte.

"Mrs. Gaszynska, I know about your husband and son."

Her sad face lit up. "My dear Maria, tell me, how are they? What has happened to them?"

"I heard them talking only last night. They are in Monte, on the third floor. They are both all right. They talk to each other every night, though the damned Germans have separated them. They receive parcels every Thursday.

The woman thanked me sincerely and knelt down to pray.

"What work would you like to do?" Anna asked me.

"Nothing, if it's for the Germans."

"Well, we must work at something. Look, here is a large tablecloth that has to be embroidered. It can't be finished before the end of the war, so choose that."

Soon I had a circle of friends: the tall Alicia, the slim Cesia, the plump Paulina. They wanted to verify the many exaggerated stories circulating about me. I satisfied their curiosity and told them story number two of my "big joke."

In the afternoon, the German prisoners walked in the yard and I was shocked when I saw Alicia sitting at the window and exchanging greetings with a tall, handsome German prisoner. I asked Cesia about it, and she explained that the German was Alicia's husband and the father of her child.

"Alicia will probably tell you herself. She is sincere and honest and a true patriot."

One day Alicia took out several pictures and showed them to Cesia and me. "Look, this is my son. The baby is just beginning to walk, and I am in prison. And Siegmund, too. Only Siegmund's father got away," she sighed.

"Is Siegmund a Pole?" I asked. "Then how come he is in a cell with Germans?"

"He is there because he happens to be a German," Alicia answered unhesitatingly. "It may sound strange to you, my being married to a German, but when you hear the whole story you'll understand."

Alicia had lost a brother in the defense of Warsaw in 1939. She then became an active member of the underground and was connected with the channels that smuggled arms into the Jewish ghetto.

Many German factories, working for the war effort, employed Jewish workers, who cost them practically nothing. One of these factories had belonged to Siegmund's father, who was from Brazil. He had responded to the call of the Führer for all Germans to join the fatherland and had moved with his whole family to Germany. He gradually became disillusioned with Nazi methods and aims and organized the factory for the ghetto.

The son Siegmund, who had been educated in the United States, had enough basic attachment to the principles of freedom and democracy to act wholeheartedly against the Nazis. He volunteered in the SS, was employed by the Gestapo as an investigator in Warsaw, and acted there for the Polish resistance.

He supplied the partisans in the ghetto with arms and ammunition, as well as with valuable information. He even took part in some of the ghetto fights and helped Jewish fighters to escape from the ruined ghetto.

Prior to this, Siegmund and Alicia had met and fallen in love. They were married clandestinely, with the help of a Protestant pastor, since Siegmund, being an SS man, couldn't marry without permission of SS headquarters and was forbidden to marry a woman not of German descent. So they became husband and wife before God and man, but not before German law.

Toward the end of the ghetto rebellion, somebody had spied on Siegmund's activities and he was arrested. Then Alicia, too, was arrested. The father was lucky. Smelling danger, he had escaped to a neutral country.

The charges were serious and Siegmund would have to face a general court-martial of the SS. The outcome could be only one. High treason, cooperation with the enemy, illegal marriage to a Polish woman—enough to sentence him to death. But Siegmund hadn't lost his courage. He was trying to eliminate the most serious charges, with the help of an SS general, and hoped to delay the trial.

The story sounded terrific, especially to me. Later I asked Alicia, "You mentioned a rebellion and fighting in the Warsaw ghetto. What was that? I have never heard about it, or about any Jewish fighting."

She was surprised. "You haven't heard about the Warsaw ghetto rebellion? My God, how they can isolate a person, these Germans. The Jews in the ghetto raised a real armed rebellion and gave the Nazis plenty of trouble. I can tell you all about it, because I was still free at the time.

"There was a Jewish fighting organization in the ghetto that was preparing an armed rebellion, while the Germans went on with the extermination of the Jews. When the Germans ordered another big reduction of population, the Jewish fighters met the Germans with machine gun fire and grenades from fortified positions in houses and on roofs. The Germans were infuriated and attacked the ghetto with motorized units, tanks, and infantry, but the Jews still resisted.

"A German first lieutenant named Stroop was in charge of the fight that I saw. I saw him making fun of the Jews, sending them to die as they were brought out of the bunkers, with a satanic grin on his face. Many Germans were killed, many tanks destroyed.

"Then the German command decided to destroy the whole ghetto. They set fires, block by block. But the fighters had well-prepared bunkers, cellars, hiding places. Many Jews, mostly women and children and old people, perished in the flames and explosions. But the young ones still resisted.

"It was a horrible sight. A whole area in the middle of the city— all in flames. Continuous explosions and bursts of bombs, shells, mortars kept up for several weeks. At night a big glow of fire hung over the ghetto.

"Later, when I was arrested, I was taken to the notorious Pawiak Prison. It wasn't far from the ghetto walls, and the bars on the windows were hot from the raging blaze."

Listening to Alicia's story, my heart beat with pride. I wished I could have participated in that hopeless and bitter battle for the glory of my nation.

I became a close friend of Alicia, who felt friendly toward the Jews. She had a deep belief in telling the future through cards. She did it rarely, only when she felt inspired.

Judith Strick with her older brother, Misha.

Alexander Strick, Judith's father.

Judith's Grandmother Strick.

Rachel and Alexander Strick, Judith's parents.

Rachel Strick Pisiuk, Judith's aunt.

Judith, left, and a cousin who was killed by the Nazis.

Rachel Strick and seven-year-old daughter, Judith.

Teen-aged Judith, as yet untouched by Nazi horror.

Judith and Israeli soldier in Beersheba during war in 1948.

Judith and members of Israeli Army with whom she took intelligence course in 1951.

Israeli Army Captain Judith Strick.

Edward Dribben of United States Air Force.

Marriage of Judith Strick to Edward Dribben at Sde Boker on January 12, 1954. David Ben-Gurion, at right, gave bride away.

Judith and Ed during European trip.

Judith Strick Dribben in 1960 with her pet dog.

Days went by more slowly for me in the Monastery than back in the corner at Monte. The older women had their occupations. They mostly prayed or held séances. They used a rudimentary planchette, a small, heart-shaped board supported by two castors and a pencil. One evening, under the leadership of an older doctor, the spiritualists sat concentrating. It seemed strange to me to see intelligent, well-educated women bent over the planchette in a trance. The old doctor pronounced solemnly, "Soul of our great poet Adam Mickiewicz, we ask you to appear before us prisoners. Come down, come down . . ."

I could hardly control a giggle, but I wanted to see the comedy to the end. To my astonishment the pencil began moving slowly and then jumping wildly.

"The ghost is nervous," the old lady whispered. "There are unbelievers among us," and she motioned to Alicia and me to move away.

Then she repeated the invocation. We exchanged an amused look, but controlled ourselves. The pencil stopped moving and slid gently to the middle of the board. Then it began moving from one letter to another, pointing.

"He came, he came, he is here," the doctor announced. "Look, he speaks . . ." And she began deciphering.

"I . . . am he . . . re . . . what do . . . you want . . . women?"

"Tell us, dear Adam Mickiewicz, what will be the outcome of the war?"

The planchette stopped, then started jumping aimlessly.

"He doesn't know, or is it that we don't understand him?"

"Tell us, dear Adam Mickiewicz, what do you see on the Eastern Front?"

The planchette moved back and forth.

"He speaks," the old lady went on. "Yes, I see a . . . terrible . . . picture . . . of ruins and . . . death . . . And tell us, please, what will happen to us?"

The planchette stopped, then moved again, "Yes, he speaks. I am . . . not who . . . you think . . . my name is also Adam . . . I am a dead prisoner from . . . Auschwitz concentration camp . . ."

What could the trick be? I asked myself. Was it collective hysteria or imagination? Was she really reading something or just saying what she would like to hear?

"I was . . . tortured to death . . . by the Nazis . . ." the voice of the old lady went on, "you, here, some will . . . go to the camps . . . some will go home . . . but some will die . . ."

The planchette rapidly slipped out and was stopped by one of the women.

"He is gone," the doctor declared. "Let's wait awhile and then we'll call Grandpa Pilsudski."

We walked over to the window.

"What a lot of stupid nonsense," Alicia said. "I've never seen this foolishness before. There is always one leader who fools the whole crowd, and they really believe that somebody is talking to them from the other world."

About the middle of September, Anna was suddenly taken away on a transport to a concentration camp. Our cell commander became the docile, blonde Kiki.

One day I was sitting with Alicia and Cesia. The latter was plunged in thought. She suddenly turned to Alicia and implored, "Dear Alicia, don't refuse a small request. Please lay out your cards for me. I want to know what's going to happen to my husband and me."

Alicia wasn't too willing at first, but finally she laid out the cards on the table. She became serious and concentrated. Cesia looked on. With a sharp movement Alicia swept the cards from the table and, looking bored, said to Cesia, "I don't feel like handling the cards today. I'm not in the right mood for it."

Cesia walked away without saying a word and picked up her sewing. Alicia sat down with her back to Cesia and motioned to me. When I came closer she seized my hands. Her teeth were chattering and her hands trembled.

"It's terrible," she whispered. "I saw it as soon as I laid the cards out. Cesia is on the threshold of death. She is going to die, in a couple of hours maybe, shot the same way as her husband. I saw the ace, the ten, and the nine of spades . . . it is death . . . Oh, God don't punish me with foreseeing such terrible things."

"Alicia, what nonsense. How can you be so silly, to believe in a pack of cards. Forget it:"

About three-quarters of an hour had passed when the key turned in the lock and a Ukrainian policeman entered.

"Czeslawa Miodowska," he said.

Alicia, petrified, stared at the policeman. Cesia stood up, her arms hanging down helplessly. She turned very pale.

"Put together your belongings and come with me," the Ukrainian said.

Several women helped Cesia and gave her bread for the trip. She said good-bye faintly and walked out with the policeman.

We were all confused and frightened. What could it be? The transport to the concentration camp had just left an hour ago. There couldn't be another one. Where were they taking her? We ran to the windows. Under the shadow of the big trees was a big empty truck, and four heavily armed SS men stood near it smoking and talking.

In front of the entrance we noticed Sanders, the fat, brutal prison secretary.

After a short while Cesia appeared, following the Ukrainian.

Sanders shouted at her, "So here you are, Czeslawa Miodowska, you damned Jewess, fooling us so long, you Sarah!"

He grabbed her long hair and kicked her.

"Get into the truck!" She was as pale as a sheet of paper, but she looked at Sanders fearlessly. She picked up the bread we'd given her, which lay on the ground together with her belongings, and walked slowly to the truck.

At the same moment many women walked toward the truck, some chained, some with the Star of David on their arms. They walked slowly and quietly. They were placed in the truck, Cesia among them. She never looked up at our windows.

The armed SS men took their places in the truck and it moved off. We were still looking out the windows when Alicia fainted. It took some time to revive her.

"I am cursed," she kept repeating. "Why should I foresee things that others don't? I'll never touch those cards again."

In the evening, Emil, a half-Polish, half-German prisoner, knocked on our door. "There was a girl taken from your cell. She was shot, together with Jewesses from the cellar, in the Sand Hills, outside town. Was she also Jewish?"

"We don't know."

The old doctor crossed herself.

Several women began praying. They prayed for the dying, for the prisoners, for liberation. They invoked God and Saint Rita, the patron saint of prisoners.

Alicia lay there exhausted.

It took us several days to recover from the tragedy of our cell mate Cesia.

In October of 1943, we heard terrific news. The Allies were in Naples. The Russians were approaching the Dnieper line. But why hadn't they reached Poland?

We began darning our clothes. The better-dressed prisoners helped out the others. I was given a dress, a skirt, a pullover, a pair of shoes, and some underwear, as my clothes were in deplorable condition.

It had been a whole year since my arrest. A year—what I had experienced in that time. I thought of my mother and younger brother. What about them? Were they still safe on Yadwiga's farm? And my big brother? Where was he? And my father?

Soon darkness fell and we slept. But not for long. It must have been about midnight when noises from the corridor and the yard awoke us. We heard steps, voices, the opening and slamming of doors.

We sat up on our mattresses listening. Someone ran to the window and told us there were many SS men in the yard, carrying flaming torches.

"I'm afraid," someone whispered, but a firm sharp voice shut her up.

Soon the noise moved upstairs to our corridor. We could hear steps approaching our door. Then the heavy key turned in our lock. The first to enter was Sanders, after him the head guard, two unknown SS officers, and behind them Rosa.

"Concentration camp," someone whispered.

Sanders ran over a list with his index finger. We waited silently. He began reading out names.

"Gaszynska, Anna."

"Yes."

"Korbut, Maria."

"Yes," the old doctor's voice responded clearly.

"Arsenyeva, Maria."

"Yes," I replied.

"Olshansky, Kira. Jakubowsky, Zofia. Yadviga, Leontyna . . ." Sander's voice read on and on.

When he finished, only Alicia, Paulina, Christina, the blonde Kiki, and two others remained in the cell.

"All the prisoners whose names I read are to pack their belongings, get dressed, and be ready in twenty minutes."

The Germans left the cell and the door was locked. Alicia jumped up in her nightgown, grabbed the cards, and ran to the table, leaping over mattresses and benches.

"I am going to lay out the cards for all of you before you go. First for you, Maria. I promised you that a long time ago."

While I dressed, she laid out the cards.

"Oh, Maria, Maria," Alicia whispered, "you are going to a terrible place. It will be a short trip. You will be surrounded by death, disease, torture. You'll be very ill twice, but you won't stay in that place. You'll be in a second prison but a little one. Suddenly you'll emerge from all the shells and bombs. You'll be free. Well, that's enough. Be brave and look after yourself. You'll need a lot of strength."

We embraced. Then I rushed to get dressed and to pack my belongings, which fitted into one little paper carton.

In the meantime Alicia laid out her cards for all the others, and I could hear her talking gently to them about their future.

While we were waiting, Alicia took me aside. "Listen," she whispered, "none of the others will survive. I didn't tell them, they will all die. The old ones first. I am heartbroken. See what you can do for them. God bless you, Maria. And remember to look for me after the war. You have my address, haven't you?"

Then Sanders came back to count us. We were ordered to walk in twos. I took Kira's arm.

We passed through two solid lines of SS men holding torches and then through a narrow street. We could see submachine guns, grenades, gas masks. All this for thirty or forty unarmed women prisoners.

About forty of us altogether, we were taken to a large empty cell. There were no mattresses or blankets. Some of us slept, some prayed, some whispered in the dark. Now we knew—we were on the way! But where? Auschwitz? Dachau? Ravensbrück?

Early in the morning the door opened and the prison secretary came in with the treasurer—a little bespectacled SS man. The treasurer handed back everything, or almost everything, that had been taken away from us when we arrived at Monte. I got back my mother's watch and my purse. .

A little later the door opened and Franz stood in the doorway. "Maria," he said when I approached, "so here you are." He stamped his foot in anger at the discovery.

"Franz, you probably understand how much I would like to know where we are going?"

"Yes, yes, I understand, but . . ." he turned his face away. "I don't know, I really don't know." Then he added, "You are going to the Reich, to work."

"You don't want to tell me the truth, Franz, even as a farewell gift, do you?" I said resentfully. "Even when you see me for the last time?"

"I can't tell you. The truth is too awful. I wish you luck. Be strong. You should survive even that."

He stroked my shoulders and before I could say another word slammed the door. He stood for a moment behind the door, then his steps slowly died away into the distance.

About noon we were ordered to leave the cell in twos. Again I took Kira's arm and we walked toward the yard. Then Wehmayer noticed me. He came over with a man who held a leather quirt.

"Look, Alfred," he said to his companion, "do you see this girl? A very dangerous Russian spy and paratrooper. She might run away from the transport."

"Don't worry, Wehmayer." He interrupted the commander before he could mention the name of the place we so much wanted to know.

"Since I have been appointed transport commander, not one prisoner has escaped alive. Depend on me."

"I bet," Wehmayer said, "as much as you desire to leave Monte, Maria, you will be longing for it as for a lost paradise."

"You're wrong. Any place under the Nazis is a piece of hell," I replied. Both Germans found it amusing. "She is a tough little nut," Alfred smiled. ""They'll soften her up over there," Wehmayer laughed.

"Your curiosity will be satisfied within the next two hours," Wehmayer continued. "Good-bye, little darling, and don't forget me."

I whispered to Kira, "What a bastard." After a short while our turn came to climb into the big covered truck. Three heavily armed SS men took their places, checked and loaded their submachine guns.

We crossed the city through several suburbs; then we were out on a wide asphalt road. It was the only road of its kind in the whole of western Poland to the Reich, and everybody knew that Auschwitz lay in that direction.

The convoy moved fast. Everything was gray, wet, foggy. After half an hour we left the highway and turned down a side road.

Later we crossed a railway line, a little deserted station, then a big road with two rows of huge old trees. We could hear the croaking of frogs and see patches of slimy water. It was swampy. Then another side road.

We saw a group of men working, all of them in striped blue gray clothes and caps, two guards behind them with rifles and dogs on leashes. They were digging a ditch. They didn't stop or look up when the convoy passed.

The convoy halted. Through the window in the back of the driver's cab we could see an iron gate. There was a wooden barracks to the left, several SS men standing outside it. There was a big inner courtyard surrounded by brick buildings. I saw a huge inscription over the gate:

ARBEIT MACHT FREI

IN THE SHADOW OF
THE CHIMNEYS

12

We were shocked by approaching crews of women with shaved heads, dressed in impossibly dirty khaki pants and blouses, with big crosses painted crudely across their backs. They were wearing the black Star of David. Jewish women, and in what a deplorable state! But their presence in the concentration camp comforted me a little, as it meant that not all Jews had been exterminated on the spot.

After a while we got our caldron of tea. It seemed more like boiled manure and rotten straw. We walked quickly to the barracks. On the way we were accosted by some old hags who wanted to dip their containers into our caldron. Our barracks commander carried a big stick and chased them away.

"Get away, you dirty trash," she yelled. "Keep your shitty hands away from our caldron! You miserable whores, you Muslims!" And she struck them mercilessly, knocking down the dirty containers.

While we were chewing our portion of bread tasting of potatoes, sawdust, and mildew, two women came in.

I heard someone asking in Polish, "Is there anyone here from Montelupich Prison, from Krakow? We heard a transport from there came in today."

I jumped up and recognized Laura and Christina Makowska, although Laura was without her fancy hairdo and minus a few front teeth, and Christina was thinner and smaller and her hair was very short.

"Maria, my God, you're here," Laura cried, running toward me. We kissed and embraced and I shook hands for a long while with both my prison mates.

"What are you doing here? Is it possible to live in this place?"

"Live? You mean survive, don't you?" Christina said.

"If you can work, stand the cold, the roll calls, the diseases and mistreatment, the poor food. I was strong as a bull. Look what typhus has done to me. I almost died. But with God's help we'll go on. The main thing is to keep strong, not to give in or turn into a Muslim."

"A Muslim?"

"I'll explain what that means. A Muslim is someone who has lost her courage, who becomes subhuman. She can't fight back anymore."

"On what are the prisoners working here?" I interrupted. "It seems to me I saw factory chimneys . . ." I stopped because both of them gave me a horrified look.

"Factories!" Laura burst into unnatural laughter.

"Nobody knows about it outside the camp," Christina said, "but these chimneys belong to furnaces or crematories where the Nazis burn people alive."

To turn my mind away from this horror I asked, "And what has become of our friends, Wanda, Zofia the cell commander, Zofia the teacher, Lubanska, the blonde Wanda?"

"All of them dead, except Doctor Kosciuszko. They all died of typhus. You don't know how they die here, young and old, fat and thin. Remember, Maria, if you want to survive, keep yourself clean, don't eat trash, if possible find steady work, and be as inconspicuous as possible."

"Well, Maria," Christina said, "we'll have to go now. We have to be in our barracks before lights-out. I live in Block 10 in B Camp, and Laura is a nurse in Block 28 in the hospital. We will do everything we can for you. Come and see us."

"Come over, Maria," Laura said. "In the evening they permit visitors in the hospital area. Remember, Block 28."

"Wait a minute. What does block mean?"

"Block means barracks." The two of them disappeared into the darkness. I stood outside my barracks still stunned by all that they had told me.

One of the most terrible things in a concentration camp was the absolute lack of privacy. The most intimate things had to be done in a crowd in the presence of many other women—living, sleeping, eating, washing, showering, going to the toilet. There was no place where a prisoner could be alone.

There was one place—the isolated dark cell somewhere in the Bunker—the name of the ill-famed camp prison, in the men's camp. A prison within a prison.

Slowly we began to realize where we were, how the whole camp was organized and ruled. The women's camp was called Birkenau. The men's camp, Auschwitz. We began to observe the SS men and women who ruled the camps. And we began to know the prisoner functionaries, the "job prisoners."

This seemed to be the ultimate disgrace—that prisoners were ruled indirectly by SS men and directly by other prisoners. It wouldn't have hurt quite so much to be mistreated by the SS.

The whistles and gong summoned the prisoners to roll call. "Be glad to have a morning without roll call," the block leader said. "The worse the weather, the longer it takes."

"What happens at the roll call?" a new prisoner asked.

"They have all the prisoners in fives before the barracks, and then they keep counting us until our backsides freeze and bladders burst. Or until the Muslims faint or collapse."

We had only black water for breakfast, were ordered to have our belongings ready and wait.

It was still dark when I went out to search for the toilet and a washing place. The whistles announcing the end of roll call died in the cool, foggy morning air.

During the night we were not allowed out. We had to take care of our needs in buckets. Many women could not overcome their embarrassment and suffered till morning.

The block leader mocked them. "Look at these delicate ladies.

Ashamed to shit and piss among their own friends. That's something. If you're that delicate you'll die very fast."

The latrine was a long gray narrow building with small windows and a long seat from one end to the other. When I came in the place was overcrowded, and there were queques in front of every squatting woman.

For the first time in my life I saw a mass of human beings taking care of their most elementary needs at the same time. Standing in line, I made some distressing observations. Many of the prisoners were in a deplorable state. I could see skinny legs, completely emaciated buttocks and bellies. Many of them had diarrhea. Their clothes were filthy. There was no toilet paper. Some used rags.

Every so often, a well-dressed, clean-looking female would push away a squatting prisoner and take her place, cursing and slapping everybody around. Nobody protested.

In the washroom was a repulsive-looking woman with a big stick in her hand. She observed the prisoners as they washed and deliberately and cruelly struck their heads, backs, and arms. In this way, she made sure that nobody used too much water. Who could she be? I looked at her rough face, big strong hands and arms, and listened to her cursing. She had a number with a black triangle inscribed on her dress. I didn't know its meaning at the time.

I walked back to the newcomers' barracks. Somebody yelled, *"Achtung."* A strange group entered the barracks. First a tall SS man with a slim girl. She wore a black dress with a red armband embroidered in white. She had a number with a red triangle. Six other girls followed, similarly dressed.

Several small tables and chairs were brought in and the girl with the red armband began reading names from a list. She ordered the newcomers to stand in lines before the tables.

Then the black-robed girls ordered the newcomers to bare their left arms. They dipped needles in bottles and applied them to the prisoners' arms. There were shrieks of pain, and I could see black stains on the extended arms. When my turn came, I asked the young Polish-looking woman what she was doing.

"If you must know," she whispered, "a personal number has to be tatooed on every prisoner. Here one becomes a number." Then she asked my name and checked it against her list. She found it immediately.

"Menard, Marie-Josephine?" she asked, surprised. "Your name sounds French, you speak Polish, and you are Russian. Well, your number will be 63578."

"Quite a long number to remember," I said, baring my arm, "and are there really that many female prisoners in this place?"

"Must be." She prepared her tools, consisting of two needles set in a wooden handle and a bottle containing black China ink. "I came here at the beginning of the year and I am in the twenty-five thousands. I have to survive somehow. Forgive me for doing this."

She looked well fed and well cared for. She had good clothes and shoes and a beautiful kerchief on her head. This job must carry special privileges, I thought, while she incised the number on my arm. I wiped off the black stain, but the ink was tattooed deeply under the skin and the number showed clearly.

Was it a brand or a stigma? Or just to mark off a prisoner so that she couldn't get lost in the crowd? Quite a good idea, I thought. Once the number was there, there was no chance to escape. It bound us more strongly than any chain. It was something that could only be replaced by another piece of flesh.

When they had finished with our group, we were marched to a big room with many tables.

This was the second part of the concentration camp matriculation. Here they took away everything we owned except towel, toothbrush, soap, and comb. They carefully noted what they confiscated, and the prisoner even had to sign a form that listed every item of her confiscated property.

So there we were, the entire transport from Krakow, young and old, stripped and waiting.

The slim girl in the black robe and red armband came in, asking for Maria Menard.

"That's me."

She gave me a kind of badly fitting housedress to put on and told me to follow her.

She led me to another part of the building and knocked on a door. Inside were two SS men, a sergeant and a corporal.

"Leave us alone, *kapo*," the older one told my escort, who immediately left the room.

"So you are the so-called Marie-Josephine Menard," the sergeant said, "the bogus Frenchwoman and genuine Russian. Not bad looking."

"Not bad, rather interesting," the corporal said.

The sergeant continued. "We have been ordered to keep you in good shape. The Gestapo is *very*," he emphasized the word, "is very interested in you. And they might need you later. In this place, a prisoner's life isn't worth much and nobody gives a damn if there are a couple of hundred prisoners more or less. I hope you understand that. All of you are going to get haircut 'zero.' But we'll leave your hair. Not all of it. We'll give you a short cut. When you've gone through quarantine you'll get a good job, so that you won't have much difficulty surviving and keeping yourself in good shape. Understand?"

"But I wouldn't like to be an exception," I said.

They exchanged a surprised look.

"Do you have a girl friend you'd like to keep near?" the older one asked.

"Yes."

"Her name?"

"Kira Olshansky."

"Hoffman," he turned to the young corporal, "see to that. And as for you," he gave me an almost friendly look, "the orders in this camp are given by us. Remember it and don't get into trouble. I'll see you at the end of your quarantine."

I walked out with the corporal and was returned to my group.

In the meantime the women had been arranged in lines for shearing. A beautiful young girl with long curls came in and ordered Kira and me to follow her. She took us to the "barbershop." The floor was covered with thick layers of blonde, black, brown, and red hair.

"Come here," the girl said to us. "You're lucky. All the others will look like monkeys. Let me give you both a nice modern short cut." And she picked up her tools, in apparent enjoyment of her work.

In a second room, girls shaved our hair under the arms and between the legs. When we complained, one of the girls said to us in Russian, "Don't get excited. You should be glad we're doing it. When we got here the job was done by SS men."

Later, in the shower room, the shaved women with their bare skulls all looked alike. Only their bodies announced their age. Later we recognized them by their eyes, noses, chins, cheeks.

A plump girl entered. She wore good clothes, a sweater with a red yellow Star of David, and an armband embroidered "*Sauna Kapo*."

She demanded in German, "Who is ready for the next room?"

The women started crowding around the door. Suddenly the girl produced a big belt. She began beating the naked bodies and heads, leaving red welts.

"Keep in line," the girl yelled.

Next to me were some Polish women. One of them said, "The Jews rule again, in the concentration camp."

"We can't help the Germans mistreating us, but we should do something about the Jews," said another.

"You'd better keep your mouth shut," a third declared. "I don't care who beats me. I've already heard there are *kapos* of all kinds— Germans, Slovaks, Poles. Somebody talked about a Polish *Lagerkapo*."

"What does a *kapo* mean?"

"Just a kind of leader."

Not far from us stood a tall, white-haired Italian woman. For some reason she had attracted the attention of the *Sauna Kapo,* who hit her with the belt on the face, neck, and breasts. The woman became furious.

"*Disgraziata putana* ('disgraceful whore')," she shouted.

Before we could grasp what had happened, the *kapo,* helped by two other well-dressed girls, dragged her down and kicked her until she lay bloody and silent on the floor.

In the next room, we stood in line in front of tables piled high with clothes. I received a striped dress and jacket, striped underpants and undershirts, rough stockings in different sizes and colors, two odd shoes that didn't fit, and a piece of string to hold up the stockings. Everything was wrinkled, the underwear was stained and smelled of disinfectant. But there was no time to think about all this, because we were hurried to the Political Department.

We were just getting hungry when a caldron of steaming liquid was brought in with bowls and several spoons. Again we had to form lines to receive our food. I was given a bowl of a bitter yellowish gray concoction. It tasted awful. Naturally the bowls and spoons were not washed, just passed from one prisoner to another. And if somebody had an infectious disease? But I pushed that thought away and looked for a faucet to wash my hands and rinse my mouth.

Then we arrived at the Political Department. Behind a small table sat a dark-haired SS corporal, busy with a pile of papers. A *kapo* checked my number, then gave me a piece of cloth with a red triangle printed on it, an *R* superimposed on the triangle, and my number, 63578.

"Tell me, please, what does the red triangle mean?"

"The red triangle is for political prisoners, the green one for criminals, the black for antisocials, violet for Bible explorers, and the star for the Jews." The answers provoked fresh questions. But I kept silent and waited.

A girl with a round Slavonic face noticed me and called out, "Are you Russian?"

"Yes."

"Come over to my table. I take care of the Russians."

Before filling in my questionnaire, she whispered, "We have already heard about you. Will you come and work with us?"

"I don't know."

When she had finished with me, I was called to the SS corporal's table.

"Here is your *Schutzbefehl* ('order of protective arrest')," he said and handed me several forms pinned together. I read the top one with the heading "The Supreme Security Department of the Reich. Order of Protective Arrest: Marie-Josephine Menard, alias Maria Alexandrovna Arsenyeva, born November 5, 1918, in Leningrad (so attested by prisoner), for having affected the security of the German armed forces and general security of the Third Reich, has been sentenced to protective arrest in concentration camp Auschwitz for an indefinite period of time." And below: "The Gestapo is entitled to cancel or change this order at any time." Underneath it was somebody's unintelligible signature, and at the bottom a blank for the "protected prisoner's" signature.

"Are you dreaming?" the SS corporal interrupted my study of this impressive document.

"Not dreaming—just surprised."

"Surprised?"

"Well, what does it mean, 'indefinite period of time'?"

"Indefinite? It means until the end of the war. Understand? And now sign the order, right here."

"Sign the order? Sign my own verdict? I don't want to."

The German looked menacing and raised his arm.

"Sign it, what difference does it make?" the *kapo* intervened.

I took a pen from the German's desk and signed with big letters in Russian characters across the corner, half illegibly, "Death to the Germans." Nobody paid any attention.

Afterward I joined my companions in the sauna room, now emptied of tables and clothing. All the newcomers, shaven, washed, dressed in camp clothing, registered, and numbered, sat in groups on the floor of the big room in the early fall twilight.

There was not much talk. It had been an eventful day and needed digesting.

We were arranged in fives, counted, our numbers were checked, and then we were led to Block 3.

That was to be our first home in Auschwitz.

Block 3 was a big wooden prefabricated barracks, apparently intended as a stable. A stove in the middle ran across the room. The interior was filled with wooden beds, in three tiers and divided into compartments. A *Stubova* was in charge of each *Stube,* or room.

On each side of the entrance hall there were two rooms occupied by the block leader.

Our *Stubova* was an attractive Polish girl, Yanka. To our surprise she was friendly. She distributed blankets and told us we could get into our beds as soon as the roll call was over.

Kira and I occupied a top bed that had a very thin straw mattress. We arranged it as best we could. We were given two blankets. One we spread over the mattress, the other over ourselves. We placed our belongings under our heads, because we had been warned about thieves.

We felt glad in the dark, but soon the fleas and bedbugs found us. We went to sleep feeling devoured.

It seemed we had hardly slept at all when there was a bellowing of *"Aufstehen* ('get up')." We woke up groggy. It was still dark and nobody knew what time it was. We dressed quickly, wrapped our belongings in a towel, and made our bed. When we moved the mattress, the women underneath cursed volubly, as it was full of dust and straw that fell on them.

We barely had time to run to the toilet, which was already crowded, and we could not get into the washroom, as it was locked. We came back just as the job prisoners were chasing everyone outside for the morning roll call.

Then we stood for our first roll call, arranged in fives, in front of the barracks. As far as we could see and hear, the same was happening all over the camp. We heard shouts from all directions.

SS men and women walked back and forth. It was cold and damp. A furious wind blew from the direction of the mountains. The ground was wet and slippery, and the sticky mud clung to our badly fitting shoes, making them heavy and even more uncomfortable. We shivered in our poor clothing, while most of the old prisoners—we recognized them by their numbers—had warm clothes, scarves, and good shoes.

"To organize," "organization"—we heard these words repeatedly. "To organize" in concentration camp slang meant to get something illegally. It meant to steal, to exchange, to find, to take away. "You'll learn to organize things," the old prisoners told the newcomers. But in the first roll call we froze in the wind and it seemed to us that even the weather was collaborating with the Nazis.

Our block leader, Vera, a Jewish Slovakian girl, ran around busily with her second-in-command, the tall, sturdy Bozka. Vera was a good-looking girl, about twenty years old, with curly black hair and an intelligent face. She was a gentle girl.

The hard work was done by several aides. Vera wore a striped dress and jacket, good leather boots, a scarf, gloves.

The job prisoners counted us over several times, told us to button our clothes, discard any rags. Then we waited a very long time. Daylight appeared slowly, battling the fog and dark.

Yanka, who was standing in the next row, explained things for us. She pointed to an SS man. "He is *Rapportführer* Taube. A devil. And this black-haired girl is Stenia, the *Lageralteste*—the top prisoner of the women's camp. And this is the *Lagerkapo*, the queer little German. They call her Leo because she is more man than woman."

Two SS women approached. Someone asked who they were. "They are the *Aufseherinnen* Irma Grese and Drechsler. The little blonde sets dogs on woman prisoners. And she decides who is to be whipped and who is to go out through the chimneys. And the one with the big teeth? Another vampire."

At last there was a harsh "*Achtung*" and we stiffened to attention while two SS men and two SS women, and the *Lageralteste* and *Lagerkapo*, counted us off methodically.

I followed the group with my eyes, and for a moment I met those of Stenia. She gave us the same attention she would give the counting of electric posts or bales of straw.

A whistle dismissed the roll call, and work columns started marching toward the gate.

First the camp orchestra hurried down, playing a German march. The musicians were well dressed. A dark-haired girl conducted the orchestra.

"Do you see the conductor? That's Alma, a famous musician from France. A lucky Jewess . . . Yes, she arrived on a transport from a French camp and was intended for the chimneys. And delicate also. She told the camp commander who she was and that she could organize an orchestra. The commander liked the idea, and now she is the music *kapo*. A great artist, you must admit. And a good girl. She has saved prisoners from the chimneys and helped many others."

"The red kerchiefs are the clothing store detail, Canada. Here is the ammunition factory detail, and here the punishment detail. Look at the red and white rings on their backs. They have been caught smuggling, carrying on with men, stealing, trying to escape. They work like hell all day long at the worst kind of work. But they are given a bigger food ration—the Nazis are a strange lot."

Vera appeared and told us in German that we would spend two weeks in quarantine. Then she dismissed us.

We wanted to go inside but were chased away. I walked, with Kira, to the "prairie," the space behind the barracks and toilets.

We met many prisoners on the way. Crowds of women of all ages, speaking all possible European languages, were walking in all directions. We finally reached the prairie. It was full of green puddles; the smell was putrid.

We talked to a group of five red-triangled, low-numbered Russian girls. They had been sheared but wore kerchiefs and good shoes. They told us they had been sent to work in Germany at a metallurgical factory in the Ruhr, where they had worked from twelve to fourteen hours a day. The area had often been bombed. When the air raid alarms sounded, the German supervisors would lock them up in the factory and run to the shelters themselves.

"We were lucky," one of them said. "Our factory was not a military one, so our consciences were clear. Others had it worse, they had to produce ammunition, bombs, shells. They couldn't sleep or eat. What a disgrace! To produce weapons against our own brothers and allies.

"Then we decided to run away, so we collected food and set off eastward. But they caught up with us in Poland. Just think! We got that far."

One of the girls looked us over. "You must get kerchiefs and better shoes, and something warm under your dresses. I'll tell you what to do. Save your bread and take it to the workers in the clothing store. There you can exchange it for clothes and shoes. But remember, don't starve yourselves. One must eat here or die quickly. And be careful with the job prisoners. Better keep your mouth shut. Don't react if they slap or push you. Let it go. It is more important to survive."

Walking across the prairie, we saw a group of women squatting by one of the puddles. It was difficult to determine their age. They were faded and sickly looking. Their clothes were rags. Many of them had no shoes or stockings. They had horrible scabs. Some of them were washing rags in bowls, using the putrid water from the puddles. They must eat from the same dishes, I thought. They seemed to be speaking Spanish.

In spite of the general air of misery, many of their faces had not lost their intelligence. I approached two of the younger ones. They were talking and did not pay attention to us.

"Who are you?" I asked.

"What do you want of us? We have nothing to barter or sell. Leave us alone."

"I don't want anything, just to talk, prisoner to prisoner."

"But you are Christian and we are Jewesses," the first one said bitterly.

"We may be Christian, but we are human beings, and prisoners just like you."

"No, you are not, because they can put us in the chimneys any time they want, and they would not do it to you."

"But we're against this discrimination. Can't you understand that?"

"Even the other Jews call us dirty Muslims, miserable corpses. Well, it's not our fault, this climate kills us. We come from a warm country."

"Where are you from?"

"We are Greek, mostly from Salonika and Athens. We came here over a year ago, and now less than half of us are left. We don't speak German, and we're not like our sisters from Slovakia who get all the good jobs and walk over dead bodies. We are feminine and delicate. Our men always did everything for us. And we are lost here. We aren't enterprising enough to 'organize,' so look at us."

"But what are those terrible sores on your arms and legs?"

I couldn't hold back the question.

"Oh, you mean those scabs." She looked embarrassed. "They made us work in the swamps all summer. Then the awful sores broke out all over our bodies."

"So how do you manage?"

"Manage?" We just sit around here until they select us one after another. But don't think we are dirty by nature. Because of these scabs the block leader won't give us a change of clothes, or let us into the toilets or washrooms, or the dispensary. What can we do?" Another girl joined the group and began looking for lice in the seams of her dirty dress.

Without a word, we continued up the prairie, leaving the group and the large green puddle behind us.

We walked around the camp. We saw women working everywhere. Some were digging ditches or holes in the ground. Some carried flat wooden stretchers loaded with sand or stones. They moved slowly, heavily, but quickened their pace when they saw an SS man or a *kapo*.

On the way, we met Yelena, the blonde girl who worked in the clothing department. Yelena invited us to her block. "We have plenty of soup there and maybe some bread also. We work in a good unit, so most of us don't eat the camp soup. We 'organize' our food."

Then she advised us not to eat the camp soup, because the Germans put a powder into it that caused women to lose their menstrual periods.

"In a way it might be better," she said. "It's easier like that to keep clean. I know many girls who have missed their period for over a year. Who knows how it will affect their bodies in the future."

Yelena's block was clean and neat. Later a caldron of steaming soup was brought in. Yelana filled two white bowls of soup for us.

"Cabbage soup with pieces of meat. Don't get excited—it might be some horse that died of old age. But who cares, calories are calories, wherever they come from."

She gave us some bread, too, and enjoyed watching us eat.

While we were talking, the block filled with prisoners coming in for lunch. Most of them wore clean clothes and seemed reasonably well. They had all kinds of unusual delicacies, sausages, homemade bread, butter, eggs, apples. They even had heaters to prepare their food on.

"How do they get all that food?" Kira asked.

Yelena smiled. "You see, prisoners are allowed to get parcels. Many of them get at least two a week. They are allowed to write letters, too, once a month. But the Russians can't, and parcels sent to Jews are confiscated. Often the Germans and the job prisoners take out the best things, but those who have families in the occupied countries get enough food. This is how they manage to dress well, get jobs, survive. And whoever gets no parcels lives by 'organizing,' the way I do. Don't worry, girls, you'll learn to do it, too," she added, as we left feeling comforted and well fed.

We went back to our block. On the way we almost ran into a middle-aged Polish woman. She was running, her face distorted with fear and horror. She turned behind the next block and stopped to look back. At that moment her pursuer, a tall *kapo,* jumped furiously at the woman, who tried to free herself, but the *kapo* was stronger.

The *kapo* was a plump German wearing a black triangle. She grabbed her victim's arm and kicked her in the belly and beat her over the head and face with a stick. Wide red marks appeared on the victim's face, blood flowed, but the German *kapo* was not yet satisfied. She was raging, her face flushed with fury. "Dirty swine! Whore!" she kept shouting.

She was finally satisfied when her victim slipped out of her grasp and fell down, lifeless. She kicked her with her leather boot, muttered another curse, wiped off the stick with a piece of paper, and walked away.

Only after the *kapo* had disappeared did some women run over to the woman lying on the ground. They lifted her up and carried her away. No one knew why all this had happened, and when we asked for an explanation, the women just shrugged their shoulders or shook their heads indifferently. One said, "Who knows why? And who cares? Mind your own business, newcomers. You'll see this happening every day."

On the fifth day of quarantine, we visited the old doctor in her block. The three Yakubowsky sisters were sitting near her. They looked ugly and miserable with their shaved heads and badly fitting clothes. One of them already had camp diarrhea. Its victims were unable to control their bowels. They relieved themselves wherever they happened to be. General weakness followed. Many prisoners died of it. Too weak to move and giving off a foul odor, they simply dried up from the loss of bodily liquids.

In the evening I ran to the hospital and got some precious medicine from Laura. But when we went over next morning the old lady had already been taken to the hospital. Her condition was serious.

Before noon there was a sudden commotion in the camp. SS men and SS women were running all around, and so were the job prisoners and block leaders. Whistles were being blown all round the camp, and there were shouts of *"Blocksperre! Blocksperre!"* They were selecting for the chimneys.

Sitting in our block, we learned about the selection from other prisoners. The Jewish prisoners had to stand in line before their blocks to be selected or rejected by Camp Commander Kramer, Woman's Camp Commander Mandel, the chief physician Dr. Mengele, and the *Lageralteste* and *Lagerkapo*.

The victims-to-be passively awaited their fate. There were no rules for selection for the chimneys. A pale face or an ugly expression. A dirty garment or a sore.

Kira and I were taking a walk. We came to a barracks surrounded by a stone wall. The windows had iron bars. We heard screams and moans coming from inside. I could see hands and arms protruding through the bars.

"This is Death Block 25," a passing girl explained. "A gruesome place. They starve the prisoners here for three days. Then they burn more easily, the Germans say. Be careful. Whoever is caught smuggling food or water to them goes with them to the crematories. I hear they have roll calls here, too. Those who are still fairly well answer when their names are called out, and then the sick, the half-alive, who sit or lie in fives. Then there are the dead, they are laid out in fives, too."

The noise from inside beat at us in waves. We could hear water being begged for in all languages.

Just then the gate of Block 25 opened and a plump woman in a striped dress walked out. There was no doubt. She was the block leader. Some of her blonde hair showed under her scarf. She had arms, breasts, buttocks, strong legs. She looked a normal woman, just another woman.

We returned silently to the prairie. It was quite deserted now, especially where we used to see the Greek women.

We learned to "organize." We made contacts with other prisoners. We did not feel lost or even lonely. And we waited for the end of the quarantine, to be put into a steady work detail.

There was one German girl in Block 3 who attracted attention by her appearance and behavior. She looked rather like a young man. Everybody called her Fritz. Sometimes in the evenings she would dance with another girl. Fritz spent her nights outside the block. She had two admirers, the German *kapos* Martha and Hanna. One day Martha was attacked by the fat Hanna on the way to the block. They fought savagely. The fight ended with the arrival of two SS guards who separated them with kicks. We heard that they landed in the Bunker. Fritz felt very proud and important after the fight, and spent the night with *Lagerkapo* Leo.

Then came another *Blocksperre*. It had been three days since the last selection, so we knew that this time it meant the burning of selected victims.

The crematories worked all night. Unable to sleep well, we woke up constantly, and we could see the flare of the chimneys reflected in the window opposite.

We were absorbed into camp life. We lived from day to day. Decent food and beds, clean clothes and bathrooms seemed unreal. The images of our families and friends faded. The partisan period seemed like a movie seen long ago.

13

On October 15 our quarantine ended. "Completed quarantine"—what a joke! Typhus and malaria flourished at Auschwitz, diarrhea and pneumonia, scabies, lice, and germs.

Vera told me I was to be transferred to Block 32. She took me over to *Scharführer* Erber, remarking that he might be in a better mood after breakfast. The audience with the vicious-looking Erber didn't take long.

"You'll start work in the Political Department registering newcomers. Maybe I'll need you once in a while for translating. Do your work well and don't disappoint me. I've heard about you and know you're capable."

Back in Block 3, Vera called for me again and this time we walked all the way to B Camp, to the clothing store.

"Good morning, *Frau* Schmidt," Vera greeted a middle-aged woman wearing a red triangle. "This girl has to be dressed for the Political Department."

"Another one of Erber's gang?" The *kapo* smiled.

"I am from nobody's gang, madame *kapo*."

"Don't get excited. Oh, you are Russian, red triangle. Maybe I am wrong, but the black-robed Political Department people don't inspire much confidence."

"Maybe," I said, "but I'm on my own. Temporary employment doesn't equal surrender."

"My job isn't so temporary. I have spent about five years in prisons and concentration camps," she said proudly, "and nobody can say I have surrendered."

"I don't know about you. You are a *kapo,* but I'll just be one of the pen-pushers."

She quoted a German adage. " 'Here is where the dog lies buried.' You think you'll be just that, but that's not Erber's intention."

"Not me."

"Good luck, anyway." The *kapo* smiled in a friendly manner. "I'll give you some warmer clothes for the winter."

The *kapo* equipped me generously with a black robe, red woolen dress, sweater, warm underwear, well-fitting shoes and stockings.

"This new generation is cocky," I heard her saying to Vera. "Just think, I was already a Socialist when she was being suckled at her mother's breast."

I said good-bye to Vera, and to Kira, who was transferred to A camp. Then I went to Block 32, where Yelena and the Political Department workers lived. Another Slovakian girl, Aranka, was the block leader. She was short, dark haired, and rather friendly.

After lunch I walked toward the sauna building with Ludmila. She was a husky girl with a Slavic face. In ten minutes she had told me about her town, her family, how the Germans came, how she was deported.

We reached the sauna building, where she introduced me to Maryla and Danuta, with whom I was to work.

We exchanged greetings. Danuta's face was familiar.

"Weren't you in Montelupich Prison?" I asked.

"Yes, of course, so you must be the famous Maria with the sixteen names who was isolated in Monte."

The woman at Danuta's side had a cold, reserved face and seemed to pay no attention to us, though her eyes measured Ludmila and me almost contemptuously. She went off with Danuta.

"Did you notice that classy lady?" Ludmila laughed. "She is never at ease with Russians. She thinks we are godless, against family life, and would like to cut the throats of the aristocracy. And maybe she thinks blue blood runs in her veins. But you should see her when she gets a parcel—has she ever offered anything to anybody?"

There were already several clerks in the office. Ludmila introduced

me to the Poles Wala and Kasia, to the Greek Jewish girl Flora, and
the Slovakian Jewish girl Edith. Maryla and Danuta were in their
places.

Ludmila arranged a place for me near her. On the other side sat
Maryla. Then she explained how the questionnaires were to be filled in.

In the afternoon, Ludmila proposed that we try to "organize" something from the new transport. We walked through the sauna rooms.
There were several hundred women there.

We could move about freely. Even the sauna *kapo,* Magda, waved
to us when she passed by. We arrived at Yelena's table. She knew
why we had come. There were plenty of clothes for us to choose from.
"Made in Holland this time!" she said sadly.

I needed a warm scarf and gloves for myself and some warm garments for the old ladies and for Kira. We walked out well equipped and
hid our bundles in one of the cabinets in the office.

Soon Flora and Kasia came in with some bundles, too. They offered
us biscuits, chocolate, and sugar. All made in Holland. At first I wasn't
sure we were doing the right thing. Maybe the Dutch women would
miss their belongings when they were released.

Or they might want their food themselves. But then, the day of
release seemed so far away and the garments so unimportant if freedom
really came. And if we didn't eat this food, the SS or job prisoners
surely would.

And then the first batch of newcomers filled the room.

Kira was in one of the blocks where the camp workers lived. She
worked in the yard, carrying stones and dirt. She had a bad cold, so
the sweater and the warm shawl I "organized" made her happy. I
decided to help her find an easier job.

Later I went to see the old ladies. Doctor Korbut and one of the
old sisters were in the hospital. The first had a very bad cold and high
fever, the second acute diarrhea. I gave away all the Dutch clothes to
the other two sisters. They did no work, just sat in the mud and rain.
Their spirit was broken. They were Muslims, I thought.

Two days later we heard that a transport from Russia had arrived.
The newcomers' barracks was overcrowded, and we learned that the
people were from Dnepropetrovsk. The reception of this huge trans-

port began the next day. Suddenly Erber appeared in the office and called to me, "Come. I want you to translate my speech to the Russians. Besides that, I want you to pick out some specialists. The Russian women are the only ones who have trades and professions." He was talking to me as we walked into the sauna room, overcrowded with the newcomers.

I felt like hell, walking in with an SS man. As I called loudly for silence, I heard someone whisper, "A Russian!"

"The devil knows who she is," another whisper sounded in the crowd.

"Tell them," Erber ordered, "that this place is not bad for working people. Whoever has a good trade will get a decent job. They'll have it good."

I drew a deep breath and dared to translate, "Women and girls! This devil next to me wants me to give you a big load of rubbish about this place being good for working people. He lies like hell." I glanced at Erber with a smile. He listened indifferently, without understanding. "You should know, my dear compatriots, that this camp is a hell of a place. In plain words, an extermination camp. But we should not give up and lose our spirit. If we'll help one another and be strong, they won't destroy us. So, listen, the ones who have important trades and professions, let me know. Our women must get important jobs. It will be easier that way to help one another and survive. Have you understood?"

A whisper of approval passed through the crowd.

"What are they happy about?" Erber asked.

"They are ready to take jobs according to their professions," I replied.

"Very good, very good." Erber was all smiles. "I knew you could talk the right way. Well, first ask for doctors, trained nurses, and medical personnel. Needed badly."

After some hesitation and whispering in the crowd, a number of women came forward—doctors, nurses, a surgeon, medical students.

Then Erber asked for technical personnel. The results were a mining engineer, one electrical and one mechanical engineer, three architects, an electrician, a locomotive engineer, many mechanics, machinists, tractor drivers, one welder, several bricklayers, and two agricultural graduates among others.

The SS man got excited. "The goddamned Communists! They know how to make their women useful. Let's write down all the numbers. There are plenty of jobs."

The list completed, I said, "I'll see you soon in your quarantine. Be careful and keep strong. If you'll help one another everything will be all right. Remember, this camp is a grisly Nazi hole. Good luck. We must make it and survive until liberation comes."

"Thank you, thank you," I heard voices from the crowd. "You give us courage. We thought we'd be lost here."

Later I returned, to be surrounded by a crowd of smiling women. I talked with the surgeon Ljubov Alexandrovna, with the old doctor Olga Ivanovna, with the nurse Antonina, with the engineer Olga, and with a girl named Tamara, who told me frankly, "When you first came in with the German sergeant, we thought you were a collaborator, but we know better now."

In the evening, after a long tiring day registering the Russian arrivals, I visited Laura. I saw a camp hospital for the first time. It was a regulation barn filled with three-tiered beds. It smelled of carbolic acid and disinfectant, not of medicine and cleanliness. There were no sheets or pillows. The patients for the most part were naked.

I found Laura in a white apron taking care of a patient. We climbed to a top bunk to talk.

"The doctors here are almost helpless," Laura said. "There are no medicines, no injections, no instruments. Everything must be 'organized' or stolen. I have seen doctors in a fury of helplessness. They could save hundreds and even thousands if . . . Well, why talk, the Nazis want to exterminate people, they have been sent here for that purpose. Then they send letters to the families. Your relative so-and-so died of natural causes, or of pneumonia, or acute this or that, or of typhus. You can imagine how they lie.

"And in our block it is especially difficult. Our block leader is a Pole. God save me from such Poles. All she cares about are men and sex. Her aides have to stand guard when she has a man in her room. You should see the fancy clothes she wears and the jewels she has.

"But because of all this we can ask her men for medicines and injections for our patients. It hurts me every time the doctors have to kowtow before that bitch and beg her to 'organize' some medicine. And she insists on knowing who is to get it.

"And everyone must keep quiet because of her relation with Dr. Mengele."

Then Laura told me about the two blocks of Jewish patients. She said the Jews preferred to walk around with their diseases because those hospital blocks could be emptied into the chimneys. And then she told me about Dr. Mengele's "research."

We hadn't realized the time, so when we heard the whistle we had to run to the hospital gate. Luckily I was close to my block, and we parted silently.

While registering the next transport I felt something stinging my thigh. I put my hand under my dress and pulled out a large clothes louse.

Ludmila noticed it and said, "Kill it. We must see if there's blood."

When I crushed it, there was a smear of blood.

"Bad," she said. "It is a typhus louse. Now you'll have typhus in about two weeks from now. Don't worry, every prisoner gets it."

"But what shall I do about it?"

"Why should you worry? We'll help you. Forget about it."

It was easy to say "forget it," but I couldn't. I thought of all the prisoners dying of typhus.

When I began to feel feverish, about two weeks later, I decided not to give in and went on for several days until I felt so sick I couldn't work. Aranka, the block leader, said it was better not to walk around with typhus. She finally persuaded me to go to the hospital and took me to the infirmary.

Black patches danced before my eyes, I was dizzy, had a violent headache, and almost collapsed by the time I reached the hospital.

14

When I woke it was dark and quiet. The silence was broken now and then by moans and screams. My head was burning and I had a terrible thirst.

"Water," I called out, "water."

To my surprise somebody climbed up and gave me some. The cup trembled in my hands. My neighbor woke up and helped me drink from it. All I could see was her short hair, and I felt her naked body next to mine.

"Who are you?" she asked in a Slavonic-sounding language.

"I am Maria, a Russian."

"I am Vidosava and Yugoslavian. You seem really not well."

"Yes," I said and slept again.

There were three others sharing my bed, a Pole with typhus, a Russian with typhus and pneumonia, a Czech with high fever and a dreadful cough. Some of the patients had scabies and scratched themselves till the blood came. Lice and fleas afflicted us the whole time. We were too weak to hunt them out.

The disease was tormenting me but I had the will to live. I sipped some soup that Klavdia cooked for us and I even tried to eat the coarse bread.

After several days, Ludmila and Yelena came to visit me. That evening I felt a little better, though I hadn't yet reached the crisis.

Then Laura brought me a piece of bacon, some bread, and a piece of cake. She waited until the doctor, Olga Ivanovna, made the evening visit and asked if she needed any medicine or injections for me. The next day Laura brought an injection that Olga Ivanovna had asked for, but I was so ill I hardly recognized her.

That night I woke up in a fever and felt something cold lying at my side. It was the lifeless body of the Polish woman. I don't know how we managed it, but somehow we got the body out of the bed and onto the floor below. The night guards carried the corpse away.

We fell asleep again. And nobody worried about that dead woman, not even Vidosava and I.

About ten days later after a severe bout of fever followed by dreams of toppling houses, I woke up feeling better. The swollen feeling was gone and so was the pain in my joints. But I could hardly hear. My sight, too, was affected.

I told Olga Ivanovna about my sight and hearing. She wasn't too worried, but checked me again carefully, listening to my heart and lungs. Then she said, "You are a little horse, to get over such an illness." She added that I should get back to bed, eat as much as possible, and rest.

"Thank you, dear Olga Ivanovna, you were like a mother caring for her own child," I said, and tears filled my eyes.

"Don't talk like that, my little Maria," she said and turned away to wipe off a tear.

Several days later I began learning to walk again. I was able to get down from the top bed, but my legs buckled under me. It took me a week to learn to walk by myself.

Olga Ivanovna asked me if I felt strong enough to leave the hospital. She suggested that I stay a few more days when she noticed my hesitation.

It was good there. You could avoid roll calls, sleep whole days and nights, nobody chased you or hit you.

At the beginning of the second week of December, 1943, I left the hospital. A blanket covering my naked body and clogs on my bare feet, I walked all the way to the sauna in the cold.

Suddenly a big truck stopped near our block to pick up the dead. They were piled up high, frozen. Naturally I walked as quickly as possible, my clogs slipping on the ice. There was a pile of corpses outside each block.

The air was sharp and icy, the horizon almost clear, with the blue mountains to the south.

I reached the sauna, showered, was sprayed with disinfectant, received camp clothes and surprisingly good shoes, warm pullovers, panties, and stockings. But I was given the "zero" haircut. I was glad of it, because it was best to have my head shaved after typhus. Then the Polish block leader of Block 20 came to pick me up. I had lost my job at the Political Department.

Inside the new block were two tiers of large wooden boxes. There were eight prisoners to every box. They lived and slept in eights. I approached a group of Russian girls, as I wanted to share their box, and they accepted me.

The roll call wasn't long after supper and we began to make our collective bed. We laughed trying to work out how to make a bed for eight on two very thin mattresses with five blankets, two of them badly torn. We could only change our position in the bed if we all turned over at the same time.

Next to the toilets was a pile of stones. Our task was to carry these over to the main road. About noon, when the stones had all been carried over, we carried them back. It seemed absolutely senseless, but we didn't mind. The weather was clear and cold and the exercise made me feel good. We carried the stones over and back three times.

Our supervisor was a pleasant Polish girl who told us we were making an important contribution to the German war machine. We laughed and worked.

In the evening after supper, we sat in our boxes. There was a sudden roll call. Then a fat SS officer addressed us through the block leader, who translated for him. The camp commander wanted volunteers for the "Puff" (Auschwitz whorehouse, frequented by the SS and the *kapos*).

We were stupefied. A whorehouse in a concentration camp, on a volunteer basis! My box companions expressed their anger.

"That's really something! Only Nazi brains could think of anything like that! I wonder who volunteers for such places."

The answer came immediately. Two prisoners, one a girl, the other middle-aged, volunteered.

"Are you Poles?" the commander asked.

"No, we are both German," the older one replied.

"You seem too old for a good quality whore."

"I am only thirty-three."

"What did you do before you were arrested?"

"I used to work at the same trade."

"What about you?" He turned to the young one.

"I am only nineteen and a half, sir."

"What did you do before you came here?"

"There were French prisoners of war working on our farm—"

"Enough," the commander interrupted her. "Block leader, send them over immediately. There is a big shortage, you understand. But now what about the others? Poles and Russians and all the other trash? Tell them they will have a pleasant life. From ten to sixteen men a day. A fine job. The cream of the cream—SS men, *kapos,* block leaders, foremen."

The block leader translated all this into Polish. She got a girl to put it into Russian, who found it difficult to translate this disgusting proposal.

A very tall girl in a white scarf addressed him. "I want to tell you in the name of the Russian girls that we won't go there. We are ready to work in the fields, the factories, on the road, at any kind of work, but not there."

He was dumbfounded. Then he broke into a big smile.

"Well," he said to the block leader, "tomorrow send all the Russians from your block to outside details. They love to work in the fields and on the road. And this one here," he pointed to the girl in the white scarf, "she'll be the aide of the *kapo.* I like prisoners who want to work."

15

The *kapo,* a German prisoner with a green triangle, walked at the head of the detail. She wore a red armband, looked well fed. She had a disagreeable face, an odious voice, an ugly body. She was an old criminal, and it was said that she had murdered her mother and husband.

No hope. No courage. No spirit of friendship. Nothing. Every prisoner cared for herself. If someone was struck, you were grateful it was not you.

The attacks of the *kapo* and the *Anweiserinnen* fell upon us. They did not pick their victims but struck at random. They slapped our faces, whipped our bodies, beat us all the time without giving us time to recover.

We kept silent. Silent and angry. Worse than that—we were raging inside. We hated the *kapo,* the guards with their leashed dogs.

We walked with frozen legs and feet in our worn-out shoes. We wore only the striped clothes. We came to a large field surrounded by bare trees. Here we had to push wagons along a line of rails. They were small wagons but the effort required of us was enormous.

Were we defeated? Had we become Muslims? That was the fear that almost overpowered me. We were condemned to slow annihilation, if we did not die of disease or malnutrition.

We could not die; we wanted to live, *just to live*—this thought filled me completely, until I no longer felt the cold and the frosty wind. To exist till the Nazis lost their wars, till they didn't exist.

"Work, you stinking *Dreckscheisse!*" The German *Anweiserin* was tall and well dressed. She had a friendly smile for the guard. She was hateful to the prisoners. The rails ran up a mountainside. It was wicked work. The rails could have skirted the slope, but the Germans wanted us to go over the hill. (To us it seemed like a mountain. It was only a hill.)

I wore gloves made from pieces of wool. I had paid two rations of bread for them.

"Russian, you want to work with gloves? Give them to me. You'll get them after work." She pulled my gloves off and walked away.

Then she came back. "Your brothers are fighting German heroes." She hit me.

"Why do you hit me? Am I not working? Do you have some other complaint about me?"

"I beat you when I want to."

We could not talk, we could not help one another. We threw the stones into the lorries. We had no idea of time. At lunchtime the whistles of the *kapo* and the guards sounded along the field.

"Have you been here a long time, in Detail 117?" I asked Josepha, one of my fellow workers.

"Since I got out of the infirmary. I had typhus, you know."

Yes, I knew. So after typhus they send one to this detail, to die in the cold.

"Do they die fast in this detail?"

"We don't like it when somebody dies in the field. We have to carry her on our shoulders. It would be better if they starved in their blocks."

The soup was cold. We ate it in bowls passed from one prisoner to the next. We filled ourselves with turnip soup. We needed something warm, but it was absolutely cold. It tasted awful and contained the powder that stopped our periods.

We looked at the guards, with their dogs, warming themselves near a bonfire. They ate buttered bread and sausage. They had cheese sandwiches, real coffee, real tea.

We could only dream of such food. They gave the scraps to the dogs. They let the dogs fight for it. We would fight, too, for a little piece of meat or sausage, for a little piece of cheese, even a piece of bread.

A sergeant sicced a dog on one of us. The prisoner tried to run away. She ran quickly but tripped on some stones. The dog threw himself on her and bit her in the neck. The guards laughed and the *kapos* joined them. They ate their food and laughed at her. The guard let the dog enjoy himself ripping the girl's flesh. She was a Yugoslav. She did not try to stop the dog from biting her. She lay there passively. She was a Muslim, I thought, she wants to die to escape the suffering, weakness, and brutality.

We started work again, filling the wagons with stones, but in the afternoon the *kapos* saw the wagons weren't full.

They ordered us to push a wagon in the direction of the hill. I was so exhausted I don't know how we reached the top. Our hands were bleeding and frostbitten.

Even in Auschwitz day had an end. We lined up in fives to be counted. We had to carry the girl who had been bitten by the dog. She was almost unconscious, and frozen. It was a wonder the *kapos* allowed us to carry her in shifts. We warmed up marching, but had to slow down when a girl whispered that some of the women could not keep up the pace. We walked slowly till we passed the general assembly. From there we hurried to our block.

The block leader and her assistant greeted us with kicks. "Where have you been so long? We waited for you an hour, dirty faces, Russian faces, crematorium people! You should be sent through the chimneys, oh, yes, through the chimneys."

It was now completely dark. The snow stung our faces. We stood there an hour. It seemed that the other details were late, even later than ours. *Rapportführer* Taube and the *Lageralteste* Stenia, the *Aufseherinnen* and the block leaders, were rushing here and there. Something must have happened.

Then a whistle sounded and we entered our block. We went to our box and took off our shoes. We sat quietly resting after the march and dried our shoes and jackets. Then the *Stubovas* began dishing out supper.

One Sunday I walked over to see Laura. I hadn't seen her in a long time. She kissed me and invited me to climb up to the top bed, which was her kingdom. Oh, yes, her kingdom, because she slept in it by herself, because it was so different from the box where we lived, eight to each box, two wretched blankets and no place for our things, and no place for the food we did not have.

"How am I? Pretty well. I work in Detail 117."

"What did you say? In Detail 117? How did you get there? It is a penal detail. What did you do?"

"Nothing. I'm with Russians, Poles, Yugoslavs, all sick or recovering from typhus or something else, all of us just out of the infirmary but not quite dead. They call us Muslims, but we aren't." I stopped so as not to weep.

"Don't tell me you are in that detail. Even the strong girls don't survive. Are you working on the wagons?" She sighed. I ate a sandwich from Laura's package but it didn't taste good to me. Then Laura gave me a cigarette, and that I really enjoyed.

I left Laura to return to Block 19. On the way I heard the yelling of *Rapportführer* Taube. All the block leaders and *kapos* were doing gymnastics to his orders. He had them run, crawl, jump, and imitate frogs and dogs and croak and bark.

When I saw our block leader jumping like a frog, I laughed, and no one could beat me for laughing.

I climbed into our box. "You know, the *Rapportführer* has a pot belly."

I had a clean brassiere and a clean shirt that I had bought in exchange for the *Zulage* (the double ration of bread and margarine for the work details). I had warm panties I had bought for another *Zulage* from a worker in the *Bekleidungskammer*. I looked clean and wasn't a Muslim. Hard work will make me feel well, I said to myself.

I got under the covers and slept dreamlessly till morning.

We were loading the lorries. Before noon we had an unexpected visitor: *Aufseherin* Irma with her two leashed dogs, *Frau Aufseherin* Irma, blonde, with an angel face and snake eyes, the camp's chief torturer. We were very careful not to attract her attention. We pushed and pushed. It seemed to take us an eternity to roll the car over the hill.

The next team were unable to coordinate their efforts. They were completely unnerved by our visitor. They hesitated and lost control of their wagon. It swayed, bowled down the hill, and capsized, scattering stones over the whole area.

The prisoners were completely broken in spirit. *Aufseherin* Irma sicced the two police dogs on them. The girls tried to escape their fangs, but the trained killers easily overtook them. One grabbed a Polish woman who slipped on a rock. The other fell upon a Russian girl.

At Irma's orders, the *kapo*'s underlings beat and kicked the girls still untouched by the dogs. The *kapo* wrote down the numbers of the delinquent team.

The dogs were tearing at the girls' bodies. Irma came closer to observe what they were doing. Her eyes were bloodshot. The sight of the blood seemed to intoxicate her. She panted. She was sexually excited—everybody could see that. We stood in a trance, as at a gladiatorial combat.

Irma left the girls lying on the ground. We had to carry them back to camp. We tried not to stumble on the way. We knew they were dying.

When we returned to camp the *kapo* led us to Block 2. We were frightened. Why hadn't we been taken to our own block? Somebody said this was the block where they flogged prisoners. Although we knew there were public floggings, we had never seen one.

We came to a yard enclosed by a cement wall. We were told to line up in fives. The girls bitten by the dogs were lying there. It was forbidden to take them to the hospital. Those bitten by the dogs must die.

Six girls were called out to fetch the specially constructed whipping block, which was set up in the middle of the yard. The *kapo* read the numbers of the girls who had capsized the lorry. They stepped forward. Some of them were weeping, others trembling or silent.

Lagerkapo Leo tried the whip—a rawhide knout with three tails. Will she lash all twenty girls? I asked myself. But there were the *kapo* and her underlings, and SS people. There were a lot of people to assist her.

They were waiting for somebody. *Rapportführer* Taube, SS *Aufseherin* Irma Grese, SS *Aufseherin* Drechsler, and *Arbeitsdienstführer* Schultze arrived. Then the lashing began. The prisoners were stripped and lashed across the buttocks.

The first was a Polish girl. She fell on her knees begging for forgiveness, but *Lagerkapo* Leo whipped her across the face. The girl lay down on the whipping block. Her cries were indescribable. She was lucky to get only twenty-five lashes. When Leo got tired, she handed the whip to a *kapo*.

I observed *Rapportführer* Taube and *Aufseherinnen* Irma and

Drechsler. They were excited by the flogging. Irma smiled at Taube and said something to him and they both laughed. When there were only nine girls left to flog, they went off.

The prisoners dying from the lashes lay still. There was no sound from them. The *kapo* flicked at their bodies as if they were weeds. Then she stroked the whip handle and turned away whistling.

We carried away the wounded prisoners. The block leader said we could take them to the hospital. We had to wait till the end of the roll call. It seemed it would never end. It lasted so long that the wounded prisoners were frostbitten and blue.

We carried them to the hospital. I didn't know whether they were alive or dead. I ran to Olga Ivanovna and told her that we had brought over two wounded prisoners. Olga Ivanovna examined them and told us they were dead.

We ate our supper without tasting it. All our thoughts were concentrated on them. This was the first time we had seen a flogging.

There was silence in the blocks and the open spaces between them. Light played on the sentries cramming the towers. They had machine guns and submachine guns commanding the approach to the fence.

Did I see this, or was it only a dream? There was a prisoner hiding in the shadow of a block. She was sure that nobody, not even the sentry, could see her. She must have said to herself, "I've had enough of this hell, this filth, this shouting at me 'dirty Muslim, *Mistbiene, Krematoriumfigur.*' Enough of being kicked and beaten, enough of being a prisoner. Better if I run to the wire. I will die but have the last laugh. I'll not starve on my louse-ridden bed, or at roll call. No, I'll die well at the electrified fence or from a burst of machine gun fire. Better than wait for extermination in Block 25, and then be dragged to the chimneys."

And she slipped out of the shadow of one block and passed on to the shadow of the next. Soon she would reach the forbidden zone.

The sentry in the tower saw her. "There's a lousy prisoner approaching the forbidden zone." He aimed his machine gun. "She doesn't like this camp. She doesn't want to work. She's one more superfluous mouth. She's a stinking Muslim. Come on, my dear, come on, don't be scared of an SS man aiming his submachine gun at you!

"Come on, let me shoot you down. You won't die on the wire. The wire is here for something else. It's here to guard the camp from what's outside, from partisans, maybe, but they wouldn't come here. Germans rule here."

The prisoner ran frenziedly to the high-tension wires. Then the bullets of the submachine gun reached her. She fell, tried to get up, but could not. She had lost the dash for dignity. In a silent requiem, she was lamented by the souls of thousands dead at Auschwitz.

One day I went to a Jewish block, where the workers of the sewing shop lived. I was surrounded by women talking Yiddish. I had some *Zulage* bread and margarine, enough to acquire a pair of stockings or woolen socks.

I saw them lighting candles and knew they would pray over the lights and bless them. It was Friday. It reminded me of my mother lighting and blessing her candles on Friday, but here there was no white bread covered with a napkin beside the candles.

Someone came up to me.

"What do you want in our block? It is Friday evening and we don't do business on the Sabbath."

"I didn't know today is Friday," I said, excusing myself. "I only know when it is Sunday. We don't work that day."

"Why are you looking at the candles?"

"I didn't know that the Jews light candles in a concentration camp. What for?" What I really wanted to say was that I was longing for the candles my mother used to light every Friday.

"Because we believe in God, and we spend our bread to buy candles, but you don't believe in God. You come from Russia and probably your parents don't go to church."

"It would be better if you ate your bread. Nothing will come of your candles. Do they save you from being selected for the crematorium?" I was sorry as I said it. I spoke rudely because the woman had said that my parents were godless.

"Well, our God will pity us if we are selected for the crematorium, or for anything else that happens to us here."

Before leaving, I looked back. There were candles at every window, at every box. I felt like one of these women and I didn't feel like one of them. I didn't dare to reveal my religion for fear of betrayal. I would have despised anyone who had advised me to confess my Jewishness. I wasn't ashamed of it, but they wanted to exterminate us and I had to defend myself as best I could. Therefore I was Russian.

On the way to work, we saw men carrying beds from Auschwitz into the C plot. That was the northern part of Birkenau, past the road to the crematorium. They walked silently, followed by guards with leashed dogs at their sides.

What was the purpose of all this? Were the Germans bringing more prisoners to this camp? Weren't there enough already?

Did they want to imprison all Europe here? The women's numbers had reached ninety thousand; in the men's camp, two hundred thousand.

There, on C plot, the men were beginning to build barracks. We did not know why they were bringing the railway up to Birkenau, and as far as the Brzezinka woods. They were digging holes and ditches.

I woke up the next morning feeling very depressed. I had seen a black man in my dream. He was so hairy I couldn't see where his moustache merged with his beard. He wore black monastic garments and said something in a language I didn't understand. I told my friends about the dream.

"The people where I come from say," Josepha remarked, "that seeing a black man in your dreams means a very dangerous illness." Everyone seemed to agree about this.

On the way back to camp, I felt so ill I couldn't walk. Two friends held me up under the arms. I don't know how I got to camp, how I stood the roll call. All I remember is the moment when I undressed and stretched out on the bed. I dreamed again of the black man. I was hiding behind a tree and he saw me, and suddenly he changed into Walter Betz, wearing an SS hat with the skull and bones. He laughed insanely, pointed at me, and said, "Yes, I know you are a Jewess! You shall die in the flames of the crematorium, but you must tell me where your Jews are hiding."

I woke up coughing. It was a deep, dry cough, piercing my lungs.

"She is dangerously ill. We must take her to the infirmary, but the *Stubova* has to give permission," I heard someone saying.

I was asleep and was roused only when they took me to the hospital. They had brought me to Laura's block, the block for those with lung

illness. Oh, yes, there was the *Pflegernia* on the other side of the partition, where only the dying were put. Would they transfer me there?
When? I waited for them to put me there, because I was dying . . .

Then I thought of my father. He must be dead or he would send us
news of himself. Peter had said as much to me. And what did I know
about my mother and little brother? They must be alive, otherwise
where would I go when the war ended? To Yadwiga's house . . . They
would never know and never imagine that I was sick with typhus and
pneumonia. They must never know that I worked in Detail 117. Should
I tell them—I mean my father . . . He was goodness and charm itself.
I must tell him how *Aufseherin* Irma Grese set dogs on the prisoners
and how the block leader hit me in the face . . . Oh, that would be terrible for him—how a prostitute struck his daughter in the face . . .
Where shall we meet? In the realm of death, if I die now . . . God, I
must not die, I don't want to die before I see the Nazis retreating from
the battlefields. Even if I cannot recover fully, even if I am a cripple,
I want to live . . . Oh, God, give me the strength to live! I am so thirsty,
I want to drink, drink, drink . . . nurse, nurse, quick, come here, I am
so thirsty . . .

I was very ill with pneumonia and pleurisy. I lay in bed for many
days. My fever rose to 104 degrees at night. Maybe I talked of my
perishing nation, perhaps I told about my adventures with the partisans,
perhaps I spoke the forbidden languages, but I couldn't control myself.
I was delirious.

I saw the doctors bend over me, and they spoke Russian and Yiddish among themselves. I understood everything they said, so I wasn't
surprised when Maria Samuilovna, the doctor from the Crimea, a
Jewess, said to me in Russian, "Maria, my dear Maria, don't be
frightened, but we have to transfer you to the *Pflegernia*. It is nothing,
you are still our patient, you won't die. We won't let you die. Even if
you find yourself lying with a dying woman, you shouldn't let it affect
you."

She spoke to me reassuringly, but I understood her. I was dying. I
asked the nurse to call Laura at once. Laura came. She knew about my
going to the *Pflegernia* and was on the verge of tears.

"No, don't weep, Laura. I will not die. God will give me the
strength to live. I must be alive when the Germans say *kaput*. Oh, I will

not die, but Laura, if I lie in back of the partition, will you come and see me?"

Laura nodded her head, because she could not speak without weeping.

Josepha and Nadja, the girls from my detail, came to see me, and they wept silently, as if I were dying.

I wasn't aware of being moved, but I found myself lying behind the partition with another woman in my bed.

She is unconscious, I thought. Perhaps she will die. Here lie only the dying women. Oh, she is awake now, she wants something. I don't know what. I will ask her, but what language will I use? Perhaps Polish. She looks like a Pole to me. But she has found the glass. She coughs and spits into it, coughs and spits again. She says to me, "I spit out my lungs. I don't know if I will live much longer . . . You see, here lie the dying. Are you dying, too? So young and going to die . . ." She coughs and spits again. "Aren't you from Montelupich? It seems to me I saw you there," she says and continues coughing.

I couldn't answer her. I was too shocked to be lying in bed with a woman who had tuberculosis. Will it be death for me, too? I want to sleep . . . I became delirious again.

Nurse Wanda bent over me. "How are you? A little better? Is your name Maria?"

I was conscious and answered, "Yes, I am Maria. I feel just a little better. Isn't it wonderful when a prisoner in the *Pflegernia* gets well?"

"It is wonderful. I'll be happy to transport you back to the block. Now, let's eat." She gave me some oatmeal. I was hungry and the food tasted wonderful, but the woman next to me was coughing again and looking for the glass in which she spit out her lungs. That disgusted me and I wanted to vomit but could not.

"It's nothing to be disgusted about," nurse Wanda said to me. "They spit out their lungs because we have nothing to give them. What can we do when there are no medicines and no injections? When you were very sick, our block leader Katica 'organized' some injections for you, to save your heart. And you seem to have survived the illness."

"Who is Katica, a Yugoslav?" I asked.

"Katica is our block leader, a wonderful girl, a medical student. She has replaced the former block leader, who was, God forgive me, a nasty Pole. I shouldn't say that because I am a Pole myself, but she was an impossible bitch. Now what else do you need? A drink?"

The woman who lay next to me suddenly became conscious. "You listen," she said. "I recognize you from Montelupich Prison. You don't remember me, I was a criminal, an old criminal. I was over there waiting for a transport. For a couple of days we were locked in a cell, in Montelupich. I remember you because somebody said, 'She is a Russian with sixteen names!' " Here she coughed hard and brought up a lot of phlegm. "Don't be disgusted, it is nothing, it is the disease-ridden lungs. I am losing them . . . so I lose my life."

She coughed again, suffocating. When she raised herself, blood came out of her mouth, spilling over the bed, and she fell back unconscious. I called the nurse and helped her clean up the blood. After regaining consciousness, the woman rested a little and then went on speaking. "I am Stanislawa. I am dying. Remember my name. I know you are of Jewish descent, somebody told me. You don't have to confess. To hell with it. You can be a Jew or a Pole or a Russian. It's all the same. I have seen all kinds of people. There are wonderful Jews and the Christians can be like devils and angels. I know you are Jewish, some-body told me . . ."

"No, you are wrong. I am Russian. You must remember that."

But she interrupted me. "You don't have to confess. You are not in district court."

"I have nothing to confess, Stanislawa," I said and fell asleep.

When I awoke, it was evening. The nurse had just come to take care of us for the night. When she shook Stanislawa, she was dead. She could have betrayed me to the administration of the camp, and now she was dead. I didn't know whether I had much longer to live myself. I wasn't sure that I wouldn't be betrayed by another woman as a Jewess, and they would then take me straight to the crematorium . . .

Another woman was put in my bed. She was unconscious. She had inflammation of the pleura, I heard the doctor say.

After two weeks in the *Pflegernia* I began to feel pleasantly well. I was emaciated and was afraid to look at my arms, my legs, my breasts. I had no muscles. I had nothing that could be called flesh, but I had strength in my heart.

Maria Samuilovna, the doctor, checked me. "You are convalescing, my dear," she said in Russian.

"What disease did I have? Please tell me."

"Only pneumonia, and maybe a slight pleurisy. Too such diseases are dangerous and you wouldn't have survived without the injections. Well, tomorrow you'll get up a little."

I saw Katica, the block leader, when she walked through the *Pflegernia*. She wore a white jacket over her striped dress. She was bending over the beds of the dying. Then she came to my bed. I spoke the Yugoslav greeting, "Death to the occupiers and freedom to the partisans," in Russian and she understood. She smiled as she bent over my bed and asked if I felt all right and if I was going back to the block.

I thanked her for the injections. "Oh, there's nothing to thank me for. Many women told me to help you recover. I help the anti-Nazis first. God bless you, Maria, you must live—isn't that so?" And she looked at me with her blue Slavic eyes, so sincere and honest.

I got up at last. I walked back and forth across the barracks. I enjoyed walking—it was like living again, like fighting the Germans—I laughed—with my hands so emaciated I could hardly have pulled a trigger.

I saw Laura. She was excited to see me walking.

I was taken back to the block. I lay in bed surrounded by many convalescents like myself. We talked about the liberation. It seemed so near to us, so imminent. We wanted to be strong, to be fat, because we wanted to get out of the camp alive.

I heard the orchestra playing one Sunday in the infirmary, but with a different conductor. Alma had become ill and died. The new conductor was a Russian girl, Sonia. The musicians lost themselves in their playing. It took them beyond their despair, beyond their hopelessness.

At the concert I saw the Lilliputians—a whole family brought from Hungary. There was one man among them. They were Jewish. I also saw the twins: young girls and grown women, from Dr. Mengele's experiment department, but before any experiments had been performed on them.

I wanted to return to the camp. When I told Laura, she looked me over and was satisfied.

"If you feel that well, you should go back to the camp."

All that evening we sat at her place. We recalled everything, all the women we had known in prison and in the concentration camp. We remembered everyone who had died, and it was a staggering number, maybe several hundred women.

"Now you are leaving the hospital, maybe forever. I hope we do not meet in this place again. I want you to be strong and healthy."

We kissed. I left the barracks the next day, in the early morning. It was the end of March, 1944.

I was assigned to Block 17, B Camp. Our block leader was an intelligent Polish woman, a former teacher. She herself and those working under her treated us as friends. Everyone felt free to approach her.

She gently rebuked the prisoners who behaved badly. This had more effect than a beating. One word from her and we were all won over.

All the work in the block was done quietly, without raising one's voice. In the other blocks where I'd lived, our ration of bread had always been smaller than it should have been because the block leaders pilfered while we starved. But this block leader was honest.

On arrival I was called to the block leader's room. I was frightened at first, and then pleasantly surprised. She invited me to sit down and asked my name and number. I answered in Russian, although she spoke Polish.

"But you know that I am Polish. Why don't you speak my language?"

"How do you know I can speak Polish?"

"I know why you were arrested and sent to a concentration camp. Tell me, is it true that you knew Christina Makowska in prison?"

"Yes, I knew her. We were in the same cell in Montelupich, and I met her again here."

"Christina is no longer here. By the time I got here she had already left. She was caught writing letters to her father and her fiancé. She was deported to Ravensbrück. I knew her outside. For me she was a symbol of Polish resistance."

I told her all I knew about Christina. She was very much affected when she heard about the torture Christina had undergone.

"Why are you so interested in Christina?" I asked.

"Because she refused to recognize me in the Gestapo lineup. I'd been working with the partisans and she rescued me. I pray to God to spare her." She crossed herself. "And now I want to help you. I was told by the Society of the Patriots of All Nations that you were an anti-Nazi. I won't ask you what you did, but I want to help you. I would advise you first to work in the sewing shop, and afterward, when you get stronger, I'll send you to work in the flax fields. All right?"

I was deeply moved by this block leader's behavior. The Society of Patriots of All Nations—what was that? A mutual aid organization? How did they know about me, and how had they gotten me into this block?

I began working in the sewing shop.

Our block was occupied by Poles, Russians, and Yugoslavs who lived quietly together—a welcome change from the hatred that the Nazis fanned.

At the end of April, 1944, the site of the crematorium was surrounded by a wooden fence covered with branches and shrubs. It was impossible to see the buildings except for the chimneys and roofs. Nobody was allowed to walk there.

That first night hell broke out. The locomotives whistled so close to the barracks that we woke immediately. In the dark the SS men herded the transports. There were crowds of men, women, and children. The *Rampa* was alive like a big railroad station. We heard them shrieking.

We wanted to see what was going on. The *Stubovas* and the barracks guards, with tears in their eyes, begged us not to go, because the SS men had ordered anyone shot who went out.

No one could sleep. We looked out through the doors and windows. Women prayed in almost every European language. The noise on the *Rampa* was terrifying. Before morning the four chimneys were pouring out the smoke of dead bodies, nails and hair, crushed bones.

In the morning we were taken out of the block, which was situated near the *Rampa*. We were forbidden to look at the *Rampa* and the crematories.

Nonetheless I saw thirty freight cars filled with people. Then fifty. Then fifty-six. Then seventy. And trains with up to one hundred cars. We counted them every morning, and there were prisoners in the camp who knew how many cars came in every day.

The massacre of people continued. Only a small number were diverted to the camp. They were the best looking, the healthiest, the best guinea pigs. These were saved from the crematorium, but not from Dr. Mengele's experiments. They didn't know what had happened to their loved ones. They were stunned. No one told the truth to the people in the freight cars. No, we could not say anything to them because the SS men were everywhere. The doomed did not know they were to die.

We walked around in a daze. Only one thing was real, the smoke and the flame. The flame shot out from the chimneys, and it was yellow red in the darkness, and it was bright during the day. The blaze was continuous. The smoke hung like a hard, heavy, immobile mass, and pressed between the barracks, in the empty spaces and above the roofs. It was clear weather. There was no wind to blow it away. It irritated the throat, the nose, the lungs.

There was enough food then. We would find the transport's bread, its plum and strawberry jam, in our ration. We got the lard and the goose fat brought there by the doomed. We found jewels in toothpaste and in tubes of cream.

The SS woke the orchestra at night. The Germans wanted them to play and sing songs. The SS forgot it had ordered us not to look at the chimneys, so again we used the toilets and washrooms on the north side. We saw three SS men standing on a hill, sorting out the new arrivals. They called out, "To the right! To the left! To the right!" Right was death. Left was life. How rarely they said "left" and how often "right."

We were so tired we could no longer watch the people getting out of the trains. We had seen French trains, Hungarian and Czech trains, Russian and German trains.

We lived in a nightmare. We couldn't sleep. We couldn't breathe. We couldn't eat. We prayed to God in every language to stop this massacre.

Some women didn't care. One girl said, "I am glad to eat when they kill the Jews. I don't care about them."

"The Germans *should* kill them," said another, "but what will become of us Christians? We will be killed after all the Jews are annihilated." But most of the prisoners couldn't condone the murder of so many people. No normal mind could condone it.

Finally we asked our block leader to allow us out of camp during working hours, and we began working in the flax fields. We left the camp in the morning and returned in the evening. During the day, the smoking chimneys temporarily disappeared from view. We rested pleasantly in the fields. We picked vegetables and green fruit. Nobody disturbed us.

One quiet night in June, 1944, the Nazis took all the men and women from the *Familienlager* where families from Czechoslovakia were interned. Nobody heard anything, but in the morning silence hung over that camp.

Several weeks later Auschwitz was awakened by an uproar from the gypsy camp. The gypsies were running about, fighting the SS men with their bare hands. They resisted but the SS men overpowered them. Then they burned them.

Near "Mexico" camp, near C plot, were sickly-looking women with pernicious diarrhea. They were dressed in rags, their naked bodies showing through. They were on the way to the crematorium, going to their death quietly, as if it were nothing!

One day, as we returned from the flax-fields, our detail was called to A Camp. The *Arbeitsdienstführer* said they wanted to examine us for scabies. We were being chosen for some kind of work, it seemed.

I went with Lisa, Wjera, Dragica, and all of us were chosen. We all looked well after our work in the fields.

"How long have you been here?"

"Since October, 1943," I replied.

"How well she looks. She's been here too long. Have you had any diseases?"

"No, nothing," I said. I knew it was better to say I had never been ill.

They wrote down my number. At roll call, our block leader called our numbers.

"We are going to part," she said, "I am happy you are leaving this camp, even if it's only for Germany."

Nothing could please us more than to leave Auschwitz.

I said good-bye to the block leader, and to Laura, my only friend from the prison days who was still alive. She gave me her address. I promised to write to her if I lived until liberation. We kissed and I left. I thought, to whom else should I say good-bye? I realized there was no one, except the dead.

In the morning we received clean striped clothes, striped underwear, new wooden shoes. We were given a loaf of bread, margarine, and a piece of sausage.

About noon we were loaded into a train, forty girls to a car, the very cars that had brought victims to the camp! We didn't really believe we were leaving Auschwitz until the train actually moved.

We were traveling west, that was clear. We saw men and women dressed like free human beings—a woman in a German dirndl with a white blouse and black apron.

Was it possible that a girl could still dress to please?

Lisa, Wjera, Dragica, and Katja were in the same car. We were a group of Russians, Italians, Yugoslavs, and Poles. I told the girls that my name was Lydia and I was Russian. I kept my father's name and became Lydia Alexandrovna.

The train skirted Vienna, continued south through Baden. After two days of traveling it stopped at a big building that looked like a factory. We got down from the train and an important-looking civilian came up and looked at us appraisingly. Another civilian addressed us in German. He told us we were to work in this munitions factory. If we worked diligently we'd get prizes but if we were lazy we'd be sent back to Auschwitz. We were marched through Hirtenberg, a picturesque little town, till we arrived at an ugly camp consisting of eight barracks. It was located near the slave workers' quarters, and all the workers crowded around to take a look. Compared to us, they were free.

The *Unterscharführer* questioned us about our knowledge of languages. A Polish girl, Sonia, said she knew German and Polish, adding that she could make herself understood by Russians, Yugoslavs, and Italians.

The girls urged me to tell him I knew many languages, as they wanted me to have an important job. I stepped forward and said, "I know German and Russian, Polish and Italian, if you wish to use me as an interpreter." He asked the Polish girl who she was. She said she was

Sonia Butkiewicz. "I am German-Polish. My father was a true German."

"I'll take you," pointing at Sonia, "as *Lageralteste,* and you," he pointed at me, "you'll be the camp clerk."

I asked the girl in Polish, "If your father was German, then where did you get your Polish name?"

"What I said is true. Only my mother was of Polish descent, and from now on you'll have to take orders from me and from the *Unterscharführer.*"

"I think it should be orders from the *Unterscharführer* and then from you." She looked at me with undisguised hatred, but didn't say a word. The girls who surrounded us listened to the conversation. Dragica said, "Lydia, you put that bitch in her place. She says her father was a German. Who knows how she will treat us?"

Lisa, Dragica, and Katja were sent to the kitchen, with Katja as their *kapo.* Wjera was chosen as a block leader, along with five other girls. We slept in barracks. We got two blankets each, and it was a joy to have a bed to myself!

Sonia found Katarzyna, a Polish woman who had been a prison-mate of hers. She was eager to make the bed for the *Lageralteste* and wanted to make mine, too, but I said I didn't need her services. I would make my own bed.

Then I went to see my friends. We discussed Sonia's strange attitude toward the prisoners and the girls expressed their fears.

Sonia was looking for me. The *Unterscharführer* wanted a report on the prisoners, and she told me to list their names, numbers, and nationalities, and then take the list to his room outside the camp.

"Come in," a voice called out when I knocked on the door.

The *Unterscharführer* was sitting on his bed shirtless.

"Prisoner 63578 has brought you the report on the prisoners," I said, standing at attention.

"That's good. That is very good," he mumbled and took the paper from me.

"May I go."

"Why do you have to go? Don't you want to stay with me?"

"I don't stay with Germans."

"You don't believe a German has the same thing a Russian has?

You should take an example from your *Lageralteste*. I love girls who don't bow to the power of the Germans. I must tell you I don't believe in the Führer's dogmas. I don't believe . . . I am . . ." I realized he was drunk.

I excused myself and returned to the camp.

Next morning we were up at five. We washed in a clean washroom. Everything was new: the barracks, the toilet, the kitchen. The guards were new at their task, we at ours. Breakfast was wonderful: ersatz coffee and a piece of bread with margarine.

The *Unterscharführer* had a talk with me. "You will have to give numbers to the prisoners. Now I have to explain something to you. This camp belongs to Mauthausen concentration camp; we are an external camp of Mauthausen. This is also a concentration camp, but you will work in a free factory and the discipline will not be as strict as in Auschwitz. You should be happy you are no longer in Auschwitz. Well, to continue. You will have to write a report every day to Mauthausen. I'll send it through the mail—not you. Not even the *Lageralteste*. If I listened to your *Lageralteste* I'd be very cruel to the girls here. But I am going to listen only to myself. Then I'll be an angel, oh, yes, an angel."

Our girls in the last block got in touch with the Russian men who lived in the slave workers' camp. They promised to contact the girls in the factory, for they also worked there. They said the Americans would be coming from Italy and the Russians through Poland, and we should be patient—we didn't have to wait much longer, but we must wait quietly if we didn't want to be killed.

New staff arrived at the camp, a *Hauptsturmführer,* a doctor, and an SS woman. The *Haupsturmführer,* Karl Schroder, was a tall, thin-faced man who spoke a Viennese German. The doctor, Stephen Wieck, a little man, looked sympathetic. The SS woman looked unpleasant.

Sonia was the first to greet them. I let her go alone, even though she had asked me to come with her. When she returned she was all excited. "You ought to be sorry you didn't go with me, Lydia. I met the *Hauptsturmführer* and the doctor and the *Oberaufseherin*. They are nice, very nice. The *Hauptsturmführer* is just wonderful. He asked me a few questions. He asked, 'How is discipline in the camp?' and, oh, yes, 'How is *Unterscharführer* Kellerman doing?' I didn't know what to say."

A few minutes later the *Hauptsturmführer,* together with Kellerman, entered the office. After some preambles he said, "Sonia has just informed me that she wants a carpenter to make a room for you two, and a store. Would you like to share a room with the *Lageralteste,* away from the other prisoners?"

"No, *Herr Hauptsturmführer,* I would like to live with the rest. I don't need a separate room."

"That's very nice of you, but you will have to share a room with the *Lageralteste.* I want you to enjoy more authority in the camp."

Then he went over various administrative details with me.

The girls returned from work, marching and singing a Russian song. Sonia met me outside.

"Why are they singing a Russian song? It is forbidden."

I looked at her, surprised. "What do you mean, forbidden?"

"It is forbidden to sing Russian songs in a German concentration camp. I'll tell them, don't worry. I'll order them to shut up."

I laughed and went to meet the girls. They were tired after twelve hours of continuous work. Later they complained to me that they had been worked hard, driven by the German foreman. They didn't get a minute's rest and weren't allowed to go to the latrine.

I wanted to take these complaints to the *Hauptsturmführer,* but Sonia stopped me. "You're not allowed to go to the officers, Lydia, without my permission."

I wanted to go anyway, but Katarzyna took me aside and said, "Be careful with her. She talks to the officers, and then boasts about it, and they laugh at you."

That upset me. "Tell me, Katarzyna, were you with Sonia in prison? I have heard something about it."

She had been sweeping the floor and stood there with the broom in her hands. "I can tell you only if you keep quiet about it, Lydia. She was imprisoned along with a German. She was accused of stealing jewels from a Jewish business. And she was also accused of seducing this German and many other Germans. She is a whore, just a whore. She sells herself to many men. She wanted to be an *Anweiserin* in

Auschwitz, but they caught her—excuse me, it will disgust you—they caught her making love to a woman, another whore like herself. But I have to warn you. She hates you terribly. She wants the same discipline here as in Auschwitz. She misses the chimneys."

It was the end of summer, 1944. Every day, at about 10:00 A.M., Allied bombers passed over our heads to bomb some Nazi target. Then at 2:00, 3:00, or 4:00 P.M. they flew back. We prayed that they wouldn't bomb our camp, only the hateful factory producing bullets for the Nazis.

The only news we had came from the slave workers. They told us that the Allies had taken Rome in June, 1944; that they had made big advances in France and were approaching Paris; that the Russians had retaken the Crimea and the Ukraine and were now in Poland, on the San and Bug rivers. We must wait.

Every Friday we took showers in the shower room of the slave workers. It was ordinary enough except for the inscriptions on the frosted glass windows: "Mother, don't forget me," "I am a slave worker in Germany." And names. Family names, first names, sweetheart's names . . . just names. We added our names on the window: Italian names like Angela, or Slavic names, Nadja, Marusia, Hannaka. All the names had the same lonesome look, scratched on the glass.

Sausages, margarine, and cheese were given to the *Lageralteste* to distribute to the prisoners. Sonia welcomed this opportunity to organize some of the food for herself.

I told the girls about it. I suggested that they take their portions to roll call and show them to the *Hauptsturmführer*.

After roll call, one of the girls stepped forward to show the *Hauptsturmführer* her diminished sausage and margarine.

Sonia tried to bluff her way out. But the *Hauptsturmführer* was angry. "You'd better give the sausage to the block leaders to distribute, and you, Lydia, keep a check and report any thefts to me. It's disgusting to steal from the prisoners' food."

After a month in this camp, I felt I was a woman again. My periods had returned after the lapse of a year. The Auschwitz powder had lost its effect.

Olga, a Ukrainian girl and an engineer, drew me aside one day.

"We've decided to sabotage work in the factory. I've worked out a way of damaging the bullets. It's a crime for us to produce bullets to be used on our brothers. What do you think of the idea, Lydia?"

I thought about it. Could the Germans discover the sabotage? Could they trace the dud bullets to this factory? I was all for sabotage, and if I were working in the factory I would do it myself.

Tanya got worse and we were afraid she would die. Antonina came and asked me to call Wieck. He came with me to the dispensary. She was lying on her bed, her face livid, her breathing inaudible. Wieck took her pulse. After a few seconds he dropped her wrist, took out his stethoscope, and listened to her heart. We did not have to ask what he heard. We saw it in his face.

What a pity she had to die so near the end of the war. How could we write to her parents? Wieck's face was sad. He told us we could bury her the next day.

It was the first funeral and, we hoped, the last. We carried her on our shoulders and buried her in a simple grave. The cemetery was forbidden to prisoners. We took a piece of board and inscribed it with her name and date of death: the girl from the Ukraine, who died in the camp.

It was dark when we dug her grave, and the slave workers couldn't see where we buried her. We sent them a letter that Tanya Onistchenko, from the Poltavian region, had died, and we hoped they would bring flowers to her grave. We asked the Poltavians, men and women, to remember her name and her grave, in the vineyard at the foot of the Austrian mountains.

One day Sonia took a Polish girl out of the line of prisoners and struck her hard on the face. "Why didn't you work?" She slapped her again and again.

"Why are you beating me? The SS beat me in Auschwitz, now the *Lageralteste* beats me in Hirtenberg."

Just then *Unterscharführer* Kellerman came into the yard. Startled, he asked Sonia, "Why are you beating her? What has she done?"

"I beat her because I received a report from the factory that she doesn't work well."

The *Unterscharführer* looked at Sonia and repeated, "Why do you beat her? Did someone give you permission to do that? If I don't beat the prisoners, why should you? Do you understand, *Lageralteste?*"

"I understand, *Unterscharführer,*" Sonia answered, her face red.

"Don't call me *Unterscharführer!* I am *Herr Unterscharführer.* Is that understood, *Lageralteste?*"

"Understood, *Herr Unterscharführer.*"

16

The air raid sirens screeched and the guards rushed to their posts. I thought about the girls in the factory. The Germans locked them up in the workshops and then went to the shelters. I wanted the planes to destroy the Germans, but not to hurt my friends in the factory.

There was a tremendous roar from the other side of the mountain. An ammunition dump must have exploded. The barracks seemed to rise in the air, like a bouncing ball. In the middle of all this, Sonia came running through the snow toward us as if her life were at stake.

"If the planes drop leaflets, bring them to me immediately," she said. Wjera, Lisa, and I looked at one another, our mouths agape. Had she run to us through this hell to tell us *that*? When I recovered my composure I said, "*Lageralteste,* would you object if we read them first?" We all laughed.

A guard told me some officers had arrived and were talking to the commandant. I was worried. Maybe they had come about the sabotage. Olga had been destroying the powder. And the girls weren't lacquering the pistons. Maybe our luck had run out.

I sat down to type out the lists of prisoners, as I did every third day. Sonia was in her room. A guard came in and asked the *Lageralteste* to come at once to the *Hauptsturmführer's* office.

I went to tell my friends that something was wrong. I cleared a little frost from the window and sat watching the commandant's office. One hour, two hours. I went back to the typewriter, typed out the lists again, with more mistakes than a child would make. Suddenly the door flew open and Schroder, the *Hauptsturmführer,* came in with another officer. I stood at attention.

"What are you here?" the officer shouted.

"I am just a clerk."

"What is your nationality?"

"Russian."

"Oh, a Russian. We should kill all the Russians, all of them. You are not working in the factory?"

"No, only here in the office."

"Who is working filling the bullets?"

"All the girls from the camp: Poles, Italians, Russians, Yugoslavs."

"Russians . . . Russians. I don't care about the Italians and the Poles. They are ignorant scum, all but the Russians, isn't that so?"

"I don't know, *Herr Offizier,* they are not Bolsheviks. They just work."

"You're not a party member?"

"No. First, I am too young; second, I am not."

He quieted down a little. I saw a friendly look on Schroder's face. "They have discovered an act of sabotage," Schroder said. "We suspect the Russians. What do you think, Lydia?"

"How can that be? There must be a mistake. They are simple girls. They had no education. They wouldn't know how to carry out sabotage." I was certain they didn't know Olga was an engineer.

"There is sabotage in this factory, and I'll find out about it, if I have to beat every girl to death."

Then they left. I went to Wjera and told her all I had heard.

When I came back Sonia asked me where I had been. "In the toilet," I said. Sonia looked at me suspiciously.

When the girls returned from the factory, all the prisoners were dismissed except the Russians. The officer started shouting at them, "Russians, scum, I know about the sabotage, I mean s-a-b-o-t-a-g-e. You are guilty of sabotage. I swear I'll have you all hanged on high trees. All of you!" He almost choked with rage.

"You can stand here till I dismiss you." Then he went off.

We stood in the frozen air. The snow began to fall. The girls warmed themselves by taking turns to go to the toilet. At midnight Kellerman came and dismissed us.

"Tomorrow you'll work packing rockets. The Russians won't have anything to do with bullets anymore." He turned to me and said, "Thank God, I am leaving here. There will be a new *Rapportführer*. They say I am too lenient."

I went to see Olga and told her that we'd probably get a real Nazi murderer now. She was worried, too, but her mind was on the sabotage. "Lydia," she said, "we are going to sabotage the rockets. How, I am not sure, but we'll do it."

The new *Rapportführer* arrived. He was a small, ugly man with a prominent chin. I was sitting at the typewriter and didn't rise, as Kellerman had never asked it of me.

"Don't you get up when the *Rapportführer* comes into your office?" he shouted. I stood up stiffly and replied, "Nobody ever asked me to. If you want me to, then say so, and I will stand to attention."

"I have said so, that is enough. You are the clerk, aren't you?"

"Yes, *Herr Unterscharführer*."

"Where is the *Lageralteste*?" He picked up a sketch I had made. It showed the barracks with the fence and the vineyards in the rear. "Did you make that?"

"Yes, *Herr Unterscharführer*, I did."

"Will you make a picture for me?"

"Yes, *Herr Unterscharführer*."

"I'll be waiting for it."

At that moment Sonia entered. She seemed pleased to meet the *Unterscharführer*. "I am Franz Walter," he said proudly. "I come from an aristocratic family. My father was a baron's bailiff, so I received an aristocratic education." He went on talking to Sonia as they walked out of the office.

That evening, after roll call, the new *Rapportführer* was walking along the road with Sonia when a small Italian girl came along. He stopped her. "You are a cranky sow. You know what that is?"

"I don't understand German," she said, frightened.

"And I don't understand your filthy Italian language! You betrayed us in the war! You are a stinking sow!"

The more he screamed the more excited he became. He knocked the girl to the ground, picked her up, slapped her violently. The girl's screams mingled with the noise of the *Rapportführer's* blows. I thought of the *Haupsturmführer*'s description of him: a man born of the inbreeding of rascals.

I had to rewrite a letter to Mauthausen that the "aristocratic" *Rapportführer* had written in the language of an illiterate. It ran, "I, *Unterscharführer* Franz Walter, came to Hirtenberg camp and have 'disappointed' all the prisoners that were 'depraved' by *Unterscharführer* Kellerman."

I showed him all the mistakes in spelling, sentence structure, and vocabulary that I had underlined with a red pencil. He wasn't offended.

"You know German pretty well, don't you?"

"Yes, I do, and I have a good command of *Hochdeutsch*. You should use my services. Your writing is impossible."

"Lydia, I forbid you to tell anybody, even the *Hauptsturmführer*. You understand?"

"If you don't want me to, I'll keep quiet, *Herr Unterscharführer*," I said.

"Don't annoy me with your *Herr Unterscharführer*. I don't want to hear it anymore. You will write all the reports for me, won't you?"

Wieck said, "Sonia is the most wicked woman I have ever seen! She encourages Franz to mistreat the prisoners. She told him—and I heard it with my own ears—that he should kill some of the prisoners. Franz said, 'You are a very good *Lageralteste*.' Then I left the room. I was afraid I would get into a fight with him, and you know what it means to get into trouble with an old party member."

I went to my office, but I didn't feel like typing. I took a piece of paper and began sketching. I drew a winter landscape of our camp, the trees and vineyards covered with snow. It showed the courtyard and barracks, white and neat-looking, and prisoners. The painting expressed my loneliness.

The *Rapportführer* came in and looked over my shoulder.

"Very nice, Lydia. Is it for me? I want to have a picture of the camp in which I work."

"I'll make a better one for you if you will buy me colored pencils or water colors. I can make you a much prettier drawing." I did not want to give him this one.

"Do you want me to buy you paints? Is that what you want?"

"Exactly, *Herr Unterscharführer*. If you get me the paints I'll make a much better painting for you."

"All right, but you must promise that I will get all your paintings, Lydia."

"All right."

He switched to another subject. "I want you to tell me anything you hear said by the *Hauptsturmführer,* and from *Unterscharführer* Wieck. I want you to be an informer, to tell me everything they say against the Nazi party and against the Germans. You understand, you are not stupid! To Schroder we are no more than *Piffkes*—that's a nasty name the *Ostmarkers* call us."

"How dare you suspect *Haupsturmführer* Schroder! Don't you know he is as good a member of the party as you? And Wieck also."

"If you tell Schroder, I'll torture you. You are nothing, just a prisoner. You told me that you worked on a farm! That's a lie! You were a partisan, spying on the German army and the Third Reich. I read your file. If you want to get out of this camp alive you'd better pray to me as to Christ! You should be a carcass in Auschwitz, in the chimneys of Auschwitz!" He slapped my face.

He turned away and walked out. I saw him through the window, pacing back and forth. The he stepped into the office again.

"Lydia," he said apologetically, "I order you to do this. You must tell me everything they say. I order it! You won't forget? Well, we are quits. Isn't that so, Lydia?" He went out.

The Germans had a tunnel under the factory, dug for them by the slave workers, to be used during air raids. Naturally, the prisoners were forbidden the shelter. During one raid, the prisoners were locked in their workshops while the Germans went down to the shelter as usual. That day, a bomb landed on the factory, went through the roof and the four stories of the building, and exploded in the German shelter!

The girls sabotaged the rockets. Olga said they were giving the red rockets green labels and the green rockets white ones. It didn't seem very much, but it gave the girls satisfaction to know they were doing something.

Natasha came to me to say the girls wanted to put on a play, *Natalka-Poltawka,* a love story about Ukrainian life. We had many talented girls in our group—singers, circus performers, artists. The declared purpose of the play was to celebrate the New Year, but its real purpose was to contact the slave workers and to get their help in case the Germans decided to exterminate us. I asked the *Hauptsturm-führer* if we could put on a show. He thought it a wonderful idea. At the rehearsal Sasha sang a folk song about a garden. We could almost see that garden.

Larissa, the gypsy, danced. She seemed to be somewhere on the steppes far away from the camp. She moved to the rhythm of the guitar and the violins that weren't there. Her eyes shone, and we could see her dressed in the gay colors of her people. Her tempo quickened. Then she stopped suddenly and bowed to the group. We were in a dream. Then we awoke.

Alla, the circus performer, twisted her body in a thousand ways. She lit a match with her toes. She did handstands and contorted her body into a bridge. I was afraid she would break in two!

We were sure that we would have a great show—and contact the slave workers.

One day Franz heard three Italian girls cursing Sonia. He brought them to the office. Sonia whipped them and then Franz had his pleasure. When he was through, he said to me, "I would like you to hit someone someday."

"Do you want to poison Sonia?" Wala asked me. "Tina the nurse has some rat poison. I can let you have some."

"Yes," I said. "She should die like a rat. Once she's dead, there'll be no one left to egg on Franz."

The New Year's show was attended by the *Hauptsturmführer,* the *Rapportführer,* Wieck, the guards and SS women, and all the prisoners. While everyone watched the show, several of our girls talked through the fence to the leaders of the slave workers. The play was a great success—the slave workers promised their help, not only if there was trouble but if we wanted to escape.

The red-haired Maria, and Sasha with the beautiful voice wanted to escape at once. The quiet, blonde Evdokia also dreamed of freedom. She couldn't wait any longer. I warned them that if they were caught they would be executed, but they laughed and said, "If they get us, they can shoot us, but if not, we'll be free."

17

One day Franz brought back from Vienna a light brown boxer. We thought he wanted it as a watchdog, but the dog wasn't vicious. He fed it the garbage from the kitchen—better food than we received.

After a week Franz said, "I'm going to slaughter this dog. He has a fine layer of fat. Wieck said that dog fat is as good as any. My lungs are not in a good state. I need fat." He stroked his belly. "It will be a feast for me. I'll make a Vienna schnitzel from the dog's ham, and I'll eat the liver fried with onions. It will be a banquet. Eh, *Lageralteste*?"

Sonia agreed wholeheartedly.

He killed the dog, skinned it carefully, and hung it up like a butcher's joint. He took the fat to the kitchen and rendered it himself.

Evdokia, Maria, and Sasha told me they would make an attempt to escape the following night. I took another look at the rat poison. Tomorrow night Sonia would get special sugar in her tea! I didn't sleep well that night. I dreamed that the girls were captured and beaten by Franz. They had asked me to join them. They said they had a good plan that was sure to work, but I preferred to make my own plans.

That evening it was particularly quiet. "Sonia, you want a cup of tea?"

"Yes, Lydia."

I heated a little water in a cup and dissolved the red grains. I took some of the herbs we used instead of tea and boiled them with the rat poison. It looked like tea, but the smell was vile.

"Aren't you going to make me some tea, Lydia?"

I made her a cup of this tea, sweetened with sugar from her secret hoard. Sonia thanked me and went to sleep.

I was awakened by her shrieks.

"Should I call Wieck, Sonia?"

"Get me the bucket, quick."

I jumped out of bed, ran to the office, and brought her special bucket. I was too late. She had spewed all over the floor.

"I'm dying. I'm dying." She spewed into the bucket.

I left the office. She could die by herself. I walked through the cold winter night until I came to Wjera's block. She gave me a place in her bunk. The warmth and Wjera's body relaxed me, and I fell asleep.

In the morning I went to the office as usual. To my astonishment, Sonia was still alive. She had big bags under her eyes and was still vomiting. This time I went to call Wieck.

"I am afraid you have a contagious disease, Sonia," He announced after examining her.

The girls carried her on a stretcher to the isolation ward. Wieck winked at me and said, "I think she will enjoy lying alone for a couple of weeks. Perhaps I should inject her with phenol?"

"What is phenol, Wieck?"

"It is an injection—how shall I say?—from which she wouldn't wake up." His face showed his hatred for Sonia.

I laughed and walked away.

The *Hauptsturmführer* appointed me *Lageralteste* temporarily.

The following night the three girls disappeared. Their escape was discovered at the morning roll call. Franz was frantic.

"Where are the girls?"

"I don't know, *Herr Unterscharführer*," I said. "Perhaps when the detail goes to the factory, we can make a more thorough search."

"You're right." He sent the detail to the factory.

How I envied the three girls! Walentina and I had to report at once to the *Hauptsturmführer*.

He sat in his chair and stared at the ceiling. Franz, who was also there, was the first to speak.

"If I thought either of you knew anything, I would shoot you both."

Our camp commander continued to stare at the ceiling.

"It would give me pleasure to eliminate you."

"*Herr Unterscharführer,*" I broke in, "does it make sense that prisoners planning an escape would say anything about it to those in authority over them? I thought you were more clever than that."

"Lydia," Franz said, "I would like to believe you, but the *Lageralteste* is sick. You must know something."

"Stop growling at me! If you don't trust me and Wala, then send us to the factory. Then I wouldn't have all this thankless responsibility."

Schroder spoke up at last. "I see you girls are not guilty."

"You should blame your guards and not us. It seems strange the girls disappeared without anyone firing a shot."

"I'll punish them," Franz said, "yes, the guards. Lazy sons of bitches."

"*Herren Offiziers,* may we go?" I asked politely.

The relief was short-lived. Sonia was back in a week's time.

"I'm sorry I didn't give you enough poison," Tina said.

"So am I, but she'll get hers yet."

Spring was in the air. The spring of the last gasp of the Third Reich was approaching. We were awaiting our liberation. It was March, 1945.

The raids stopped. There was nothing left to bomb. Planes flew by overhead. Where they went or what they bombed, we did not know.

The *Hauptsturmführer* and Wieck showed themselves rarely. Franz stopped beating the girls. Sonia became silent and her leather belt was nowhere to be found.

I was typing the morning report when Franz came into the office. He looked around the room suspiciously and closed the door.

"Why do you close the door, *Herr Unterscharführer*?" I asked, trying to keep calm.

"I don't want anyone to disturb us. I want to make my will. Do you understand? I want to make my will, my testament. Lydia, don't tell anyone about it."

"Oh, no, I wouldn't tell anybody, *Herr Unterscharführer.*"

"Oh, just call me Franz. I am your friend. Isn't that true?"

"Yes, you are . . . Franz! And you want me to do it for you?"

"You know German much better than I do. You will do all the

writing. I want to leave my property to my friend, a very intimate friend of mine, Gertrud Blaschke. She has lived with me for many years, ever since my wife died. The German army has been defeated, but will recover, maybe today! And we will have the new weapons, the V-3, that will destroy all the allied countries, all at once. And now please start writing. I want to make my will because I'm disgusted. I don't know whether I will live that long—to see the German victory. Write that I leave her my house on Himmler Street in Nissen." He walked back and forth across the office.

"What shall I write at the beginning? I must indicate the state of your mind, but I can't because I am a prisoner and you are SS man. What shall I say?"

"I don't know. Write what I told you. I will send it to her and she will remember me forever, even when I am dead." He did his best not to cry.

Work stopped on March 11, 1945. The management of the Gustloff Werke ammunition factory disappeared. The machines lay idle—no more bullets and rockets for the defeated German army. The slave workers and the prisoners sat in their barracks waiting for liberation. Their suitcases and baskets were packed. The slave workers sent us notes asking if we needed help. They would defend us if the SS decided to kill us.

Sonia brought an order from Franz that we were to leave the camp in two parties. First would be the Russians, who made up half the camp, with me as their leader, along with Franz and some of the guards and the SS women. The Poles, the Italians, and the Yugoslavs would make up the second party, with Sonia as their leader, and accompanied by the *Hauptsturmführer* and the remaining guards.

The prisoners were lined up in fives. We were given bread and margarine and a piece of sausage. We wore civilian clothes under our camp uniforms.

I said to Wjera, Lisa, and Antonina, "If I see anyone on the road I know, I'll try to escape; if not, I'll march to Mauthausen."

The *Hauptsturmführer* came out drunk and said he hoped we would be nice girls and would all meet at Mauthausen.

We knew it was a long way to Mauthausen, too long. The slave workers shouted, "Run away, girls, it will be easy for you."

They dispersed when the guards aimed their rifles at them. The road was crowded with troops and refugees. Franz took command. He was drunk.

We marched and marched. We passed endless lines of refugees and soldiers. There were Germans, Hungarians, Romanians, Russians, Estonians, Lithuanians, and Ukrainians. There were the remains of Vlasov's army and all the collaborators from eastern Europe. They were all heading west, where they could present themselves as refugees.

Our striped garments repelled everyone. The same sight greeted us everywhere. The towns and villages were abandoned. Their inhabitants had taken their cars, bikes, and wagons, or had fled on foot. All of them were escaping to the west.

Several times an alarm sounded. We saw Russian and American planes. All the refugees looked for ditches to hide in. Only the soldiers kept on marching.

"Who's that pushing a bike? Isn't it the girl I saw at the dentist's? Isn't it *Fräulein* Barbara?" I said, *"Fräulein* Barbara! Good morning!" She responded with a nod of her head. I was so happy! I pointed her out to Wjera and Antonina. They were surprised and said, "You'd better escape tonight, and take us and the others with you."

I didn't know how to manage the escape, but I kept on turning it over in my mind. Franz passed by. He stood there swaying backward and forward, and cursing. Then he disappeared with one of the guards and we were told to wait for him.

Franz came back riding a white horse. A white horse, just like a Roman in a victory parade. It looked silly to us. He was drunk and pressed the flanks of the horse, afraid of falling off. He rode his horse over to two sergeants in a military car driving away from the front. "Why are you running? I ask you, I ask all the German army, where have you been? You brought this disaster on us."

The sergeants looked at one another, and one of them replied, "Because we didn't have the strength to defeat the Russians. And what did *you* do? You wreck of an SS man, you guarded and beat these girls! Who knows why they are in prison? Shut up, or . . ." and he reached for his pistol.

At the same moment Franz reached for his. "You Wehrmacht face!

You talk like this to me? I am Himmler's guard. I guarded the spies and bandits." He started crying.

The two sergeants looked at him as if he belonged in a mental asylum and drove on.

I would escape tonight. Franz wouldn't take me to Mauthausen! We'd escape tonight because it would be more difficult later. Franz would sleep a drunkard's sleep. I would talk to Zellermayer, our sentry. I hoped he wouldn't stop us. The SS women were quite inoffensive. They were just young girls from Austria who longed to be home with their parents.

I walked over to Zellermayer. "And what will happen if we want to escape? What will you do, Zellermayer?"

"What *should* I do? I don't know. I am just as miserable as you. I don't know what has happened to my wife."

"Zellermayer, you won't shoot? Or if you must, then don't aim directly at us. Just over our heads in the air."

"I will shoot. It is my duty. I would be executed if I didn't. But I won't aim at anybody, I assure you."

I thanked him in the name of the girls.

We must escape tonight.

Franz went to sleep with one of the SS women and abandoned us to the care of the guards. The other guard didn't hear too well and had a stiff neck. He slept most of the time.

I had no fear that Zellermayer would aim at us. He could not aim in the dark even if he wanted to. We lay down but soon got up. There were perhaps ten or eleven of us. None of the others had moved.

Then we began to run. We heard Zellermayer's shots, but they were wide of the mark. We ran wildly. I saw a fenced-off church. We ran into the yard. I lost the girls behind me. I climbed over the fence, jumped over the graves. Then I came to another fence. It was covered with barbed wire. I scratched myself, but I climbed over it. Then I hid myself in a wood on a mountain side.

After I had got back my breath, I tore off my striped garments and stood in a blue sweater and long pants. I climbed the mountain and rested on the other side. Then I heard someone calling, "Where are you?" It was Tamara.

"Yes, here I am," I cried.

No one was pursuing us.

"What do you think, Lydia? What shall we do now?"

"I think we should retrace our steps. We'll head north till we reach the front."

We came to a stream and drank for a long time. We walked for a long time through the woods. We passed empty houses. There was no one around. No dogs barked at us, and in the houses there were no signs of life. We wanted to rest, but it was too dangerous. I didn't know whether they were looking for us, and we were still not far from the camp. We kept going till sunrise. Then we decided to sleep. We slept and slept and slept. I didn't dream at all but just slept quietly, my first sleep in freedom.

I scattered flowers over Tamara's face and hair. She woke up, rubbed her eyes, hardly recognized me. Then she said, "Oh, Lydia, are we really free?" And she wept. I also wept, wondering if I would see my mother, my father, my brothers, Peter.

We turned eastward, following the road. Everybody else was heading west. Our clothes hid the numbers on our arms. Some German soldiers told us we were going in the wrong direction, but I explained in German that we were on the way to our parents in the next town.

The column of refugees suddenly ended. There was only the dung of animals, the tracks of tanks, and a lost blanket nobody cared about.

We now heard the roar of artillery from the east.

It could be very dangerous for two girls there. We hid behind trees and bushes when we heard anything moving.

We saw a hilly village far off. We found it deserted. Entering a house, we found shelves of tomato puree. In the corner stood a barrel of sauerkraut. We were delighted and filled our hungry stomachs. I found some eggs in the yard. Eggs! We hadn't seen eggs for two and a half years. We ate them raw.

We ate the tomato puree and the sauerkraut and we were happy. Time passed and we were eager for time to pass. It began to get dark. I collected some more eggs from outside. It was quiet and we went to sleep. That was the second night of our freedom.

Sometime during the night the village was shelled. We didn't know what time it was. The Germans had left the place and the Russians hadn't yet entered. It was no-man's-land, and yet it was being bombarded.

Then we heard a German platoon in retreat.

The night was nearly over. The Russian artillery began again, but this time the target was not our village. In the morning, although we remained hidden, we opened the door a little so we could catch every sound from outside.

There was sudden movement in the house. Many men were rushing in, kicking over furniture, creating a terrific racket.

Tamara said, "I am afraid. I think they are setting up a machine gun nest."

Just then we heard the striking of a clock. It sounded five times.

And then we heard someone shouting in Russian, "Andriusha! What time is it?"

IV

THE HOMECOMING

18

After my escape I was interned in a Hungarian castle. I was free to walk around inside the castle, but not to go out. I had twice been interrogated and had been promised that the account of my past activities would be verified quickly. I waited. It seemed to me the war was far away. The newspaper on my lap was full of news. I longed for reunion with my parents, with Peter, with my brothers. At night I had disturbing dreams.

Some of the castle cells held prisoners who had been Nazis, Russians in German uniform, Hungarian SS men. The guards treated them roughly.

The trim elderly major stood up. The young captain remained seated at his desk, playing with his fountain pen. They averted their eyes. Had something gone wrong with the investigation? The major took my hand and shook it warmly. "I have the honor to greet a former partisan of the Lvov unit. We know everything about you. There is no need to give us any particulars. We know how you held out against the Gestapo. And we have greetings for you from Willy." And he kissed me on both cheeks, Russian style.

I was choking with pride and my mind was flooded with memories. I couldn't say a word.

The major handed me three letters. The first was from the Lvov police. It said my father had disappeared and had probably been murdered by the Nazis, no one knew when.

The second, from the Red Army, said Peter had been killed in a battle with the Nazis in Czechoslovakia.

The third was a letter from the Ministry of Security in Poland. It ran as follows:

"We have investigated Yadwiga Deren. She stated that German soldiers of the SS appeared on her farm three weeks before the Russian army occupied the territory, searching for Jews. She had been betrayed by someone who knew they were looking for a woman with a boy. They searched the house and found Mrs. Romana Skowronska, alias Rachel Strick, and accused her of being a Jewess. She did not deny it. The boy, who was in the barn, saw the Germans taking his mother and came running to her, saying that at such a moment he would not leave her."

"They both went with the Nazis," Yadwiga was quoted, "and the SS men told me to stay home. I heard several shots and after a few minutes the Nazis came back. They accused me of hiding Jews, and the penalty for that was death, but they proposed to me to have intercourse with them. I was so scared that I let them do whatever they wanted. Then they robbed the house and left. I found out later that they had infected me with syphilis. In the evening my husband came home and I told him the whole story. We went to look for the bodies. Mrs. Skowronska lay on the ground with bullets in the back of her head. The boy lay near her. He was shot through his hands, which covered his face, and also had bullets in the back of the head. We buried them in the place where they were murdered. . . ."

I sat down. Before my eyes my mother appeared, with a country bandanna on her head, looking at me with love, sadness, and anxiety. And my father, my handsome Sashenka, with his smiling face, speaking to us quietly before his disappearance. And Peter, my beloved, always saying, "When the war is over, everything will be fine," and Arthur, my brother, who came to my bedside every day and kissed me good morning. I was now alone among strangers. Should I kill myself? Or try to make a new life?

The major broke into these thoughts.

"You must pull yourself together and tell me what you want to do in the future. A young girl like you should think of making a new life for herself. You have had enough of prison and concentration camps. Don't think me indifferent to the dead. My wife and three children were killed in Smolensk. I lost a brother in the air force. Think it over. You will see that I am right." His words had a strong effect on me.

"If you want to go home," he continued, "we will transport you to Rovno. Or do you want to serve in the army? You know so many languages, the Soviet army needs you."

"Will I be allowed to serve in the army? I would like that. I don't want to go home, to an empty house of memories. How could I be happy there? I want my revenge. Promise me, major, that I'll take an active part in the attack on some German city."

"How can I let you get killed now that you've survived the Nazi hell?"

"How can I live without paying them back?"

The major hesitated for a moment. Then he said, "I promise."

The garden was deserted. I sat on a bench beside some trees that had been neglected during the long war. I looked at my dark green uniform and I was content. The next day I was to join a tank regiment at the Third Ukrainian Front. The Russians had predicted the conquest of Vienna within a few days.

I watched the ants carrying grains to their nest. Was it good to be an ant? The ants have no nationality, religion, race.

I emerged from my gloom. Now I was in the army and must accomplish something.

The ants were out in large numbers. If they had voices, would they argue and push each other around, I wondered. They were swarming around dry grass and dry branches. Was it all so important to them?

We crossed the Danube over a pontoon bridge, following the artillery barrage. Thousands of heavy cannons, howitzers, mortars roared monstrously. Lightning from the Katiushas shone on the horizon. When the bombardment ended, we entered the suburbs. The major had put me in the rear guard. Soon, the first prisoners appeared. Burned-out buildings greeted us. When I saw the charred bodies of those Germans who had obeyed the order "Vienna must remain German," I thought, "Your might has passed. Now it is my turn."

I was a machine gunner in a T-34. Our tank had seen service from

Stalingrad to Vienna. It had been burned out seven times. Twenty-two men had died in it. On the chest of Vanya the commander were displayed the Order of the Patriotic War, the Order of the Red Star, and the Red Flag, given for bravery beyond the call of duty. Other medals commemorated the liberation of Stalingrad, Sevastopol, Odessa, Kursk, Warsaw. He even had a ribbon for all his wounds in battle. I looked at them and envied him. How many Nazis he must have killed! And how many battles he had fought.

We advanced into the city. Through the open hatch I saw a German soldier stumbling toward us. I noticed his black collar with the SS insignia.

Vanya shouted, "Shoot him! What are you waiting for?"

I waited until he came nearer and squeezed the trigger. I saw his distorted face as the bullets ripped through him.

I could not speak to my comrades about the pain that racked me. They were mostly from deep Russia, from Georgia, from Central Asia. They, too, hated the German invader. How I envied them. They had fought for their Mother Russia and their ideals. They could sleep at night.

"What are you thinking about?" The tank commander brought me back to reality. "Is it about the Nazi you killed? That's nothing. He'll be put on the list of Fascists who fell to the Soviet army." And he grinned, showing his white teeth in a broad smile.

We continued to advance. My stomach turned from the stench of the rubble, of burning wood, paint, and human bodies decomposing.

Machine gun bullets began to pepper our steel sides. Our tank turned, like an indignant monster, and rumbled forward, picking up speed rapidly. About two hundreds yards in front of us I saw a strongly fortified gun position. Our 85-millimeter cannon bashed away and soon the concrete structure collapsed and human bodies and parts of weapons rose and fell in the air. My own machine gun rattled away, and in a matter of minutes there was nothing left of the bunker and its defenders.

Through the slit in the armor I saw the silhouettes of German soldiers in flight. I cut them down, but two managed to veer to the right and out of range. I was furious at their escape and in my anger fired a wild burst in the direction they had taken. The commander said, "I understand. You are trying to repay them for your family and your dear friend."

The wireless brought us the latest news: "Vienna is ours. The enemy surrendered. Long live the Red Army!"

Vanya grinned ecstatically. He was a handsome man. His weather-beaten face and neck bore several deep scars. The gunner in our tank was an Armenian youth, and he shouted something in the language of his province. The driver, a stocky blond Ukrainian, stood up and the tears flowed down his face. He didn't bother to wipe them away.

We stopped in a ruined square and opened the hatch to see what was left of Vienna. I heard screaming. A soldier with a savage Mongolian face caught a girl by her blonde hair and threw her down. Her hair mopped the street. Vanya shook his head and laughed. "The spoils of war: the killed, the hanged, and the raped. I wouldn't stop him even if I could. Let him have his pleasure and his venereal disease!" Then he became serious. "I am against all this. You have probably been told that the Soviet army does that after every victory, but it's not true. It is the backward minorities. According to their code, when you conquer a country the women are yours—pretty, ugly, young, or old— it doesn't make any difference to them."

Later I walked alone through the streets of Vienna. The Germans were in hiding. The city seemed deserted. Only groups of Russian soldiers, armed to the teeth, and a few tanks roamed through the city. I stopped at a ruined shop sign, "Music Shop." I walked in. I saw a sheet of music under a charred table. It was a Chopin Concerto for Piano and Orchestra. I began to sing the melody and was so lost in it that at first I did not hear someone moving behind me. Quickly I turned. My submachine gun hung from my shoulder, and my finger was on the trigger, but it was a Russian officer.

Recognizing the melody, he accompanied me. We stopped at a long, difficult passage. He said, "I wonder what my playing's like these days. Could I recapture my former technique? My hands have gotten used to a trigger, and to throwing grenades. When I get home I will practice ten hours a day. It is time for the weapons to be silent and for music to be played instead."

I looked at my rough concentration camp hands. How would I ever regain my own technique?

To celebrate the conquest of Vienna, all the tanks of our regiment met at St. Karl's Square. We fired off a salvo. The men threw up their helmets and kissed each other, Russian style.

"Long live the Red Army! Long live our leader Marshal Malinovsky! Long live our teacher, our father, our shining sun, Generalissimo Iosif Vissarionovich Stalin! Hurrah! Hurrah!"

When the commander shouted to his troops, "You fought well for the Soviet Union!" the regiment shouted back, "We serve the Soviet Union!"

Vanya, the tank commander, was standing near me. He, too, threw up his helmet, revealing his light yellow hair, but he frowned at the cheers and muttered, "We serve the Russian people, and those who died in the Nazi occupation."

"Blessed is the Lord, our God. I will exult in the work of Thy hands. Lord, give me courage to enable me to punish Thy enemies. May it be so!" Thus did Major Kurmangalin pray.

In the shade of the pine trees, all was quiet.

"Russians are . . . shit!" hissed the SS officer. He was lying on the ground. His lips were dry and his face distorted. He groaned as the bayonet dug deeper into his intestines.

The Mongolian profile seemed luminous in the semidarkness. Major Djemal Kurmangalin was sitting on the prostrate SS officer like an Oriental, his feet crossed, as if he were patiently squatting in the marketplace. The major was a tank officer. His face was pockmarked and flat. He spoke Russian with a heavy Kazakh accent. On his chest was displayed an enormous number of medals, going back to the Japanese-Soviet incident on Chalchin-Gol.

The Nazis had killed his three brothers, and to a Kazakh blood vengeance is sacred.

The SS officer twisted and writhed. The major whispered through the darkness, "Perhaps you are the one who killed my brothers." His face was calm, without cruelty. The western horizon turned dark red.

I remembered how the major had come in when I was interviewing one of the prisoners. "I want an officer," he said commandingly.

"You can choose anyone you want, major," I replied.

These were the last defenders of Vienna. Their uniforms were ragged and dirty. They had stripped themselves of their insignia, as they were part of an SS unit.

Major Kurmangalin barked at them in his horrible German, "Is there an officer here?"

They pushed forward a man, who was trying to fend them off with kicks and blows.

"He is an *Obersturmführer*. He is trying to hide."

"Yes, yes, let him suffer, because he is an officer," the other SS men shouted.

"Shut up!" thundered the major, and there was silence. Then he looked straight into the eyes of the SS officer, with the insolence and pride of a victor. The SS man turned away.

When I reached my quarters that evening I overheard a discussion about him.

"He is a Kazakh. He has his own laws and he will follow them to the bitter end." A voice with an Uzbek accent sounded firm.

Another voice, speaking pure Russian, replied, "But his laws are of the past. Let him kill the German but not torture him."

"Yes, but I saw him when he found his brother with a wound cut out on his back in the shape of a five-pointed star. Even if he is a party member, when it comes to revenge he is only a Kazakh."

I thought about it for a moment and decided to visit the major and ask him about his code of vengeance.

In response to my knock, he opened the door and asked shyly, "What is it? Do you want to see me?" He was out of uniform.

"I just want to talk to you. I want to know what you felt when you waited for the death of the SS officer. Was it satisfaction? Happiness? Enjoyment? Or maybe nothing at all . . ."

The major looked at me searchingly. "Does it interest you that much?"

"Yes, very much. You must know that the Nazis killed everyone I loved—my family, my lover, my nation, everyone." I spoke calmly, but rage flickered under the surface. He showed no emotion or even curiosity as he puffed his cigarette. "I know what you did to that Nazi," I continued.

"You mean my illegal torture and murder of the SS officer?"

"Is it the law of vengeance of the Kazakh nation, and perhaps sacred?"

"What I wanted to do was something quite different from what you say. For me, he was a Fascist, a torturer. I wanted to show him something of what the Soviet people have suffered from the Germans. Of course, I know the regulations, but the authorities won't touch me. In fact, why don't you take a couple of German prisoners and show them the same thing, show the bastards how they, too, can be tortured and put to death, let them feel what it's like. But, no, you are a good girl and wouldn't dare do such a thing. What would our country have done without the Kazakhs who never stopped fighting and killing the enemy?"

"You are right. I also have killed Nazis, in the conquest of Vienna, but it was no use. It was an empty revenge. The dead are not revived." Unconsciously I repeated the words of the elderly major, because they seemed so true to me.

He stood like a prophet, his Mongolian eyes turned to the ceiling. His index finger was raised. "Nobody is dead. They live, maybe somewhere else, but they live. Of that I am sure. Their life is without sorrow and filled with happiness. Maybe your mother is this pink white blossom of the apple tree, and your little brother a nightingale. Your lover may be a gray white eagle on the mountaintop, and your father a lonely wolf living on the steppe. I can easily visualize my brothers as a family of lions in the desert." He stopped, dropped his prophetic pose. "That's the way it is," he said prosaically, "and those who hold to the letter of the written law don't interest me at all."

I remained with the tank regiment until the Germans surrendered unconditionally. The army celebrated. For me it was the end of the war that had begun in 1939.

Major Trofimov came to see me. "How are you, Dittochka? The war is over for you, too. I want to have a serious talk with you. The Red Army is in great need of experienced interpreters, and you have been working with prisoners. Intelligence said you were a good interpreter, and I suggest you work with the commander for Lower Austria. I have a friend there, a very nice man."

I interrupted him. "You suggested other things to me, that I should study, grow up."

The major laughed. "But you insisted you wanted to serve the army.

Then you have to serve until you are demobilized. Did you only want to fight?"

"Yes, I only wanted to fight, and I don't know whether I'll make a good interpreter, because I am prejudiced against the Nazis."

"We need just such interpreters, who know why they hate the Germans. Will you go to this friend of mine?"

"It's all the same to me whether I serve the commander of Stalingrad or Vienna. Excuse me, major, you once passed on to me greetings from Willy. Could I see him or get in touch with him?"

"No, you cannot. I will betray only part of the secret. Willy is now serving against the most powerful enemy we have, and he has changed his name."

I was startled. "But our most powerful enemy has ceased to exist."

The major roared with laughter. "That is the secret. I think there will be no more meetings with Willy. I am sorry. Oh, about the Nazis you mentioned to us, our security forces have reported that Betz is no longer in Dresden. He disappeared in 1944. And von Korab is not in Vienna. Apparently they followed the example of all the Nazis who could escape to the west. It seems they weren't too enthusiastic about life under the Russians. By the way, I have a letter for you."

It was from Wjera.

"I've been in Dnepropetrovsk three weeks now. I was happy to get your note and to know that you are in the army, as that was your aim. I found only my mother. My father was killed by the retreating Nazis, and my brother fell for our fatherland. My mother remained alone and I can't tell you how happy she was when she saw me. Our house was destroyed. We now live in a dugout. We have one room, but we are happy. We both work and have enough money for our daily bread. The city is in ruins. They are now rebuilding Stalingrad, and our city is on the list. Don't write to my old address, but just to the post office, as our dugout has no number.

"You should have seen how Franz cursed and swore when he learned that you had escaped with all the other girls. Franz was the one who shot down three women—Maria, the sweet one from the Crimea, an Italian woman, and a Polish girl. I cannot hold back my tears when I think about them. Massacred . . . and never reached their homes and the people they loved so much, as I love my mother. Are your mother and father alive? Is your lover alive? You don't write about them.

"When we reached Mauthausen a terrible sight greeted us. Just like another Auschwitz. Men and women, starved, sick, Muslims. There were Russian Jews, Poles, American and English prisoners. Only Franz and Sonia ate well, issued commands, and did all the beating. It was a happy day when we were released by American troops. They forced the SS to bury the dead and carry the sick. We couldn't hold back. We tore Franz and Sonia to pieces. The Americans looked on, but didn't stop us. They allowed us to take our revenge, and even cheered. We were repatriated. None of our girls wanted to remain with the Americans. We all believed that our families were waiting for us in Russia.

"I must tell you the story of Rachilka Fiodorova. All of us stayed together because we were afraid of the soldiers. Some of them were drunk and after the girls. They thought of us as whores who had served the Germans and betrayed our country. They didn't understand that we had been in German prisons and concentration camps, that we hadn't worked for the Germans and were there against our will, but I don't have to explain all that to you.

"Rachilka wasn't as careful as the rest of us, and she paid for it with her life. The soldiers raped her to death. I still weep when I think of her fate.

"I am interested to know how you are getting along. Have you met any of our old friends? A concentration camp friendship is the strongest friendship there can ever be—Wjera." I was shaken. What was the meaning of all this? And Rachilka's death? Tears came to my eyes.

"Have you finished your letter, Dittochka?" asked the major.

"It disturbed me terribly."

"You must live for the future, Dittochka. Bury your memories. They belong to the past and the past is finished. I am going to give you a posting to this interpreting work in Austria. You'll have my recommendation to go with you."

"Thank you for everything you have made possible for me. I am happy to have known you."

It was summer, 1945. I was serving under the command of Lieutenant Colonel Abramov, an energetic and resolute man. He was something of a dandy and smelled faintly of eau de cologne. He was a party member of twenty-five years' standing.

"I think you will do well in this work. I don't love the Germans any more than you do. I am for prosecuting the former Nazis, and we can accomplish a great deal here. My friend Trofimov knew what I needed. We have the Austrians here and I would say that ninety percent are Nazis. We respect the former prisoners of the Nazis, the Communists and the Austrian patriots, but politically we don't trust them. You will see for yourself. Trofimov writes that you know German quite well. If you translate everything for me, if you can get at their thoughts and everything hidden behind their words, I'll be satisfied."

I was alone in this city that was not far from Vienna. I knew no one. While I was eating my lunch, an officer came in. He was dark haired, wiry, sharp featured. Without introducing himself, he addressed me. "Who are you? The new interpreter?"

"Yes. I am to begin work right after lunch."

He looked me over. "Where do you come from? What did you do during the war?" he asked crossly.

"I came from a concentration camp." I told my story briefly, without mentioning my partisan activities.

He shrugged impatiently. "I don't trust you. Why did you stay with the Germans? Why didn't you escape to Russia? We know your type."

I got angry. "Why don't you read my record before you make such accusations?"

"I think I will," he replied and finished his lunch in silence.

As he walked out, a major came in. "I am Konstantin, the second-in-command for political affairs. I hear that you are our new interpreter. It's nice to have a former partisan working with us. Abramov showed me Trofimov's letter. We have a number of Austrians and Nazis to investigate—I don't see much difference between them—and I will need a good interpreter who knows German well. I understand a little, but I am no linguist."

"Who is the captain who went out when you came in?"

"Oh, Fiedya? He is our special service officer."

"Does he have anything to do with repatriation?"

"He has, but this isn't the place to talk about such things."

Just then a soldier came in and said I was wanted immediately by Lieutenant Colonel Abramov. Without finishing my desert, I followed him to a conference on the various Austrian parties, Social Democratic, Communist, and National. The subject of the conference was assistance for widows, orphans, and POWs. It was not an easy task to translate everything said, but I did my best.

"You translate splendidly," the lieutenant colonel said to me in fluent German. "I understand every word they say, but that's my little secret."

I smiled because I realized that this had been my first examination.

Gradually I learned the duties of the various officers and their attitude to the people we were investigating. The Russians did not trust former Soviet citizens who had been forced to work for the Germans. They were accused of treason and of collaboration. The same applied to Soviet prisoners taken by the Germans. It was considered a disgrace to have been taken prisoner by the Germans. Of course it was always debatable whether they had surrendered to the Germans or been overpowered by them, but in any case it was felt they should have killed themselves with a grenade or their last bullet rather than be taken prisoner.

The same applied to the women and girls forced to work for the Germans. The fact that they were made to work against their will, suffered in prisons and concentration camps, and sabotaged the German war effort didn't count. I was one of these women. The thing that saved me was that I had been a partisan, though some of the officers still showed their distrust.

I worked with Konstantin on the case of the burgomaster with a cache of rifles and grenades in his home. Sasha, the operation officer, was with us. When he found weapons concealed all over the house, he was incensed and gave the Nazi a stinging blow.

Konstantin turned away disapprovingly, and in the car he said, "Our party line changed long ago. We do not do such things to the Nazis any longer. By the way, I did not see you at the last party meeting."

"I don't care, Kostia. In my hometown, Melitopol, they massacred my parents and raped my sister. That's something I'll never forget. They are monsters and I will never forgive them as long as I live."

"You do whatever pleases you, Sasha, but not in my presence. I will forgive you this time, but if it happens again . . ."

"I will disappear forever," Sasha said.

"No, I didn't mean that, Sasha. You are mistaken."

The burgomaster was arrested, sent under guard to the commandant of Vienna, and, Konstantin told me in secret, would be given a "heavy measure of social punishment," which meant execution.

One day, after we had become well acquainted, Sasha said to me, "Kostia can go to hell. Such a nice fellow, a real fighter, and yet how he talks. I don't understand him. He would be willing to betray his best friend. I only know how to fight and to be an operation officer. I love my Mother Russia, but we simple people don't understand politics. One day they say to us, sacrifice everything you have for heavy industry, even your family life; another day they say the family is a fundamental cell of life. One day they say, kill all the Nazi invaders; another day they forbid us to hurt the murderers of our people. I am a party member because without it I couldn't be what I am now, but I am a passive one. I don't talk. I just agree to everything."

I had to ask him, "What do you think of Stalin? All I know of him is that he is the leader of the Communist party and the 'Father of the Nations.' "

Sasha's expression changed. He replied angrily, "What! You are asking me what do I think of Stalin? He is the teacher of Marxism—Leninism, the leader and the shining light of all the world. Generalissimo Iosif Vissarionovich Stalin! That is what I think. You should never ask a friend what he thinks of such leaders as Lenin and Stalin! Tell me the truth, did Konstantin take you on as a spy? If so, I won't even talk to you."

"Oh, no, he didn't have anything to do with it. He regards me as a product of Polish capitalism. He doesn't trust me. It's lucky for me I was a partisan."

"I know your story, but I still don't understand you, asking about Stalin. You must be naïve or crazy. Or maybe you are a spy for Kostia." He laughed.

After that, I kept quiet and never asked such questions again.

Fiedya was briefing me. He also had his doubts about my past and worried about the contacts I had made in the course of my work.

"We are after a Nazi living in the American zone." (Vienna and Austria had been divided into Allied zones in the summer of 1945.) "He belonged to our zone, and you can prove yourself by fetching him back. You'll have a Communist in the Austrian police to help you, and follow my orders."

Later I learned that Fiedya's prejudice against girls who had lived in Nazi Europe went back a long time. His girl had gone around with German officers and escaped with them at the end of the war.

Soon after this, Abramov, who had been away several days, returned from Vienna with the beautiful Yekaterina. Abramov had a wife and a fifteen-year-old son in Moscow, but Katyenka was his "campaign love." She had been a slave worker till the Red Army liberated her.

When I asked her if she had been investigated by the NKVD she was astonished. "I was taken by the Germans, and I was liberated. Then I met Abramov. Why should they investigate me?"

I began to lose my faith in the NKVD.

I was now working on the capture of the Nazi in the American Zone. I went to Vienna in civilian clothes, accompanied by an Austrian policeman, and we watched the house where he lived. He was working for the American army, having concealed his Nazi past. Out of pride, Fiedya didn't want to ask the Americans for help.

The Nazi had a confederate named Franz, so one day I went to him with a message that Franz wanted to meet him near the brewery in Schwechat. He didn't suspect me and followed me into a car in which Fiedya and the Austrian policeman were waiting for him. When he saw the two strangers he hesitated, but the policeman's Viennese accent reassured him. The policeman explained that Franz had to see him immediately.

When we passed the brewery and continued on the road to the Russian Zone, he asked where the meeting with Franz was to take place. The Austrian answered him with handcuffs.

I was the interpreter when he was investigated. The charges included sending Jews to be butchered, taking their diamonds and gold teeth, and aryanizing Jewish property. He had become the proprietor of a Jewish factory. It was decided he should be court-martialed.

I felt my place was with the Russians because they were working against the Nazis. But what was to come later? Should I be repatriated to Russia? Did I have a future in Europe? My thoughts turned to Palestine. I had no information about it. The Russian papers ignored it. I couldn't find any Jews who were not Russians, and for a Russian Jew it was the crime of crimes even to think about Zionism.

Two of the newspapers we read in the army were *Pravda* ("Truth") and *Izvestia* ("News"). There was a joke about them: "There is no news in *The Truth* and there is no truth in *The News*."

My grandfather lived in Palestine. How could I have forgotten such a thing! I even remembered his address—92 Rothschild Boulevard, Tel Aviv. Certainly I couldn't forget my grandfather, with his little beard, his glasses, his forceful personality. I remembered how in 1939 he had shouted at the whole family, "Now that Hitler's taken Czechoslovakia, Poland will be next, and you will perish if you don't come to Palestine!"

He took my grandmother with him and returned to Palestine. But there was no way of reaching him. I couldn't think of using the army post office. It would be a fine thing if they found a letter addressed to Palestine.

I kept thinking about these Jews with weapons in their hands. I remembered how helpless I had been when I was unarmed. One day, in Vienna, I walked by the Rothschild Hospital. I heard someone speaking Polish. I stopped when I saw two youths who looked Jewish. "Are you Jewish boys? Where are you from? I'm also from Poland."

"We are Jews who saved ourselves from the Nazis. There are several thousand Jews in Vienna. They are coming here from all over Europe. But most of us were exterminated."

"Where do you live?" They pointed to the Rothschild Hospital.

I became terribly excited. They were alive and waiting for a visa to Palestine. And I, in a Soviet uniform, I, too, dreamt of emigrating to the Holy Land! If the Russians knew it!

Katyenka soon returned and I had to go back with her. In the car she said, "If you are free this evening, will you come and translate the film for us? It may be interesting for you. A very handsome major is accompanying us, a distinguished man, with a past anyone could envy. He is younger and much handsomer than Abramov—I could fall in love with him myself."

That evening I was introduced to the major. He was brought along by Abramov and Katyenka. He was a strikingly handsome man, with a jagged scar down his face. He shook my hand firmly and introduced himself as Misha. That was my brother's name.

There was a flutter of excitement in the hall as we walked in and took our seats in the box reserved for the Russian commandant of the area. The film was about the rise and fall of the German Reich. It was in English, with German subtitles.

The next evening, after a long and grueling day, I was eating my dinner in the mess. I was very tired, and as I sipped a little vodka my eyes closed for a minute. I felt someone sitting opposite me, and when I looked up I found slanting emerald eyes upon me. A jagged scar ran from the forehead down to the corner of the mouth. A snub nose was underlined by very red lips.

"Good evening! I wasn't sure you would recognize me, Miss Interpreter. I've been looking for you."

"Well, here I am."

"Then why are you only a sergeant major? Generally, interpreters are at least lieutenants. Do you know German well?"

"Yes, I know German very well. As for my rank, I've only been in the army since April, 1945, when I escaped from a concentration camp." Then, impelled by some curious desire to boast, I added, "Incidentally, I speak French, English, Polish, Ukrainian, and Italian, and I can understand Czech, Bulgarian, Serbian, and Spanish."

"You must be a very valuable interpreter." He laughed sarcastically, the scar twitching downward. "Where did you learn all those languages? Where do you come from?"

"I'm from Rovno, western Ukraine. Does that surprise you, major?"

"No, not at all. You probably come from a wealthy home, bourgeois parents who gave you the best education, the best teachers. And somehow you lived through the German occupation . . . and everything."

"Not 'everything,' if you don't mind! I went through what I went through, and it has all been checked by the NKVD."

"No offense meant, but consider, the Russians took over your city in September, 1939. Then you were under German rule from 1941. Suppose you were taken to do slave work for the Nazis, you didn't have a choice, until the Red Army liberated you. And now you are an interpreter!" He laughed.

I flushed with anger. "What you are saying, major, is not true. As I told you, the NKVD investigated my case and I have been officially thanked for my work with the partisans."

"I am not going to argue with you about what you did or didn't do, but I am inclined to think that if you fought the Nazis it was out of personal hatred for what they had done to you. It was not a Marxist kind of hatred. A true Marxist kills only out of hatred for the Fascist regime."

"Do you mean to say that you fight only for an idea? Don't you feel any personal hatred for them?"

"Our way of thinking is different. You come from the capitalist regime of Poland. I come from the workers' and peasants' regime of the USSR. I do hate the Nazis, but because of the terrible things they have done, not to me personally, but to a whole people."

"Maybe you should finish by saying, 'Hitler will be wiped out and the German nation will live' "—I was quoting from Stalin's speech.

"That's a genuine idea from Leninism-Stalinism."

"Still, you couldn't object if an ordinary citizen fought the enemy out of personal hatred?"

"No, I couldn't object. After all, that is the way most people think. But the truth, the real truth, the workers' and peasants' truth, lies in my way of thinking, though I must say you have a convincing manner, even to a true proletarian and Marxist like me." His laughter irritated me. "Sergeant major," he continued in his incisive voice, "let me tell you that in the tank corps I am the political second-in-command, but in private life I am the editor of a newspaper. I am interested to hear your story, but as a private individual, not as a commissar or even an editor."

"But you couldn't be a private individual. You are always a commissar, whether in uniform or out of it." It was my turn to laugh.

"I am really not as terrible or as frightening as all that. Let's try."

I couldn't help smiling as I nodded in agreement.

Three days later I knocked on a door inscribed "Michael Bogatyrev, Guards Major." That meant he had fought at Stalingrad, for Guards was the name given to the divisions that had fought there.

Major Misha opened the door for me. He gave me a powerful handshake. Though my hands were not lacking in strength, his grasp precluded participation or resistance.

He lost no time and began asking questions almost at once. I responded at some length and talked freely, holding nothing back. Occasionally he scribbled something in a notebook. When I talked about Peter I could hardly hold back my tears.

"You are still in love with him," he remarked. "After all, he is dead."

"But I love the memory of him. He is dead, but for me he is still alive."

"You are talking nonsense, Dittochka. He is dead." He said gently, "You received word from the Red Army and there can be no doubt about it."

"Then why isn't my brother Misha alive? The Red Army notified me he didn't fall for the fatherland, he wasn't in any hospital. Yet he isn't in any unit of the Red Army."

"You forget your brother was mobilized in 1940 and the war started in 1941. I am sorry to say the army has no accurate records for 1941, 1942, or even 1943. They just don't know what happened to him."

"And neither do I. Now the war is over and everything is just wonderful. All those whom I loved are dead, and I suppose I should be very happy."

"You shouldn't be so sarcastic. Why does it make you so terribly unhappy? Everyone in Russia has someone to mourn and terrible memories to live with. There's no reason to cling to them. Stop thinking about the dead. You should be in love with someone who is alive. I know what I am saying. Marxist science says that whatever dies becomes extinct. It disappears and is no more. Live in the present, or for the future. I wish I could create an earthquake in your mind that would get rid of all these thoughts you have." He stood there before me as though he were about to do just that.

His white shirt suited his deeply tanned skin and even his ugly scar. But I was a stranger to him—a daughter of the bourgeoisie. Children of the bourgeoisie were highly suspect. They couldn't join the army.

His hand touched mine. "Wake up from your dream. What were you thinking? I'll gladly give a ruble to know."

"My thoughts are my treasure and nobody can take them away from me."

"You can keep your treasure for yourself. No one wants to take it from you," he said contemptuously. He went to the cupboard and, with outward composure, took out a bottle and two glasses. I felt that inwardly he was boiling.

"Let's drink to the friendship of a daughter of a capitalist regime and a son of the Marxist science of the USSR. Do you find that amusing?"

"No, not amusing. Dangerous." My heart skipped a beat as I said it.

At that, he roared with mad laughter. He was indeed handsome in his ugliness, with his bronzed face, the terrible scar, and the impudent look in his eyes. Finding his face astonishingly attractive, I turned my eyes away.

Several days passed, and we met again. We walked toward the lake in the park. Gulls flew along the edge of the water and alighted to rest. The trees looked dark green in the mirror of the lake. I was at a loss, not knowing what to say to him. He seemed lost in gloomy thoughts.

Finally I broke the silence. "You haven't told me anything about yourself. You promised you would."

He sighed. After a pause, he said, "Generally, I don't like to talk about my past, but since I promised . . . I was born between 1913 and 1915. It may sound strange to put it that way, but actually I don't know. I have no birth certificate. Maybe there was one, but I have no parents or anyone who knows the date. I am not much concerned about it, but I was concerned about being a *besprisornyi*—a waif. Don't look at me with such dismay. When you were a child you had parents and maybe a governess, if I am not mistaken. I lived in the street. Without a home. Without food. And what's worse—without love. I am still envious of loved children. Anyway, we were waifs during and after the civil war. We lived in gangs. We stole and cursed and smoked cigarette butts. We had terrible gang fights. Bones were broken and skulls bashed in. Then, after the revolution, I was put into an orphanage. It was called *Dietdom*—children's home—a corrective institution for street children. The discipline seemed worse than a prison to us. Many escaped, were caught, tried, and sent back. I did not know my name, so the teachers gave me one, and they gave me everything else, even love. We were educated at government expense. Now I am director of a high school and editor of a newspaper. Perhaps that is the source of my faith in the Soviet government, in proletarian thinking, in Marxist science. It served as mother and father to me. I have been in the thick of the worst battles. I started four years ago as a corporal and today I am a major. The scar is a fresh one, from the Battle of Vienna. Can you now understand why I revere our leader Stalin and why I am proud to be a real Marxist? And you. Don't you want to tell me about your childhood?"

"Why not? I could." And I told him the story of my happy childhood with my parents and brothers and the old governess Zinaida Pavlovna. I told him about my attendance at the university, how the war started, my brother was mobilized into the Red Army, my parents died. I told him about my love for Peter. When I reached the end of my story with the three letters that Trofimov had handed me, I was overwhelmed with grief. Misha took out his handkerchief and, giving it to me, said, "You shouldn't cry, do you hear me?" He shook me so hard I stopped. "It hurts when a friend cries. Let's talk about something else."

We met a few times more. One rainy day, he came to my office. "I came to say good-bye. I am going back on leave to see my wife and children. You are surprised? Here's a notebook of mine. I'd like to leave it with you. You will find quotations in it from my favorite authors. When you have forgotten about me, send it back to me. My address is inside. Promise?" He smiled and handed me a small package, neatly wrapped.

My heart sank and I could find nothing to say.

"I've been in love with you, Dittochka, but there's no use talking about it. I have my family. I am not asking for your photograph or for you to write to me. But you will always remain in my memory as a brave girl and one who pleased me. But we won't meet again, I assure you. Be well and give your love to a man who has never known what love is. *Proschayte!*" He kissed me for the first time, twice on each cheek, and left.

The notebook, I later discovered, contained quotations from Tolstoi, Pushkin, Mayakovski and Makarenko. Makarenko was an educator and a teacher of homeless children.

"Get ready, Dittochka, we are going to visit a textile factory. The directors have some fabrics they want to give us." Abramov winked.

We went to the factory. The Austrian directors were extremely polite and kowtowed at every word Abramov uttered.

When we returned to the office, Abramov asked me to sit down. "Did you say you are really Jewish?"

"I wouldn't lie about my nationality, comrade Abramov."

"Your face isn't, and your character isn't Jewish either." His tone seemed sarcastic to me.

"As for my face, let the masters of the human race, the Nazis, worry about that, and I don't know what you mean by Jewish character."

"I've known many Jews. Some were liars, who played dirty tricks. Others were honest, warmhearted, brave. You seem to be the second type, but why do you hide your true nationality? There must be some secret about you. You must be the daughter of White Russians, or Ukrainian nationalists."

"Surely you have known me long enough to know that that couldn't be true. You amaze me. Besides, I was checked by the NKVD and they cleared me."

"I bow deeply before the NKVD, but still. Why didn't you take any fabrics? They are very expensive."

"They're all dirty Nazis, and yet they were able to open a textile factory. Excuse me, comrade Abramov, are you saying all this out of anti-Semitism?"

"Anti-Semitism is forbidden to a genuine party member like me. I like all the nationalities of the USSR."

"Then I'm a pure Russian Jew. Does that satisfy you?"

"I was only joking. You get indignant too easily. You're too young to be so serious."

Before leaving I said, "I want to study diplomacy. Would you give me your recommendation?"

"Yes, certainly."

Later, I walked out on the street. The ruins of many houses and of a Catholic church, the clouded sky and the gray avenues did not cheer me up. Why was I still in Europe? This Europe was beginning to get on my nerves. Did I really want to study diplomacy? What was there for me to do here? To serve in the army as an interpreter? All the prominent Nazis had been arrested, the little ones had gone into hiding or hidden their past. One of the Austrian policemen had told me that soon mail would be going abroad. I picked up a pine branch and was pulling out the needles, one after another. I was so absorbed that I didn't notice a master sergeant of infantry walking in step with me.

"Excuse me, sergeant major, may I talk to you?" he asked politely.

I looked up to see a tall man with a striking masculine face. Long lashes framed his green eyes. He was handsome and he pleased me. His chest was covered with medals, among which shone the Star of Glory, given to sergeants for bravery beyond the call of duty.

"Perhaps you hesitate because we haven't been introduced, but I want very much to talk to you. I know your whole story. I too was captured by the Nazis."

"Is that why you want to speak to me, to find out which of us suffered more?"

"No. Not because of that," he said with a pleasant smile.

"If you like, you can come to see me at my office."

He looked straight into my eyes and said, "You will see me soon."

We became friends. I liked him, but at the same time I was afraid of him, not the way I had been afraid in the Gestapo prison, but a strange kind of fear that I had never before experienced—I had the impression that he was an overtense spring that might snap any day.

One evening, Oleg—that was his name—came to my quarters. He was silent, thoughtful, then suddenly blurted out, "I would like to tell you everything that has happened to me in my short life, though it seems to me I have lived a never-ending length of time . . ." He stammered a little, the consequence of a brain concussion suffered at the beginning of the war.

He lighted a cigarette and his hands trembled slightly, the consequence of another concussion during the Battle of Berlin. "I was a bomber pilot once, many years ago, in 1941. Then I lost everything—my country, my self-esteem, my glory—because I was captured by the Nazis and held as a prisoner of war." He stopped and looked at his lighted cigarette.

His words astonished me. What had happened to his rank? He was now only a master sergeant and decorated. He had his glory, and his country. What was this about his self-esteem? It was I who didn't have a country, who had always served other countries, a Jew without a fatherland . . .

His voice broke in upon my thoughts. "Even though I was wounded and unable to escape, it made no difference. I even had my military papers and party membership card on me, which could betray me easily to my captors when my plane crashed in enemy territory. What happened to me was the very thing we had always dreaded. Our Soviet commandant was convinced that anyone taken alive by the enemy probably wanted to be taken prisoner . . . he must be 'anti-Communist' and probably 'leaned toward Fascism,' was a 'coward' or a 'traitor' . . . for a faithful armed citizen would surely fight to the end, or shoot himself, or blow himself up along with his captors. Yes, we were constantly haunted by this possibility . . . the plane would crash, or burn, and we would have to bail out into enemy territory.

"After all, there are circumstances when a soldier has no choice but to surrender. But that was not what the Soviet government told us. 'Never surrender! Better to blow yourself up! Not one step back!' They were afraid everybody would surrender to the Nazi devils. But I . . . I hated the Nazis bitterly . . . for the invasion, for destroying our happiness, our dreams. I hated them for their senseless slaughter, for the hatred they brought us. I tell you frankly, I hated them for personal reasons, too, because they killed my parents and my brother, who was a partisan. Ah, these personal things, you can't escape them. And you, too, lost everything . . ." At this point his hands trembled so much that he lost his cigarette and bent down to pick it up.

"I understand, Oleg. It is terrible when your government thinks that only cowards are in the army. It is hard to believe that any soldier in the Red Army would ever refuse to fight, or willingly surrender. How could they think that only cowards or traitors are taken prisoner? Every nation recognizes that sometimes it is inevitable. Of course the Nazis didn't honor the Geneva Convention with Soviet Russia, so I can imagine what it meant for a Russian soldier to be captured by the Nazis."

"But I doubt that it would have been better for me to blow myself up rather than be captured," Oleg replied, frowning. "Let me tell you all about it so you will understand.

"I was then a first lieutenant. My plane was hit by flak, and when I saw that one motor was on fire I gave the order to bail out. Then I was struck by a splinter and lost consciousness as I jumped. I awoke in a German hospital, covered with bandages.

"Some days later, officers of the German Luftwaffe came to see me. They smiled and asked in their terrible Russian how I felt and when I would be up. I could follow their German when they talked among themselves and knew what they were after, so I played dumb.

"One day I was called to their office. On the table were vodka, bread, good things to eat, but I refused. I took only a few cigarettes. Then began the questioning—what were the bomb objectives, how were we to bomb, how were we told to behave when captured. I said I didn't remember the orders. They laughed in my face and waved my military papers and party card in front of me. They urged me to be reasonable, not to get myself shot. When I still refused to open my mouth, they called in a couple of privates, who beat me up and took me to a POW camp.

"That camp was a terrible, unforgettable place. Prisoners were in an awful state. Many had wounds, without dressings, just covered with strips of paper bandages. There was no water. They were parched. They were cold at night. They had no clean underwear, no blankets, nothing. They were starving. A bit of miserable soup and a crust of sawdust bread were all they got. Many had dysentery, with no medical help, and the strongest men were dying like flies. I'll never forget it, so help me God!

"When I realized what I was up against, I chose two fellows who were willing to break out with me and go back to the front. They were strong as bulls and faithful as dogs. They believed in me, somehow. I was a pilot and knew the territory well. We managed to escape and cut across the country to the front line. It was then our real trouble began, first with the German and Romanian troops and then, worst of all, with our own troops.

"We were taken by the guards to an officer. He transferred us to an NKVD officer, who arrested us at once and put us in separate cells. They wanted to make sure we could not communicate with each other. That was our happy return to the Soviet army! We were interrogated day and night by different officers. They did not torture us, but to hear their accusations was enough to make your hair stand on end. We were called 'Vlasov army men who surrendered at Hitler's orders.' We were accused of being 'dirty spies,' 'bloody collaborators,' or 'Trotskyite renegades.' I kept repeating the same thing to the major in charge: that I had been wounded, that my plane crashed in enemy territory, and that I could not escape any sooner than I did. If what I had done was an offense to the Red Army, I wanted to wash it away in blood, but I couldn't see what I had done that was wrong. Then the major asked me what I had done with my military papers and party card, perhaps I had torn them up before being captured. He believed that I had given myself up to the Germans.

"I rose up mad with rage and asked him to call my unit, to check on my physical condition then and now. I cried out that I hated the Nazis, that they had killed my parents and my brother, and that I didn't care to live unless I could fight them.

"After this outburst, the major calmly told me that the Red Army would forgive my treason—'treason,' he said with a nasty laugh—and that they would take me back, but as a private in the infantry and not in the air force. I would have to restore their faith in me through my courage and my blood. I wouldn't be permitted to wear my medals, and a letter would be sent to my commanding officer that I was a suspected traitor and must be watched.

"I agreed to this. Otherwise I would have been assigned to a punishment battalion and no one would have cared if I perished. Anyhow, I fought through the rest of the war under these conditions. I fought madly. I rose to the rank of master sergeant. I have the medals of the liberation of Stalingrad, of the Kursk battle, of the liberation of Odessa, of Sevastopol, of Warsaw, of the battle for Berlin. You can see, I have the medals for Patriotic War, for Bravery, and the Glory Star, but there was always the gnawing pain that I couldn't fly. Flying is my real passion. I long for it as an infatuated man longs for his beloved—even more. I used to watch our bombers buzzing toward the enemy positions and I cursed my fate aloud, shaking my clenched fists. If I were a woman, I would have wept aloud. . ." He wiped his face with his trembling hand. I had a strong urge to take those trembling fingers into my own, but I resisted it.

"That was the reward the Red Army gave me for escaping and returning to its ranks. I was accused and condemned in a secret one-man court-martial. Well, at least I have my life and whatever I have earned with my strength and temerity, but nothing in the world can repay me for the loss of flying. Now, I can no longer fly—too many concussions of the brain, my leg broken in several places, shrapnel in my hip and thigh, contusions and bruises all over my body. I couldn't even apply for a civilian flying job. I am such a cripple . . ." and he stammered badly.

I felt an overwhelming pity for him and tried to comfort him. "You have fought enough for one lifetime. You should think about other things. Maybe you could train pilots. We, the generation of World War II, have to forget all these terrible things. It will be difficult, I know, but we must look to the future."

Oleg lit another cigarette. "Yes, you are right, Dittochka, I possess only my life. Have you read *How the Steel Was Tempered* by Ostrovski? He says that life is the most precious thing in the world. It is given only once to a man and he has to live it regardless of the aimlessly lived years or the disgrace of a past. What makes me angry, though, is the recollection of the man who sentenced me to serve in the infantry, who wanted me to be killed or be so mutilated that I could never fly again. I can't forget that."

"What do you want to do, Oleg?" I asked.

"That is a straightforward question. I'll answer it the same way. I want to escape to the west." He said this so decisively that I was startled. I could not help looking around to make sure no one had overheard. I could not understand. Why should he want to escape, a decorated veteran of the Red Army? He could have a job and receive compensation for his wounds.

"Shut up, Oleg, please," I whispered. "I am a real friend, but how do you know no one has overheard? We would be lost. I want to escape also, for other reasons, but I hold my tongue."

"It's true," he said with difficulty. "I ought to keep my mouth shut." And he looked ludicrously docile.

"And if you escape to the west, what will you find there?"

"I don't know what I'll find, but at least I'll be a free man and nobody will arrest me and sentence me for years to a concentration camp."

"So you'll be a free man, so what?"

"I don't know. I'll be safe, I guess. I want to sleep quietly, and work or be idle as I please. I don't want any more reprimands and propaganda talk telling me what I ought to do."

"And how do you expect to earn your living?"

"I don't know how to do anything except flying and fighting. That's all useless in peacetime. Also, I stammer and tremble and nobody will take me on. Although I can drive a car and repair engines—that's something. I am quite an educated fellow. You see that, don't you?" he said with calm self-mockery.

"Yes, I see."

"And perhaps write a book about a bomber pilot who was captured by the Nazis, who escaped and returned to his army, was convicted in a one-man trial, and how he became disgusted with his own fate and his own country."

"Oh, you'd be rich, a millionaire," I laughed. "There was once a GPU agent who deserted to America and now he can't count all his money!"

"I heard about that, and I'll end the book with the Marxist-Leninist science that gets into your soup, whether you like it or not. Yes, Ditta, go to the west. What good is it for you to go to a school for diplomats? What's the good of studying diplomacy? You'll never be able to think of policy. It will always be stated very definitely for you—no discussion or thought about it. You'll be forced to think what the government wants you to think. You'll have to have your speeches checked in advance. If you wish to be that kind of diplomat, then change your name into a Russian one, get the best marks in Marxist-Leninist science, and fall neatly into step."

"Why should I change my name into a Russian one?"

"Because with a Jewish name you would never be admitted to such a school."

"I thought there is no discrimination against the Jewish nationality?"

"Not officially. But there is discrimination. Do you know that there were no Jews in our air force regiment? Or in the tanks? Sure, there were many Jewish heroes in the infantry, in transportation—they fought like mad against the Nazis, and there could be no suspicion that they would allow themselves to be captured. But let's forget about it and talk about making our escape."

"I must think about it, Oleg."

"Very well. When you've finished thinking, report to me." He said good-bye and gallantly limped off on his wounded leg, straight, tall, and stubbornly upright.

I had learned that one could send letters abroad now and had written to my grandparents. One day my landlady brought me a telegram: "WE ARE HAPPY YOU ARE ALIVE. LETTER FOLLOWS. PISIUK." I wrote another letter enclosing my photo.

One evening I was called to the office. There were two British soldiers there, arrested on a train without proper papers.

As I entered the guardhouse, I saw two dark-complexioned men with big moustaches, wearing khaki berets. My first thought was that they must be from one of the British colonies.

"Who are you?"

"We are from the Palestine Brigade."

That was a surprise. When I examined their books I found them stamped, in English and Hebrew, "Palestine Brigade."

"You are Jews? From Eretz Israel?" I asked in Hebrew.

"You speak Hebrew! It's sad to see a girl like you serving in a foreign army and not settling in her own country!"

That made me angry. "You, too, are serving in a foreign army, the army of your British masters. Does that make you happy? And just wait till I get the chance to come! And now what were you doing in the Russian Zone without proper papers?"

"We were going to Hungary and didn't know the train passed through your zone. You can see, we got our papers in Paris. Our families come from Hungary and we wanted to trace them."

I remembered only to well the trains that had arrived every day at Auschwitz, with their children and old people who didn't even know they were to be gassed. My heart grew softer, and I didn't tell them what I knew.

"Maybe you will find them. I wish you luck." At this moment Sasha entered the guardhouse and I told him the whole story. He shook hands with them.

"I like fighters. Before I release them, let's invite them for a meal."

Our conversation was mostly about Palestine. One of them was a member of a kibbutz, the other a farmer. They talked about wheat fields, citrus groves, vineyards. They told me about bloody encounters with the Arabs and the British, about illegal immigration.

"You should contact the soldiers of the Palestine Brigade," they advised me privately. "They can help you escape from Europe." They told me about the Palestinian paratroopers who had gone to Hungary to save Jews and perished there themselves. They drank vodka, clinked their glasses with Sasha, and shook hands with us when they left.

Finally the long-awaited letter came. It was not in my grandfather's handwriting.

"Dearest Ditta, It is your Uncle Samuel who is writing to you. I was arrested by the Russians at the Lithuanian border and spent two years in prison camps. Then I got to Palestine with the Polish army. Yours is the first voice we've heard from Europe. Everybody else is dead. My children perished in Rovno. I was beyond despair, but every Jew has victims to mourn. Your grandparents died in 1942, but I will receive you as a daughter. I met my wife in a Russian prison. She will be very happy to have you. If you could get to the American Zone of Austria, I would send you the immigration permit that I got for my dear daughter. With regards from all your relatives in Palestine, Uncle Sam and Aunt Anna."

That destroyed the secret hopes I had still cherished. Somehow I had never believed the news I was given about my family, but now I knew the truth. Now I knew I was alone.

After my meeting with the Jewish soldiers I went through a radical change. What was I doing in Europe, with the long-forgotten graves of its victims and its new graves for war criminals?

I made up my mind to go to Palestine. The fact that I would be exchanging my luxurious life in an army of occupation for that of a DP didn't bother me. I didn't want to be a homeless Jew anymore.

A few days later Abramov said to me, "I would like to introduce you this evening to an important friend of mine, a lieutenant general. You can talk over with him your notion to study in the school of diplomacy." That evening the car carried us through an avenue of linden trees to the baroque villa of Lieutenant General Kowalenko.

The general was a tall, elderly man, clean-shaven and well-groomed. In spite of his gray hair, his face looked young, with its protruding chin, firm mouth, light blue eyes.

We had a quiet meal. The orderly was a quick and efficient waiter. From the conversation it was clear that Kowalenko was an old friend of Abramov's. They talked of victories and retreats, and they recalled with sorrow their dead friends.

After the meal, we adjourned to the general's study. The chairs we sat on looked like museum pieces.

"What would you think of the plans we have for my young lieutenant? She wants to study for a career in diplomacy."

"I like a young woman to think about her education. It is admirable, my young lieutenant—excuse me, I've forgotten your name. Ah yes! Ditta Alexandrovna, such a foreign name. I know you studied law before the war, and during the war had the education of a partisan, even of a spy. You have also acquired an education in a Gestapo prison and a concentration camp. Isn't this enough for someone as young as you, Ditta Alexandrovna? Why do you want to study diplomacy? Tell me the truth." He looked at me sternly, but I detected a fatherly look in his eyes. I answered that I knew many languages and thought myself suited for the profession.

"I think you are too clever to be a diplomat. Don't you want to be a doctor or a surgeon? Or a mathematician? Or a botanist? I don't want to hurt your feelings, but I must come right out with it. Do you belong to the Young Communist League? What is your background? You have a capitalist past and a bourgeois heredity. I know your war record, that you were an active partisan and that you fought well in our army, but even so the heads of the school would not accept your application. Why don't you choose something else? Something non-political? Unfortunately, you belong to a national minority. Abramov and I have nothing against you, but the school management . . . They would respect you as a member of a national minority, but they wouldn't like your background. We don't want you to suffer. You would never be admitted to such a school. We can get you into any university in Russia, but not the school for diplomats. Ditta Alexandrovna, aren't you interested in medicine?"

This blunt reply clinched my decision to leave the army and Russia. All I thought of was the return to my homeland.

My discharge orders arrived. I was to proceed to Kiev in the Ukraine. I sat in the office, fingering these papers, but my thoughts were only of my escape.

That evening I packed my suitcase quickly. I left my greatcoat, uniform, and medals. "I am leaving in the morning," I whispered to myself.

Before sunrise, I locked my door behind me and put the key in my jacket. A fine mist rolled in from the Danube. It was drizzling. I saw a military police patrol not far from the station. If the patrol saw me I would be arrested and court-martialed. The train was just about to leave. I found a compartment, said *"Guten Morgen"* in my best Austrian accent, and sat down.

An elderly woman dressed in black sat near me. She sighed as she said to her companion, *"Frau* Grete, I'm thinking constantly about my son Heinz. He was captured by the Bolsheviks. Yesterday I received a letter from him in Siberia. They are working in the woods there. I am sorry he wasn't captured by the Americans."

Frau Grete replied, "Our prisoners are miserable wherever they are. They fought the war for Hitler. They have to pay for that, but why should we be so badly off? We don't have enough bread, or meat, or lard. Do you know how much a kilo of swine fat costs? Three thousand schillings."

Opposite me sat a middle-aged man with an empty sleeve. He gestured with his surviving hand, as if to say, "They don't know what they are talking about. I know the truth." He was smoking some horrible-smelling tobacco.

The train stopped at Vienna West. American military police checked the documents of all military personnel. I walked out of the station and saw an old man wearing a green Viennese hat with a feather. "Pardon me," I said, "can you tell me how to get to the Rothschild Hospital?"

There was an inscription over the hospital entrance: "Sons of Israel, let us ascend to our homeland!" This was the watchword of the first pioneers from Russia, the Bilu.

A skinny man conducted me to the office of a young Palestinian in battle dress.

"*Shalom,*" I said.

"*Shalom,*" he said. And then, in German, "What can I do for you?"

I replied in Hebrew, "My name is Judith Strick. This morning I was a lieutenant in the Red Army. My discharge papers had come and I was to go to Russia, but I want to go to my fatherland."

"Your story is interesting, very interesting. Do you have any papers you can show me?"

I handed him my army pass and the letters I had received from Palestine.

He examined the papers for a few minutes, then said, "I cannot read Russian." He called out "Abrasha!" and a young man appeared. "Translate these papers for me."

Abrasha did so. "They're authentic. And her uncle writes to her from Tel Aviv. She is one of us."

The young Palestinian said, "You are a deserter from the Russians and still in danger. Luckily, there's a train leaving after midnight for the American Zone, and I'll give you a pass for the camp in Linz."

"Thanks very much."

"My name is Arthur. Perhaps we will meet in Palestine. *Shalom.*"

There were clean and airy cattle cars at the railway station. I compared them with those provided for the Final Solution, when people were herded together without water, with no place to sit, crowded, and sent off to Auschwitz. We waited and I lit a cigarette. A woman near me, with a sleeping child on her lap, asked me in Yiddish for a smoke.

"Where are you from?" I asked her.

"I am from Warsaw. And you?"

"I am from Rovno, and here begins our road to Eretz Israel."

"We have suffered enough," she sighed.

The young people opposite me started to sing in Hebrew *"Anu Banu Artza.* ('We Return to Our Homeland')!" I joined in. It recalled for me the atmosphere of the Zionist High School in Rovno.

I felt young again, without sorrow, without worries.

If only it hadn't taken so many years. If only I weren't alone.

The train began to move.

The sun was shining when the train stopped in Linz, in the American Zone. The station was crowded and noisy. Austrian boys were selling American cigarettes and candy. Many American soldiers were about. They all smelled of cleanliness, of toothpaste, of after-shave lotion, of tobacco, while the Russians had smelled of cabbage soup, of shoe polish and tar, of oil for cleaning rifles, and the officers had reeked of cologne.

Soon a man in a gray suit introduced himself to us as the camp commandant. "Brothers and sisters," he said, "you are welcome to the New Palestine camp. We don't know how long you will have to be here, but we hope it will be a pleasant stay."

Formerly this camp had been occupied by the German army. It was surrounded by pine groves and there was a garden that nobody tended. In the heaps of rubbish behind the houses, I saw scraps of red German flags with the swastika, and pictures of Hitler and his generals. It was amazing that they had weathered the heavy rains and snows of the winter, but then, the Germans always knew how to make fast colors.

The next day I walked into the office, where a friendly Polish woman in uniform questioned me.

"What is your name? Where do you come from?"

"I am Susan Pisiuk, born in 1926 in Rovno. I come from Russia."

It annoyed me that I had to change my name. When I had changed it because of the Nazi occupation that had been understandable, but to to be obliged to change it so that the British would allow me to enter my own country—that annoyed me.

I was assigned to work in the office. What strange people these Americans! They chewed gum, put their dirty feet on the desk, read comics instead of doing office work! Private First Class Cook had a pile of magazines on his desk, and he was reading a tourist book about Vienna. "Sarge," he said, "I want to visit Vienna. I can't go home without seeing that city."

"There is nothing to see there. It is an old, burned wreck," Sergeant Perres answered. Then he looked over his papers and handed me one, saying, "Miss Susan, please type this page in triplicate."

January of 1947 arrived. My passport was ready, with the British visa for Palestine and the French transit. The Vienna-Linz-Strasbourg-Paris express stopped at the station. A large group of my companions came to see me off and gave me letters and regards for many people, from Galilee to the Negev. I said good-bye and thought with pity of all the people who had to remain in the camp for an indefinite time, but I couldn't help being happy about my own fate.

On February 19, 1947, at noon, I boarded the ship *Providence*. In an hour I would be leaving the French shore.

The pale blue Mediterranean sky stretched above the harbor. A warm sun irradiated the greenish waves as through a thin veil. The many sounds of the port combined into a deafening uproar. The clanking of anchor chains. The squeaking of winches. The ship's horns, sometimes piercingly sharp, sometimes a hollow roar. The shouts of sailors and stevedores; the swish of the waves, whitecapped and dirty with rubbish, as they beat against the sides of the ship and broke. The port of Marseilles was crowded with men, some in uniform, some in overalls.

I looked down from the deck upon this hubbub below. I could see the old port, ruined by the Nazis, with its burned buildings and parts of sunken ships. Two pilot boats began to tow the ship and it turned from the pier, slowly heading out to the open sea.

At last I was leaving this continent on which I had suffered and survived all the disasters of the horrible war. Did I hate it? No and yes. No, because there were many places I would like to visit again. Yes, because there wasn't a single person who had been dear to me who remained there. Even though I knew that death was a law of nature, something within me rebelled against it—perhaps because it had come to me so early in life and with such murderous force. I couldn't shake off the thought that never again would I see my father's happy smile, or the serious expression on my mother's face, or Peter's blond unruly forelock, or the long dark eyelashes of my little brother.

At night there was a storm, and the next day everyone was seasick. I sat at the table with two priests, a Polish woman, two nuns, and a young Britisher on his way to Egypt. The jolly young French waiter said to me, "You are not seasick, mademoiselle, so I'll bring you a double portion of red wine."

There was an elderly woman on board, with broad shoulders and big hands accustomed to heavy work. "You must be an old-timer in Palestine?" I asked in Hebrew.

"Yes, you are right. I am from Metulla." I knew that was a settlement on the Lebanese border.

"Is it a village or a kibbutz?" I asked.

"It is a village. And who are you, speaking such good Hebrew and not knowing what Metulla is?"

"I am from the Ukraine and I am going home for the first time."

"Oh, I'm also from the Ukraine, but I traveled for the first time eighteen years ago. There was peace then, and I was a young girl like you. Oh, time passes. I remember when I first set foot on the soil of my homeland, I said, 'And to bring thee to the place that I have prepared.' Perhaps you don't know this prayer. My grandmother taught it to me."

The night before landing I could not sleep. The next day at six in the morning our ship was to reach the port of Haifa. I was restless, could find no place for myself. In my cabin the women were snoring as if it were just an ordinary night. I climbed to the upper deck. It was hot and sultry. The moon looked strange to me, with the crescent upside down, not at all like the moon that shone over Europe. We are in Asia, I said to myself. The waves were breaking slowly and gently on the sides of the ship, their foamy crests fluorescent in the darkness.

The ship moved slowly. I saw the eastern sky become lighter, turn orange and light yellow, with a silverlike mist covering the whole horizon. Sea gulls appeared from the unseen shore.

It was just before sunrise. The east glowed crimson and scarlet. The waves whispered like a sleepy child. Warmth came from everywhere, from the mist, from the water, from the cloudy haze. I strained my eyes in an effort to see Haifa but couldn't. All I saw was a thick, heavy mist.

Suddenly from the top of a mast a sailor shouted, "Land!" and at once I saw Mt. Carmel bathed in sunrays as the mist quickly lifted. I saw the port with its dark buildings, with ships and freighters, with British battleships. I saw the houses on the slopes of the mountain, the buses climbing the roads. And it was our Haifa, our port, our land . . . I had come to my native land like the Israelites who wandered for forty years through the desert. I, too, had left a desert behind me.

Two pilot boats began to tow our ship, and the English flag was on them, but it didn't matter to me; these were our boats, our sailors. I didn't pray, I didn't weep. It was like a dream come true.

I saw a crowd of people and the noise of the harbor reached me, the whistles of the ships, the buzzing of the winches, but it was our noise, our whistles, our winches. It didn't matter that in the crowd I saw khaki uniforms of British soldiers and the dark blue uniforms of the police. They were merely the occupiers, but these were our people, our workers, our women.

Then I saw a little boat and in it stood a man. He waved his arms frantically and shouted, "Ditta! Ditta!" and tears were running down his face. It was my Uncle Samuel! I can't remember what I shouted back. All I knew was a longing to be with my relatives, at once, this very minute. At the same time, an indescribable feeling of loss overwhelmed me, irretrievable loss.

With dry eyes, with a dull ache in my soul, I descended the wooden stairs. I put my feet on the concrete of the pier and felt that at that moment I was stepping on my own soil, from which no enemy could ever drive me. A Jewish policeman, with a moustache and red cheeks, stood there greeting us, "You are welcome to Eretz Israel. *Shalom!"*

I fell into the arms of my uncles. My eyes filled with tears, which I did not bother to wipe away.

We were in a taxi driving to Tel Aviv. On one side of the road was the sea, on the other the hills of Carmel. I sat between my two uncles. How Samuel had changed. His hair was graying, and there were many wrinkles around his mouth. Then I looked at Uncle Simcha, who was twenty years younger, tall and good-looking, smartly dressed. He was the lucky one. When he was thirteen his father had brought him to Palestine and put him in school, and he had never returned to Europe.

The taxi was now passing through orange groves. For the first time I saw the "fragrant citrus" with cypress and pine trees forming a border. Suddenly a British convoy approached—tanks, armored cars, Bren carriers—and our taxi was ordered to stop.

I whispered to Uncle Simcha, "What are the British doing? I thought I had come to a peaceful country."

"The British are in continuous war with the terrorists," my uncle explained. "You will know more about it later, when you have been in this country more than two hours."

Finally the convoy passed and the road was clear. The driver turned on his radio and we heard a woman's cool voice announce in Hebrew, "The British army forces have imposed a curfew on the Tel Aviv region because of terrorist activities. The population is instructed to buy food and stay at home. The curfew begins at four in the afternoon."

We reached Tel Aviv a half hour before curfew. My Aunt Anna greeted me warmly. "You will be our daughter, Dittochka," she said.

Then we went to buy food. The streets of Tel Aviv looked modern to me, with fine houses, flowering trees, and clean asphalt. Everyone was rushing with baskets to buy food. I heard Hebrew all around me. I was introduced to the storekeeper as a new arrival. I replied in Hebrew and it seemed to me I had never spoken any other language. I saw the advertisements, the movie posters—all in Hebrew. If only I had come here with my parents before the war . . .

I sat at the table eating the cake that had been baked for me, drinking coffee with milk. There were my grandmother's cups and china. Everything in the house, which had been the home of my grandparents, reminded me of them. The old silver Hanukkah lamp, their photos, the vase that I remembered, and my grandfather's library. On the desk stood a photograph of three happy young girls taken before the war, cousins—the blonde Esther, the tall, dark-haired Susan, and me . . . There were smiles on all our faces then, but now only one of us remained.

My uncle called me into my grandfather's library. "Ditta, my dear, you have suffered enough. Promise me you will not join the terrorist organization. It is very easy to die in Palestine. If you want to, join the Haganah. They are not crazy like the Stern Gang. Promise!"

He reached out his right hand to me and there was nothing to do but clasp it in mine.

19

On a February evening, I walked alone on the dark streets of Tel Aviv. As if from nowhere, three masked youngsters appeared, carrying a pot of glue and some posters. Quickly they glued a poster on a wall and disappeared.

I read: "NATIONAL MILITARY ORGANIZATION—IRGUN. The British hold Tel Aviv, Ramat Gan, and Petah Tiqva guilty of the latest terrorist actions. They have been placed under military control. The cities are not guilty. Only the terrorists are guilty."

Someone ripped the poster down, saying, "They are crazy. I'm sorry the Haganah boys weren't here."

"They are an illegal organization, so what can you expect from them?" said a woman.

I stood there listening. It was difficult for me to understand the people's reaction to partisans—instinctively I used the same word as under the Nazi occupation.

As I walked along I noticed a newsstand. Many papers were displayed, among them *Davar,* the Labor party paper. I stopped to read: "They, the outcasts, the terrorist organizations such as the IZL and the LEHI, are breaking up our national unity. They are defeating our security measures. They are against self-restraint toward the Arabs. They harass the British outrageously. The Haganah forces and Palmach, the kibbutzim and villages, remain calm under Arab provocations. They are the pioneers who will give us the long-awaited freedom."

Perhaps because I had been educated in the partisan school of Europe, I believed that only by fighting for it would freedom be won.

On a quiet Sabbath eve in March, the family was at the dinner table. In the west the setting sun was painting the sky pink, crimson, and purple, while in the east it had already turned turquoise blue and gray.

I wasn't interested in the gefilte fish and the roast. I was impatient to speak to my cousin Avraham, who was sitting opposite me. When we finally reached the tea and cake, I asked to be excused and walked with Avraham into the library, in which stood a bronze bust of Jabotinsky, the leader of the Irgun.

"I remember, Avraham, when we met in our house in Rovno. You told us then that you were active in the Irgun. I want to join this organization. Can you help me?"

Avraham seemed disturbed by my request and began pacing the room. Then he stopped in front of me and, looking straight into my eyes, he said, "Ditta, you have survived hell. Is it not enough for you? Why don't you join the Haganah?"

"Don't play games with me, Avraham. I want to be an active soldier. I am convinced that we must drive out the British and resist the Arabs. If you won't help me, I'll find some other way."

"I'll try, Ditta, but you must be patient."

Through the closed door we could hear the Sabbath songs, and we joined the family around the table.

I was working in an office for three lawyers, but the work did not satisfy me. I was restless. I dreamed of becoming an Israeli partisan. Finally Avraham brought me the news.

At eight o'clock sharp I was waiting on the corner of Tchlenow and Kongress streets. In my hands I held a rolled-up newspaper. A dark young Yemenite with an overgrown moustache stopped in front of me. He looked me over carefully, then asked, "When does the bus leave for Jerusalem?" That was the password.

"It leaves at nine o'clock."

"Follow me," he whispered.

By the time we reached a big open space overgrown with bushes and weeds, it was dark. He handed me some glasses and said, "Put them on. You won't see anything, but don't be afraid."

I took his arm as we made several turns and finally reached a door at which he knocked three times.

As we entered, he whispered, "Follow me. There are stairs." On the landing he left me.

I didn't know where I was nor how long it was before I heard a man's voice say, "Take off your glasses and come forward. You will see a torch."

I walked in and stood at attention.

"*Shalom.* Who are you?" the same voice asked, and thus began my first examination in Israel. "Why did you come to the Irgun? Do you believe in its aims?"

"I am not concerned with the political aims of the Irgun. I believe only that every thinking youth in Palestine should join an organization that fights, and I want to be a member of the Irgun, an active soldier, just as I was under the Nazi occupation."

They whispered among themselves. A car passed and threw its lights on the walls. A cat meowed. There was silence.

"Did you ever get orders to kill the enemy, to spy, to sabotage?" another voice asked.

"Yes, and I will be happy to do the same for my country."

Again there was whispering. I strained my ears but could hear nothing. The strong light of the torch bothered my eyes. I felt completely exposed before these men.

The commanding voice spoke again. "We will have to think about your application. In a week's time you will have our answer. *Shalom.*"

It seemed to me that the voice was not unfriendly.

In May, a man walked into my office. Without raising my head from the papers on my desk, I asked, "What can I do for you?"

"For me, nothing, miss. Judith, can I talk to you privately?"

His words startled me. In front of me stood a stranger, a tall, blond young man dressed in khaki, wearing goggles. If I had seen him in a German uniform I would have taken him for a pure Aryan. Apparently I wasn't free of the German way of thinking. "I am Judith, but I don't know you. If you wish to talk to me privately, I am alone in the office, but how do you know my name?" and my heart beat a little faster.

"My name is Amichai," the man whispered. "I will be your commander in the Irgun. Tell me your home address," and he scribbled it in a notebook. "Our first meeting will be on Friday, at eight, at 30 Gruzenberg Street. At the gate a girl will answer to the words 'good luck' and will bring you to the right place. Did you understand?"

"Yes," I replied. I felt a cold sweat covering my forehead. I was happy.

At eight I was at the house on Gruzenberg Street. A Yemenite girl with a bronze face and raven hair stood at the gate. "Good luck," I said. She looked up. "Follow me," she said.

How I envied that girl. She was already a member of the IZL and had probably taken part in some actions. But I had no time for thought. Soon we were upstairs and she was knocking three times on a door. As soon as we entered, the door was shut.

I saw a simple room, with a table and chairs in a semicircle. Three chairs were already occupied. As I sat down I looked at my "brothers-in-arms"—two men and a girl wearing glasses. To my *shalom* they responded in a low voice. Another young man and a girl came in. He was red haired, and I thought how strange that he should be in a terrorist organization. He would be so easy to identify. Others came in, until we were ten in all. We waited. Finally a door opened and Amichai, still wearing goggles, though it was evening, marched in and stood at attention. We all stood up.

"My unit," he breathed, "form up!"

We lined up and stood at ease. Then Amichai addressed us. "Unit, stay at attention. I am called Amichai, that is my nickname. I want each of you to give me his name, address, and place of work. You will have numbers. Roll call!"

I had the number eight. Again a number! Any nickname, any false identity—but a number . . .

Amichai went on, "Your preparation for membership in the Irgun will take from four to six months. There will be lectures on political subjects, on weapons of all kinds, on the use of explosives, and about terrorist actions. And the secrecy you must preserve. Any questions? Unit dismissed."

Ora was the name of the girl with glasses. She was a sabra and worked in a pharmaceutical office. We talked in low voices.

"If my father knew where I am right now," laughed Ora, "he would go crazy."

"If my uncle knew where I am," I said smiling, "he would go out of his mind."

At eight o'clock sharp, one evening in August, Ora and I arrived at the designated house. Ten minutes later we climbed the stairs. The scent of acacias came in through the windows. Ora was excited and her eyes glittered. I was quiet, but my heart was beating rapidly. That night I was to swear my loyalty oath.

Inside the room was dark, illuminated only by the reflected street-lights. Amichai came in, wearing his goggles as usual, and called us to attention. Then a young man appeared, lighted two candles, and by their light read from the Bible: "I have pursued my enemies and over-taken them; neither did I turn again until they were consumed. I have wounded them that they were not able to rise: they are fallen under my feet. For thou hast girded me with strength unto the battle: thou hast subdued under me those that rose up against me" (Psalms 18:37–39). He brought in a revolver and a book, which he placed under the candlesticks. Behind the table was a dark curtain.

"Number one—come forward!"

While I was waiting for my turn, I couldn't help thinking of the oath I had taken in 1942, how dangerous it had been, how different the circumstances.

I was awakened from my dream when they called, "Number eight, come forward!"

I walked to the table, placed my left hand on the Torah, took the revolver in my right hand.

"Repeat after me," commanded a voice from behind the curtain, "I swear to my long-suffering nation and to my fatherland that I will execute every order from my commander . . ."

I took the oath, then walked to the curtain. "Judith, shake hands with Uzi, the commander of the Tel Aviv area." I squeezed the strong hand, which responded with a powerful grip.

Later we celebrated by going to a café, where we danced a Viennese waltz to the music of Strauss.

"I think you should meet the right people. Will you come to the kibbutz?" asked my cousin Freda, frowning.

"Yes, sure," I replied, blushing because I had told her I was doing nothing for the independence of our nation. I must look like a simpleton to her.

My cousin Freda had turned into a handsome woman from the clumsy teen-ager I had once known so well. We had grown up in the same neighborhood in Rovno, full of dreams about our loves, our heroes, our books.

I traveled south, following the groves of oranges, lemons, and grapefruit. The fruit was yellowish green, in the fresh richness of the foliage. Dark walls of cypress and pines were covered with blossoming climbers in red, white, and pink. The beauty of nature made me gasp with joy and delight. At last I was discovering my homeland! For many years I had loved my country, without ever having seen it. In my youth, I had seen my father's postcards, showing the hills of Jerusalem with their tall cypress trees and terraces hewn out of old stones, and the first villages, guarded by high walls and a tower, with Jewish sentinels in Arab headgear.

But now something new was coming to pass—I was helping to found my fatherland. I had seen it in the spring haze and in the heat of the summer sun. It was my land, my fatherland, and I loved it all, every bud and flower, every autumn leaf and fragrant fruit.

The bus stopped. The sight of the kibbutz yard engaged my attention. It was a simple yard, surrounded by tall pines with blooming flowers, crimson and white snapdragons, red and yellow roses.

Before me stood a young man in khaki. After looking at me penetratingly, he said, "Here's a young girl who was a partisan against the Germans, but who is doing nothing for her own nation. Isn't that true, *havera* ('friend')?"

"Quite true, *haver*," I replied.

"Perhaps you couldn't find the right way," he ventured.

"Perhaps." Then I decided to speak openly. "But my way differs from your way. I disagree with your ideas about the way to independence."

"How do you know my ideas?" he asked.

"I read in the *Davar* how you wait for independence."

"Perhaps you are mistaken, my dear *gvereth* ('lady'). Who will fight for our fatherland? Only the Palmach. Your people can make a hit-

and-run attack on some British policeman or Jewish traitor, but they are not able to wage a real war against our enemies. Palmach represents our youth and our fighting force, organized by the leaders of our future government. We are the striking force of the Haganah, and we have among us veterans of El Alamein, Tobruk, Monte Cassino, and even of the German front, not only from the Jewish Brigade but some from the Russian army, too. You'd better think again."

"I will. I was an active partisan because I believe it is important to fight and harass the enemy at every opportunity, even if you do only a little damage."

"You don't know anything about Palmach's activities. Perhaps you think we like the British, because we rarely attack them? Our biggest enemy is not Britain, but the Arabs, and who will fight them? Only the Palmach, which is well organized and well equipped, with even a medical corps. Who could measure up to this force in our land? I think no one. And what do you know of our friend Wingate, who trained us for the attack? What do you know of our commanders, of our men and women in the kibbutzim, in the villages, in the cities? Next time you come, you can tell me what you have learned about the Palmach." He talked as if he were seeing a vision of the future.

Then he turned on his heel and walked away. I stood transfixed. Was I ashamed of being a member of Irgun? Not at all. But what he had said about Palmach made an impression. It was true that Irgun had several regiments but no army. It was a minority, good for terrorist actions but not for a real battle. I wanted to be active, but I had not yet been called to action. How I envied these people who had been pupils of Wingate! They knew what to do.

It was pitch-dark on the outskirts of Jaffa and Tel Aviv on this moonless November night, with a strong wind that smelled of the coming rain blowing from the sea. Our platoon, armed with Sten guns and grenades, moved in a single file and advanced stealthily through an unknown street. Wooden barracks, stone and adobe huts stood deserted, their doors and windows boarded up.

Suddenly a rifle shot pierced the thick air smelling of burning rags. Then it was quiet again, but under the silence my "seventh sense" felt the hidden enemy. There were Arab snipers on the towers of mosques and churches, and behind the corner. There were British soldiers searching for arms, taking them away, leaving us unarmed to the Arabs. I gripped my Sten gun more firmly, praying it would not jam when I needed it most, and felt safer.

Searchlights of an armored car flashed through the street, swept the roofs, lowered to the pavement, moved upward to the high needle-shaped trees. We stopped. I wished the light would move away. A frightened cat jumped over the wooden fence. Three automatic shots resounded. We squatted. Once more the bullets buzzed over our heads. Then it was quiet again.

If my uncle knew what I was doing now! He thought I was working with the Haganah. He didn't know that I hid grenades and dynamite sticks in my grandfather's library.

"Follow me," whispered the soldier in front of me. I followed him into a workshop filled with many tools, all in disorder.

The rattle of the armored car sounded nearby. Then it stopped right on our street. We saw some soldiers jump out and cock their rifles. One soldier, in fatigues, moved toward our hiding place, his rifle at the ready. "Who is there? Jews or Arabs? Answer!" he bellowed, but all he got was an echo.

We waited. I ran outside every few minutes to see if the special edition of the paper was out. The mandatory radio spoke quietly in English about some exhibition of paintings. Nobody was interested.

The United Nations was voting. How would the big countries vote? And the Arab and Muslim countries? How would Peru vote?

In the evening, everybody knew. Israel would be an independent state! The streets of Tel Aviv were bursting with happiness and joy. The hora tore up the asphalt pavements. Music played noisily. Blue and white flags adorned the houses and even the trees.

But I knew . . . the state of Israel would not be served up on a silver platter. I knew there would be war, we would bleed once more, and everything horrible that war brings would come with it. There would be war with the Arabs, with the British. Was my place not in the Palmach?

Israel, my own homeland, how proud I am that I was a witness to your birth, and I'll be a soldier for you, so help me God!

In April, 1948, I was sitting on the ground beneath a rough stone wall. A blinding torch illuminated the surroundings. A lot of automatic fire buzzed around us. Whispers ran through the yard. A distant explosion shook the air. Several rattling bursts followed one another . . . mortars—I recalled the forgotten war sounds. The east turned red as a burst of shells illuminated Jaffa. I saw a church tower, roofs of Arab houses, a minaret. A real fight is beginning, I thought. Machine guns rattled away from different directions. Flames rose suddenly, and the scent of white acacias changed into the reek of scorching, suffocating smoke.

"Unit fourteen, form up!" That was for me.

Before us was a destitute Arab slum, putrified and stinking of human urine mixed with a strange scent of fragrant spices and donkey-dung smoke. Houses were deserted. Storefronts were smashed and the merchandise looted. To me, it was a labyrinth of unknown streets and lanes, but one of our men knew these slums, and he was our guide.

"Arab positions are broken," ran a rumor.

Before we entered a narrow street, two armed soldiers in helmets stopped us. "Watch out. There are Arab snipers. They disappeared that way."

A truck stopped near us and we all enjoyed a smoke. *"Shalom,* good friends," shouted a former member of our unit as he jumped down from the truck. "I am with the mortars now. We shot down many Arab positions."

He was a young Yemenite, tall, with curly black hair, usually shy, but now in fighting mood. Soon he jumped back into his truck, but as it moved there was a volley of automatic fire. A machine gun rattled away. We saw the bullets ricochet and heard them whistle over the stone pavement. We took cover. There was a burst of several mortar shells. The truck got one in its body, went forward, and suddenly blew up. It was lifted into the air, then slowly the burning pieces of truck, of tires, of wood came falling down. Our friend was dead . . .

Our commander ordered us to move. Silently we followed him. We watched our step, the surroundings, every window, every hole. We found no snipers, but in one house there were two dead Arabs. Their hands were still gripping their rifles, their white headgear lay nearby. They were barefooted village men who had come to kill the "Yahud."

Our narrow street came to an end and the ocean, with its stormy green black waves, was before us. We washed our feet in the salty water.

Then we heard the shouting of a group of Irgun soldiers. "Jaffa is ours! Hurray!"

In the brightness of the early morning, we rested. The rattle of machine guns had stopped. Rare bullets whizzed at a distance. A young man came along the shore, took off his helmet, shook out his hair covered with sweat and ashes, and remarked, "The fight in Jaffa is almost finished, but the Arab bastards shot down twenty-five of our good fellows. And when I think of our Arab neighbors on the next street, I can see before my eyes how they killed my cousin, a sweet boy he was. We found his body mutilated, with his penis in his mouth. Yes, you can kill the Arabs without pity," he sighed.

In the starlight, our heavy truck stopped in Negba. Through the darkness I could distinguish a shell-ridden tower and a broken electric post with its wires hanging down helplessly. When I looked carefully at some heaps of earth with protruding chimneys, I recognized them as the subterranean quarters of the fighters from the kibbutz. Here the ruins of some houses, there a wall with gaping holes. Then I heard the whirr of a distant explosion. I saw a ballistic curve that came up from a police building a mile away and landed in our vicinity. It blew up like thunder, and a thousand splinters scattered. After that there was unbroken silence. The Israelis kept their peace.

Another explosion shook the air, then another—a whole barrage. The tower blinked in the glow, and the shell holes shone through.

"Check your arms," came the order.

Our transport commander was talking to a tall fellow armed with a Tommy gun who addressed us, "Soldiers and friends, cock your arms, but no shooting without a special order. We are moving into Egyptian territory. We go with God's help."

We moved forward. Two armed guards opened wide the gate, which was covered with barbed wire entanglements. Before us stretched a bare space overgrown with dry grass and weeds. We could distinguish wadis and hills nearby. We moved cautiously, watching our surroundings, gripping our rifles.

How many times we squatted or lay prone I do not remember. Our tall scout rose to his full height, and our commander joined him, as we reached the main road. The road sign read, "Dorot—Rukama"— names of kibbutzim that were now in our territory.

From the road to Dorot a truck approached. The driver jumped out. He wore the red headgear of the Arab Legion, was armed with a pistol and a heavy holster, and boasted an unusually long moustache.

"*Shalom,* boys and girls," he bowed on all sides, "a jolly welcome to the new soldiers of the 'hopelessly encircled division.' May I give you a lift to the headquarters of the Palmach, Negev Division?"

When we arrived, the vast depot of Dorot seemed deserted. Sandy wind blurred the sky. Burned gasoline barrels lay scattered, with long rivulets of smoldering liquid oozing out. In the mess hall the windows swarmed with flies. I ate a piece of dry bread, with a cup of lukewarm tea that tasted awful.

"*Shalom,*" a dark-haired fellow greeted me. "Tea? Oh, no, come with me."

I asked about the burned barrels. "You are a newcomer," he smiled. "Two days ago two Egyptian Spitfires attacked. One was shot down. The other dropped a bomb that hit our fuel. Damned bastards . . ." and he put his palm over his mouth. "Excuse me, there is war, you know."

As we approached the underground wooden barracks, I heard the whistling sound of a Primus stove and a chorus of many manly voices. The room was full of smoke and fumes, and it was terribly hot and sultry. Bearded fellows sat in a circle. I was fascinated by these robust, muscular fellows. They looked like bibilical warriors.

"Why these beards and moustaches?" I asked.

"It's a sign of virility, for 'a man is not a man without a *shuarab* ("moustache"),' as the Arab adage says."

"And how should the 'Negev beasts' look? Clean-shaven? Smelling of cologne? With a neat haircut?" added another fellow. "No, we should smell of gunpowder, of sweat, of naked fear and daring courage . . . and of death."

"Shut up, Shmulik, shut up," hissed the reddish blond fellow. "Don't remind me of the dead Hilik. He was the first to mention the smell of death."

The door opened with a rush and two men entered. One wore an

Australian hat that shadowed his handsome, clean-shaven face; the other looked boyish and wore a big golden cross on his chest.

"Judith, I have the honor to present to you Moshe Shamir, formerly Geoffrey Duncan, a Scot, officer of the British Armored Corps. He came to us with a tank, to join the Palmach. And this is 'Kid,' an Irishman—'Kid with the Cross.' "

"Are you an officer in the Palmach, too?" I asked.

"I am, thank God, a private," replied the Scot, smiling.

"Wasn't the Imperial British Army good enough for you?" I asked.

"Don't you know that the Imperial British Army wasn't good enough for Orde Wingate? We fight for the same cause," he replied proudly and doffed his hat.

"I am happy to know you," I said.

"When do we fight? I'm annoyed. What a bore!" shouted the Kid, rubbing his palms.

The door flew open and a fellow with a yellow beard ran in panting heavily. "Battle alarm!" he bellowed. "Get ready!"

"Who do I go with?" I asked, seeing they were all grabbing their arms.

"You come with me. I am Dani, the medic." We got together the first-aid bandages, plasma, stretchers. "I cursed my fate," said Dani, "when in a lottery I drew this job, but I'm not sorry now."

During the night, our convoy moved, without lights, in single file. It was cool and a slight breeze blew. Cicadas sang their shrill and vibrant song. We stopped on a hill. Scouts returned from the orchards and high cactus walls and whispered their reports. As dawn began to break, I saw the adobe village, with its fences and walls, bordered with tall trees and cactus bushes.

"This is Muharraqa," whispered Dani to me.

A cannon fired several times, its sound resounding through the desert. Machine guns rattled away. We could see the white stone roofs, protected by sacks, from which the cannon blasted. The mortars shot squeaking explosions and I saw the shells hit the village. Several shots caused fires. Three jeeps sped by rapidly, firing all their machine guns. They made enough noise for a whole regiment! Then the firing stopped. One soldier came to us with a deep wound in his arm. I dressed it and gave him a drink of cognac.

A half hour later we moved into the village. The huts were deserted. Some hens and roosters were foraging for food. Two old men with long white beards and deep wrinkles answered our questions, put to them in Arabic.

"Where are the people?"

"They escaped during the night. Only the warriors waited."

I ran to see the "warriors' " white house. A crowd of "Negev beasts" was there, as well as the Scot. "Look how they escaped," he said, "like real Arabs. The Primus is still burning. Green coffee beans. Food on the table. They didn't expect us. Here, take this," and he handed me a carved teakettle. "That will be your trophy. And get away from this house quickly. I have ordered the demolition squad. *Shalom,*" and he bowed gallantly.

I looked at the heap of white stones. Heavy, suffocating black smoke was pouring out in clouds. Flames flared up from every hut. I breathed in the astringent smell of burning and felt the bitter taste of smoke.

20

"I am not satisfied, major. Commanding a crew of six girls on an anti-aircraft gun is not my idea of active soldiering. I want to go to officers' school, sir."

Before me sat a major, formerly of the Jewish Brigade, now commander of the antiaircraft artillery regiment. He made a wry face. "You want to go where, sergeant?"

"Artillery officers' school, sir."

"Artillery officers' school is one of the toughest schools in the Israeli army. There is no special course for women."

"I know, sir, but I want to go to artillery officers' school."

"Why do you want to make life so difficult for yourself, Judith? Go to the woman officers' school if you want to be an officer. I'll give you my recommendation right now."

"Sir, I must go to artillery officers' school."

"There is something behind this nonsense! What are you out to prove?"

"Nonsense, sir? My brother was in the artillery officers' school when he was killed, and I must do it for him."

"Well, Judith, the chief of artillery has to decide about that, but I'll give you a letter of recommendation. And convey my regards to him."

It was very exciting to meet the man who had full command of artillery in Israel. He was a member of a kibbutz, had trained in the military schools of the British army and come out a major.

Shmulik sat behind his desk, a tall, redheaded, freckled man with an open face. "Sit down, sergeant. I have read your recommendation, but I disapprove. There is no place for young women as artillery officers."

"Excuse me, sir, but you must hear the reasons for my request. I *must* go to artillery officers' school," and I pleaded my case.

"Sergeant, you must take into account that this school is no picnic for girls. It requires maximum physical and mental effort and efficiency, long hours of drilling, exercising, knowledge of trigonometry, high mathematics, ballistics. It would be very difficult for you. Many of the cadets are engineers, technical students, experienced artillerists."

"I am well trained in trigonometry," I boasted, "and I am determined to finish this school with the highest marks or die in the effort!"

He stood up, paced the floor, stopped at an open window. I waited.

"I'll make an exception for you, Judith, but if you don't finish the course, don't come to me about it."

The sky was gray, it was cold, and fall rain was in the air. On such a day I was transferred to a camp near Tel Aviv. I received a service cap with a white stripe under the insignia of the artillery, a helmet, a Czech rifle, waterproof pants and jacket. I thought about my brother Misha and caressed my service cap. I'll be an officer in the Israeli army, so help me God!

My musing was interrupted by a sergeant major, formerly a British sergeant, with a heavy moustache, holding a swagger stick. I saluted. He returned my salute and scrutinized me. I felt offended, but said nothing.

"I warn you that you are joining the school as a simple cadet—no laziness or taking it easy. Go and see the list of guard, and the list of lectures, and attend the next lecture. I warn you, you are one woman among men and you must behave. Understand?"

Boiling inside, I replied quietly, clicking my boots together, "Yes, sergeant major, I'll do as you say."

I became accustomed to the early rising, the distance running in the morning, the long hours of drill, the heavy curses of our sergeant drillmaster, the mud and puddles of water that filled our shoes as we dragged the field guns to unfinished exercises. I liked the lectures on higher mathematics, trigonometry, and ballistics. They took me back to my high school days. Former students of the technical university taught me the use of the slide rule. In mathematics and ballistics I rated 100 percent, and I was happy, as one couldn't be a good artillery officer without these sciences.

An armistice had been signed, but there was no real peace.

It was early morning, April, 1949, and it was chilly. We were on a four-day maneuver.

After an hour's riding, the scenery changed from citrus groves to flat wide fields where only weeds grew. We came upon destroyed Arab villages, adobe houses broken and black from fire. Fences and high cactus walls and tall tamarisks attracted our attention. On one house we read an inscription: "Regiment 7 will rise and fight against all odds, and conquer—Palmach." It brought to mind the bitter fight over the Negba police building.

Our way led through Faluja, where we found only ruins: adobe houses fallen to pieces, stone houses deserted, with broken windows. The flat fields changed into wadis and hills, all dry land overgrown with weeds and scrub. For the first time I saw Bedouins, with their herds of camels, sheep, and goats. The men wore white headgear and the women were dressed in black.

"What are they doing here?" I asked.

"They are citizens of Israel. They didn't fight against us. Some sheikhs even joined our army."

"I didn't know that. I thought every Muslim fights against us."

"There are many kinds of Muslims. They say they were born in the Negev and will die in the Negev."

Before us opened the territory of Beersheba. We saw the high tower of the mosque and a clump of eucalyptus trees. At the entrance to the city stood a large house with green shutters, a double row of palm trees in front of it. An inscription read "Soldiers' Home."

At a turn in the road appeared the famous Kassit coffeehouse where coffee was made in *fingjanim*—a black iron coffeepot with a copper cover.

I pondered upon the conquest of Beersheba: Abraham, the tough fellow of the "Negev beasts," with the red beard and rich moustache, was killed; Sasha, the blond Russian, lost his legs; and so many other young soldiers were killed . . . because this city opened the road to the south. Beersheba itself was just a miserable, deserted city.

During the night we reached the area of banana groves irrigated by powerful sprinklers. The night was warm and sultry—the climate of the Jordan Valley in the north. In the early morning an unforgettable scene met my eyes. We bivouacked on the low hills near Dgania, "mother of kibbutzim." Before us was the Sea of Galilee, its green and blue waves beating against the shore. Here arose the River Jordan— sacred to all religions—and its brilliant blue zigzagged and curved along the green bushes and sky blue flowers on the shores.

We went to see the ruins of Kibbutz Shaar Hagolan. I stood speechless, outraged, among the ravaged and demolished houses, barns, and workshops. The water tower was overthrown, full of shell holes. In front of the children's home, toys were scattered disgracefully over the bare earth. Outside the clothing store, fabrics and sewing machines were strewn about as if someone had been playing with them. It was the Syrian army that had conquered this kibbutz, and I wondered what kind of ferocious vandals the Syrian soldiers must be.

Before us was a Reynaud 35 tank that had been stopped by the defenders of Dgania. I heard the voice of our instructor, "Courageous young fellows from Dgania threw Molotov cocktails at the Syrian tanks. When the Syrians saw how their first tank caught fire and how the tank men suffocated and burned, they turned their other tanks around and ran away. That's how Dgania was saved. The Syrian army was defeated and escaped across the border."

I had an appointment with a Czech-born major, a tough and clever officer, intelligent and capable, a veteran of the Galilee battles, who ran an officers' school.

Offering me a cigarette, he said, "We have decided about your assignment. You must realize that a woman, even though she is an excellent officer, will not be accepted by any commander. Women can no longer have combat jobs. The Israeli army is now a regular army. We have therefore appointed you adjutant in the Regiment of the South. It's the nicest job you could imagine."

"I'll do the best I can, commander," I replied without enthusiasm.

"I believe you will change your attitude. It can be a very useful job."

We arrived in a town near the Gaza strip, and I was assigned a room on the second floor of the police building. From the window I could see a big yard, with a many-branched agave, and underneath it, formed of stones, I read "Field Artillery Regiment."

There was a knock on my door and the first lieutenant entered. "I have been adjutant here and you have come to relieve me. I am glad to be going home. How do you like it here? We would like to invite you to a party for the new officers."

My work entailed thorough knowledge of our regiment and its administration. I read the security orders, also the intelligence reports. These interested me most. They gave full information about the Arab armies, about infiltrators, about our relations with the armistice commissions. I in turn reported everything to Captain Shaul, originally from Czechoslovakia, who was second in command. He was a strong man, a tough commander, who showed great understanding of his subordinates, but demanded the utmost from his regiment.

We once went for battery shooting. I asked for several fragmentation shells. My target was an orchard at the bottom of a mountain. I measured the distance, the angle of sight, knew that the wind was blowing from the west. "Fire orders to battery one," I said into the microphone, "six hundreds right, angle of sight four grades, range distance fifty-eight hundred—one gun—fire!" I saw where the shell hit the ground, shot twice more, and then gave the order for target. I was lucky—the shells were right on the mark and hit the orchard with fragmentation action.

"I never saw a woman shoot so well," shouted a senior battery commander. "If you are so good in action, you should be tremendous kissing a man."

Shaul had now become commander of our regiment. One day a letter came asking if any officer was suited for a course in intelligence. I was eager to take this course. Intelligence interested me tremendously. I dreamed of writing reports, of scouting territories, of catching infiltrators. I spoke to Major Shaul about it.

He looked at me with astonishment. "I thought you were happy with your work here. You are doing a fine job."

"But, Major Shaul, I prefer combat duty. I am eager to do intelligence. If I could take this course I could help my commander with useful information. I know something about it because I acted against the Germans. I have also read many books about it."

Shaul thought for a moment, then asked, "Do you know the intelligence officer in the South Army Command? No? . . . I know him. Shall I phone for you?"

"Can I see the major?" I asked a sergeant.

"If you want to please him, don't salute," said the sergeant with a grin.

I walked in, stood at attention, and saluted. I saw a tall man, in dark glasses, with a major's insignia. He looked at me sneeringly and said, "I am not used to such a greeting. Who are you?"

"You wear a major's insignia, and I am accustomed to saluting my superiors."

He waved his arm. "Why have you come?"

"I want to take the intelligence course, major."

"Sit down and don't call me major. Call me ***," he said gruffly. "And I can tell you one thing—they do not want women in this course."

"But there is no law that says women cannot take this course," I insisted.

"If I were you, young girl, I would think only about getting married and going home."

That ended the interview.

"Major Shaul, would you please phone Moshe Dayan for me . . ."

Now I was standing before Moshe Dayan. I had never met him, but here was a man who as a sabra youngster had been photographed with Wingate, who had lost an eye in Syria in World War II, who had commanded our troops in the conquest of Lydda and Ramle. His head was bent slightly to one side, his nose was snubbed, and he wore a black patch over his left eye. He glanced at me and I saw a commanding eye and a manly, stalwart look. In conversation he was an attentive friend, although he spoke with authority.

"Commander, I have come to ask you to allow me to take an intelligence course."

"You are the first woman artillery officer I have seen, and I want to know about the soldiers under your command? How well do they obey you?" he asked.

"I am only an adjutant, and that job annoys me. If I were an intelligence officer in the artillery I could serve my superiors more usefully."

"If I am not mistaken, you are from Russia. What has brought you to our country?"

"I realized that I belonged with my own people and therefore I am here."

"How is it you speak Hebrew so fluently?"

"I graduated from a Hebrew high school, and I also speak English, French, Polish, Russian, Italian, German, and Arabic," I boasted.

"Tell me, did you sign up for the regular army?"

"Yes, commander, I did."

"Tell me about your army experiences."

I gave him full information.

"Are you married?"

"No, commander," I replied, blushing. "I have had no time for such things."

He burst into laughter. "Go back to your regiment, pack your things, and tomorrow you will begin the course. If you don't finish with the highest marks, don't ever show your face to me again!"

"I'll do my best, commander!"

Months later, the course completed, I returned to my regiment as intelligence officer. I was given a whole barracks for my work and chose my own staff. I placed a large map on the wall showing the location of the Arab armies.

As soon as I could, I went to the South Command. There I found two sergeant majors, one German-born, who had served in the British army, the other from Poland, a member of a kibbutz.

"If you want to see Hagai you will have to wait. He has gone to see the commander."

They were both intelligent and experienced in their work, and explained many things to me, who was new in intelligence.

Hagai received me in his office. He had a long, serious face, with freckles, and large, deep-set eyes. One arm was in a plaster cast. He had replaced the major who had sneered at my desire to take the intelligence course.

"Judith, your regiment is to be garrisoned in Eilat. Have you ever been there?"

"Yes, I have, but not in any military capacity."

"Oh, that is good. I like a new soldier coming to an unknown place. I don't have to give you any special instructions," he smiled.

"What makes you think I'll be so good at intelligence?"

"You are a woman, and therefore you will find out more than any man. Isn't that so?"

The military convoy moved south on the Beersheba-Aqaba road. The terrain changed into desert. The eroded land looked like twisted lace of loess. Every wind brought heavy clouds of dust from the sandy dunes. Soon we and our vehicles were covered with sand and were unrecognizable. The road led through hills and mountains, dry, with white rocks and poor shrubs, withered from lack of water. Suddenly a fantastic view appeared before us, in a reddish yellow haze. We were on a cliff and under us extended a row of little hills, with the purple and crimson rays of the sun upon them. They gradually increased in size until they became a wall of mountains. We had reached Scorpion Pass, and from there we could look into Jordan.

The climb became very difficult and we had to reverse three or four times to get up the serpentine road. In the precipice below, we saw an overturned truck from the regiment that had preceded ours.

Over the Dead Sea hung a thick fog. The hills nearby were imposing in their colors, from yellow green to blue violet. After the pass, we reached a valley, and then a little oasis with high tamarisks that were known in Abraham's time, with a murmuring well, surrounded by high poplars, pink flowering oleander, overgrown reeds, and bulrushes with brown tassels. It was extremely humid, although a light wind blew from the mountains.

We spent the night in Ein Husub. Everyone slept but me. I felt I had found something very close to my heart. The desert was the home of our ancestors, and I longed for the loneliness and peace that the vast desert brings, the land that is arid and yet full of wells, the lush jungle in the wadis. I yearned for this serenity, without people, with only animals about me, and that beloved man whom I would someday find. That was the kind of life that appealed to me, but first I must live the life I had chosen. I had fought for it—first for artillery officers' school and then for the intelligence course.

Our convoy moved toward Eilat. The scenery changed. In the east appeared a wall of blue red violet mountains and in the midst was the valley of Arava-steppe, the salty land, with tall, many-branched date palms, their fresh green bouquets of leaves on top. The dry and dusty acacias hid in the shadow of the mountains.

When the Red Sea came into view we were on the mountain. It looked like a lake, with green blue waves topped with yellow white foam. On one side the white harbor town of Aqaba sparkled in the sun. It was exciting. The wide, sandy beaches—the Israeli on one side, the Arab on the other—seemed to open up a new world. On the Israeli shore I saw an old Bedouin building with a wide roof, and below it the Israeli ships, and many boats with colored sails. This was Eilat, the pearl of the south, a historic harbor dating back to Solomon's time.

The commander of Eilat was an intelligence officer from the "beasts of the Negev" with a hard, strong face. He said, "I am happy to have an intelligence officer here. Do you know Eilat and its surroundings, the position of the enemy? Do you have a plan of action?"

"Yes, major, I have, but give me a week to get acquainted with the place. You will receive my daily reports, and I'll welcome your suggestions."

I collected a crew and set out to see the positions of the Egyptian army in Taba and in Ras-El-Naqab. Here we saw a police building that seemed to be deserted, but we knew that behind the sandbags on the roof and in the gunports were the hidden eyes of many Egyptian observers. In Taba, which was on the shore, we saw only one soldier, a black from the Sudan, sitting in the shade of the rocks with his rifle between his legs. When we neared the border, I shouted to him to come over. He was bored and glad to talk to us. He told us that next week he would be relieved and would go home on furlough. I knew that Egyptian reinforcements came by ship, so I instructed my boys to watch for an Egyptian warship.

A few days later I received word that the warship was approaching. I invited the commander. We hid behind a rock and, looking through binoculars, we saw the Egyptian destroyer come into view.

"How did you know about this ship?" asked the commander.

I told him about the Sudanese and the information he spilled.

"That's only the luck of a female. I could never get such information."

In a week I became familiar with Eilat and its surroundings. I tried to make the acquaintance of the British, but they kept their mouths shut.

Our sergeant major, Yoske, a blond fellow with a rich moustache, was a fisherman from a village near Haifa. He had been in the British army and his voice was like a horrible bark when he spoke to recruits and "bad" boys, but warm and friendly when he spoke to a soldier who needed help. He gave a party for us and served coral fish from the bay of Eilat, broiled with onions and fragrant with Israeli spices, and beer to drink. We sang many songs that beautiful night. The lights of Aqaba illuminated the sea. The lamps from the ships glared over the harbor. I thought of our ancestors who had come to Eilat and to the temple of Ezion-Geber with the copper from King Solomon's mines, "And King Solomon made a navy of ships in Ezion-Geber, which is beside Eloth [Eilat in modern Hebrew], on the shore of the Red Sea, in the land of Edom. And Hiram sent in the navy his servants, shipmen that had knowledge of the sea, with the servants of Solomon. And they came to Ophir, and fetched from thence gold, four hundred and twenty talents, and brought it to King Solomon."

I was in Ein Husub, a place that pleased me well, for a visit to our unit. In the shadow of the tall tamarisks, the purring whisper of the stream lulled me to sleep in my sack.

Someone was shaking me. "What is it? "What's happened?"

A sergeant was standing over me. "I had to wake you. My commander isn't here and you are the highest-ranking officer. Our workers on the road report that they were stopped by Jordanian soldiers and ordered to go back. The Jordanians said the road is closed, on kilometer 86 toward Eilat."

"Go and call the battery commander at once," I ordered.

When he appeared, I said, "Give me two command cars, two sergeants, with two machine guns, by order of the intelligence officer of Eilat," and felt like a resolute commanding officer.

My command car was speeding at more than sixty miles an hour. I wanted to get there as quickly as possible. An air force jeep came toward us. "Don't go there," shouted a voice from the jeep. "The Arab Legion officer allowed us to take a side road. He said our road is closed."

"It is our road and no one can tell me otherwise," I shouted back. We were climbing a hill, and as I looked through the binoculars I could see a British armored car standing near the road. I gave orders that we be covered as we approached it. Then we stopped near the barricade, which was a barbed wire entanglement with a post on which hung a sign in Hebrew, English, and Arabic: "BY ORDER OF KING ABDULLAH —THIS ROAD IS CLOSED—EVERY CAR WILL BE SHOT IF IT USES THIS ROAD."

I checked my Colt automatic, took my tommy gun, asked a sergeant to accompany me, and walked to the armored car. A head in the red and white headgear of the Arab Legion looked out from the hatch. We could hear the noise inside the car. Then the hatches were closed. I knocked with my pistol on the armored car.

"Whein fi zabed? Bi-hiatakh, rukh ('Where is the officer? On your life, quickly')," I shouted.

We heard a soldier wiring. The hatch opened. "Officer will come."

In clouds of dust, a dark green jeep appeared. From it jumped a tall officer with a reddish blond moustache and a captain's insignia. I could see he was British.

He began to speak disdainfully in Arabic and, though I understood him, I suggested, "Can't we speak English?"

Looking at me arrogantly, he said, "This road is closed by the Arab Legion, by order of King Abdullah. You can read, if not English, then Hebrew."

"I thought your king was George VI."

"When I serve in the Arab Legion my king is Abdullah."

"The order states that every car will be shot. I must remind you that we can shoot, too."

"You cannot, my lady, because your road is crossing into our land, which I am defending."

"Don't you know that the border between Israel and Jordan intersects the lowest points of the wadi Arava? And I am not so sure that you have surveyed the territory, and can state that the border is exactly where it is most convenient for you."

"For me, your road crosses the border."

"And for me it does not."

He shrugged his shoulders, took out his pipe, and began smoking.

"So long, until the first shot," I said and ordered the driver to go on the forbidden road, to cross the barricade, and return on the same road. I waved to the British officer. He didn't shoot.

I was hurrying back to Eilat and was sorry I had no wireless. My command car stopped at headquarters. Panting and out of breath, I knocked on the door. "I must send an urgent telegram. Call your signal sergeant."

"What's happened, Judith? Sit down and tell me about it."

I gave him a full account.

"That's a fine story," he smiled. "And how was your courage?"

I grinned. "I just put a bold face on a bad situation. I observed everything, took in all the details. I was going to make myself an expensive victim, so I gripped my tommy gun, but I was lucky, as usual." I wiped off the sweat that covered my face.

Two days later, after one of our battalions with reinforcements had moved toward the road closed by the Arab Legion, like a criminal I returned to the "scene of the crime." This time I did not wear the black beret of the artillery insignia, but a helmet with a white *Kafiya* ("headgear") under it. As I reached the barricade, I was more than surprised to see the same green jeep. From it jumped two Bedouin sergeants and the same British captain. I ordered two of my sergeants to follow me.

The Bedouin sergeants stood silently by, but their eyes observed everything.

"How do you do, lieutenant?"

"How do you do, captain?" I replied.

"What are you up to now, with that army?"

"I am just a lieutenant who happens to be traveling in the desert. If you want an appointment with the commander of this so-called army, I can arrange it for you."

"I am astonished that you saw fit to bring tanks, mortars, and cannons here. Thank you, I don't want any appointment."

"Then good-bye, captain," I said. He did not reply and I returned to my command car.

Another of our jeeps came along and a lieutenant colonel stepped out. "What did he say to you? I am from the armistice commission with Jordan, but he wouldn't speak to me."

"That's because you are a man and I am a woman," I teased, "and so I was more charming!"

"Come on, Judith, stop your kidding. Get into our car and tell us all the secrets."

A day later the whole incident was closed. Only one shot was fired, no one knew from where or by whom. At once the cannons and mortars opened fire and burned the armored car. A platoon of infantry attacked the barricade and carried off the trilingual sign as a souvenir.

It was the sergeant major who called me on the phone. "Lieutenant Judith, come at once. The regiment commander is here and wants to see you."

"How did you have the nerve to knock on the armored car with your Colt? You were playing with your life!" shouted Shaul.

"No, it was not nerve. I was scared, so I had to put on a bold front. I might have been killed, but I wasn't."

"Let's drink on this. You drink first, Judith, from this bottle of cognac. It's Martell with three stars."

"Lehayim!" I said and took a sip. Then the bottle circulated among the fellows.

We went out into the yard and sat around singing songs—marching songs and love songs—until Shaul stood up. "It's nice here with you, but I must reach Ein Husub before dark."

"Major Shaul, two command cars will follow you as far as Ein Husub," I suggested.

"That's not necessary. I am armed, and you need them here."

Yoske tried to persuade him, but in vain. I expressed the thought that the Jordanians were probably angry about the barricade incident and might set an ambush, but Shaul smiled and waved good-bye.

I went to sleep with a troubled conscience.

During the night I was awakened. The commander of Eilat stood before me. "What happened? Is it Shaul?" I asked.

"Yes, he was ambushed. Come with me."

In his office there was a light. He introduced me to Dani, who was the manager of a workers' camp.

"Drink a cup of strong coffee, Judith. It will sustain you. Dani, tell your story."

"I was riding to my camp after dark. I saw the silhouette of a girl. She was waving with both arms, so I stopped. She was in a stupor. She told me she had been riding with the regiment commander when he was murdered by the Arabs. She wanted to go to Ein Husub to report it to the commander. I stopped a car that was going there, and I myself came back here to report to you because I knew they had come from Eilat."

I returned to my barracks. The moon shone brightly and the stars twinkled as if nothing had happened, though a man—a commander of a regiment—had been murdered, and somewhere there was a new widow, and two lovely daughters were now orphans.

I stopped at the place where Shaul had been murdered. It was a road with many curves, with bushes and little sand hills. We called it "a sea of fleas." I visualized how they had opened fire on him, how he shot back with his pistol, how he turned away from the main road—the tracks showed it—and was shot to death in the bushes. What a waste! I vowed then and there never to travel alone through the desert, and always to be armed with something heavier than a pistol.

I finally reached Beersheba. The battery commander informed me that my work as intelligence officer at Eilat would have to end, as he needed me to help run the regiment.

"You know how I feel about that, but if I must, I will."

One day the intelligence officer of the Negev district showed me a page from his files. An infiltrator from Aqaba had been caught by an Israeli patrol. He said that the Arabs in Aqaba were talking about a blonde woman with the rank of colonel, who came from the Israeli side and brought with her a whole army of cannons and armor and whatnot.

"That's about me, but I don't have that rank and I am not blonde," I laughed.

"Don't you know the Arab exaggerations? They are not used to women serving in the army."

"I hope next time they will raise my rank to general!"

"Do you want to talk to an infiltrator from Morocco?" asked the officer.

"From where? Morocco? I haven't heard of any such."

"Come with me and you'll see one."

From his cell, followed by an armed guard, came a tall, skinny man with a black forked beard. His head was covered with a white scarf, bound in such a way that it hid his forehead and ears, then fell down his back. He wore a long, striped Oriental robe and was barefooted.

"*Ahlan-wa-sahlan! Marhabba!* ('greeting to strangers')," he said.

"*Salaam aleyk!* ('peace be with you')," I said.

"*Aleykom es-salaam!* ('peace be with you')," he replied, meaning me and the officer, lifting his palm to his forehead, mouth, and heart.

"Who are you? From what country?" I asked.

"My name is Haj Muhammad Ibn Ibrahim, from Morocco. I am a dervish."

"Have you been to Mecca, since you call yourself Haj?"

"Every year I go to the holy city of Mecca."

"What does he mean by dervish?" I asked the officer in Hebrew. "I believe they practice chastity and poverty."

"You are right. They eat nothing but unleavened bread and water."

"You know that you have crossed many countries, also the country of the Yahudin," I said to the prisoner. "Does that mean anything to you?"

He lifted his deep raven-black eyes that were as innocent as a child's. "There are many countries, but not for a dervish. For me, the whole world leads only to the Sacred Mosque. *La ilaha illa'llah Muhammadun rasul ullah* ('There is but one God and Muhammad is his prophet')," and his eyes and voice expressed a true sincerity.

"But now you are in jail and you don't know when you will get out. What will happen to your pilgrimage?"

"It is nothing to me. I can still think, and thinking is the best thing a man can do. I think about how a man should become better, should follow the prophet and do good deeds. You don't punish me by putting me in jail."

"Release him. Let him go his way," I said to the officer in Hebrew.

"*Salaam aleykom* ('peace be with you')," said the Arab, touching his palm to forehead, heart, and mouth.

"*Mayissalame!* ('go in peace')," I answered as the guard led him away.

21

"I have decided to appoint you an intelligence officer in the South Command, Lieutenant Judith," the chief of artillery said to me. "I hope you will apply all your intelligence and energy to the work, and I wish you luck, Captain Judith."

"I will do my best, commander," and I saluted. I had been promoted to the rank of captain and I was happy.

I realized that a lot of work lay ahead. It was difficult to find your bearings in the desert—all the mountains and wadis looked alike. It was only after you had seen a place several times that you could distinguish it from others.

"Judith, we are going scouting in the Negev and I think you should come along," said Hagai. "There is a special place I want to show you. I dream of living there."

"Where is this place?"

"It's a plateau between Tel Yeruham and Ovdath. I cannot describe it. I can only show it to you."

"Do you really want to live in the desert?" I asked, surprised. "Didn't you sign up for the regular army?"

"No. I came to the army from a kibbutz, and would like to create a new kibbutz in the Negev, to go back to."

"If that's the case, I want to see it."

On the second day we reached a plateau south of the Little Cavity, which looked to me like a canyon. In the north I saw a row of large hills, all dry, stony, rounded and conical. One of them was of black flint, with a white flank. In the west, a big wadi, with many curves, some slight, others deep, and again sandstone and flint mountains, covered with pinelike shrubs and leafy bushes. The wadi itself was a fresh grassland with flowers in yellow, purple, red, and white. As we continued on, the wadi broadened until we reached a wide valley, with terraces of old stones and rocks. In the south was Ovdath, the city of the Nabataeans, which from afar looked like a green blue mountain with ancient ruins. In the east, an impassable precipice with only one road, leading to the "Way of Kings." That road opened into an arid land, covered with black, tan, and white flint and brown basalt, and continued through the eroded mountains that looked like handmade lace. There were numerous springs in this territory, but only for those who knew how to find them.

We rode through a wadi similar to the others, but suddenly it turned into a jungle, with thick bushes, desert grasses, tall poplars, and flowering pink oleanders—an oasis, like Ein Husub, with a spring gushing from a white rock, its whispering splash turning into a small stream that oozed into the thick undergrowth of the desert. On a mountain opposite, a gazelle appeared, with full-grown horns, and uttered a loud cry, a triumphant male call, repeated it, and disappeared.

I thought of the people who had once lived here, grazed their sheep and camels. Maybe they were Bar Kokhba's men who fought against the Romans, or perhaps just simple shepherds who lived quietly until attacked by their enemies. And now we Israelis, after so many horrible experiences, were in our homeland. We had witnessed the birth of our state, had fought and won, and watched its development.

Hagai awoke me from my dream. "What are you thinking, Judith?"

I returned to reality and smiled. "I was thinking about the postcards my father showed me in my youth, of the first settlements . . . I like this place very much."

Hagai became serious. "You are dreaming, Judith. I know your type . . . a regular army officer, sworn to service in the army. You will give up everything in exchange for a service job. You'll never leave the army, not even for a man you love."

If only he knew how wrong he was! "How can you know that? Is my soul so open to you?" I spoke quietly because I realized for the first time how I must appear to others, particularly to men . . . and I didn't like it.

When we returned, I spoke to my boss, Joe, who was English-educated. "We have seen part of the Negev, from the Little Cavity to the Roman Canyon. In the desert everything is visible. It is useless for artillery, there is no natural camouflage. It is empty, dry, arid, eroded land that looks like handmade lace, and it is covered with flint and basalt, valleys and hills and mountains."

"You talk like a poet," laughed Joe. "Does the desert really intrigue you?"

"Joe, tell me, what do you think of me?"

"As an officer or as a woman?"

"Both."

"With no offense meant, I think you are a crazy female who has gotten it into her head that she must have a combat job. You are doing your work well, but don't your feminine feelings disturb you? Or, tell me the truth, perhaps you don't have any."

I became confused. Didn't I have feminine feelings? Was I not a real woman?

"I am a woman," I replied. "I was born one and will always be one."

"Captain Judith, have you ever been in love with a man?"

"That is a most awkward question, but the answer is yes."

"That's better than I thought, but don't you have the feminine need to love, to be a lady in your own house, to cook?"

"Maybe. But army life pleases me better. To scout the Negev, to be ready to fight . . . I feel that I am doing something that is important for all of us."

He puffed on his pipe. "You are, speaking officially, a good Zionist and a zealous patriot, but unofficially, you are an obsessed nut . . ." and he shook his head.

I laughed and left the room.

One day I was called on the phone. "Come to my office at once, Judith," I heard Hagai's voice.

"Do you want to change your job?" he asked.

"Why should I?" I asked, surprised.

"You can have the job of intelligence officer of the Negev. Do you want it?"

"You are joking, Hagai," I laughed.

"The officer is leaving for several months, to take a course, and you can take his place, with my recommendation."

"I want it very much, but what will the artillery chief say?"

The new chief of artillery was a very serious man, accustomed to command. It was said that he cared only about the artillery and did not want to hear of any transfers to other jobs.

When I entered his office, I saw before me a tall man with an honest face and penetrating eyes.

"You request to serve for several months as intelligence officer in the Negev. You want to chase after infiltrators and advise the boss of the Negev district on intelligence. This is insanity! To change the job of captain of artillery for intelligence! This is the first time I have heard such a thing from a captain. I refuse it, and that ends the matter." I felt his anger.

"Sir, why do you make a decision without hearing what I have to say? It is through intelligence that I obtained a combat job. Before that I was adjutant, and the work bored me. If I work for several months in the Negev I will gain some valuable experience. The Negev will probably be our combat field in the future and I will get acquainted with the enemy and, yes, I will chase infiltrators. Do you remember how Major Shaul—God rest his soul—was murdered? If I become intelligence officer I will not allow such things to happen."

The chief of artillery smiled. "These are fine words, Judith, but they will not help you. I don't approve your transfer. You are an intelligence officer of artillery and you will continue to serve there. Good-bye."

I stood up. "Shalom!" I saluted, feeling resentful and indignant.

I ran to Hagai with my disappointing report. Then I went in to supper. I ate my porridge slowly. The food seemed tasteless. Two officers sat down opposite me but I did not see them. I was sunk in thought.

"Judith, lift your head." I heard a familiar voice, and as I looked up I saw the smiling face of Moshe Dayan. "Don't feel so badly. Your chief of artillery will have to resign himself to your transfer because I want you to serve in the Negev for three months. Pack your things and be off. Now are you satisfied?"

I jumped up and stood at attention. "I'm more than satisfied! I will leave at once."

The operation officer, a short fellow with deep-set eyes, received me in his office. "I'm glad we meet now. Tell me, do you feel able to be intelligence officer of such a large district?"

"If you are able to be operation officer of this big district, then I hope to be able to be its intelligence officer," I said boldly.

"What are your plans for your work?"

I explained.

"You have fine plans. I hope they work out. Now you'd better present yourself to the boss."

I saluted a lieutenant colonel who sat in a room as big as a hotel lobby.

"Come in, captain. Sit down."

I sat in an Arab armchair. This man was well known and considered an able commander. During the British mandate he had participated in blowing up bridges. He had inquisitive eyes, was short of stature, broad shouldered, and very formal. Rumor had it that he was born in Austria.

"You are the first woman in artillery who wants to serve as an in-intelligence officer. What is your experience?"

I gave him details.

"Yes," he said slowly and dryly, "we'll see how you execute your plans and what you accomplish with your helpers and auxiliary means."

One of my days in the Negev included these typical problems:

An Israeli patrol hit a mine. Command car destroyed. Driver wounded. Two soldiers slightly wounded. Another mine discovered near Nir Itzhak.

Truck mined near Magen. Tracks led to Gaza border.

Military patrol shot two armed infiltrators in Raman Cavity.

In Nirim, infiltrators stole irrigation pipes and bales of hay.

In Nahal settlement infiltrators broke the fence, searched the barn, were chased by soldiers but escaped. Their tracks led to Gaza border.

In Kissufim, an ambush was set up against infiltrators. Two were shot, two escaped.

Near Shuva an army patrol captured a dozen infiltrators. Their guide had left them and returned to Jordan with all the money—so they said.

Oh, these telegrams . . . there were so many of them, from army patrols, from kibbutzim . . . the borders were full of incidents, minings, attempts to murder, stealing . . . when would all these crimes end? With enemies on every border, this armistice was wrong for us . . . we were not allowed to live quietly.

The phone buzzed. "Is the intelligence officer there? This is the commander of the armored mobile unit."

"Yes, he is."

Soon a smart-looking young sabra captain in battle dress entered the office. "*Shalom.* Where is the intelligence officer?"

"He will be here in a minute. Perhaps I can help you."

"I'm setting out to chase the hashish caravans in the Negev. What do you know about them?"

"Oh, yes, I know about them. They are bringing the stuff from Syria, through Jordan, to Egypt. They carry automatic weapons, even heavy machine guns. They use special signals: red rocket means danger, green rocket all quiet. They are well equipped for these trips. They have their own roads." I approached the man. "And they usually ride on Arab horses and camels, the white racing camels that are the fastest moving in the desert."

"Oh, very interesting, but where is the officer?"

"I am the officer. Sorry!"

"You are! Your black artillery beret misled me. I thought that you, too, were waiting to see him. I didn't know a woman could hold such a job."

"It's only temporary. I belong in the artillery."

"I'd like to give you some advice, captain. Leave the army and get married! I have known so many nice and attractive girls who got high ranks and remained spinsters. Excuse me, but why should an attractive girl waste her time in the army?"

I didn't detain him, nor reply, but an inner voice said to me, "Think about it. Perhaps he is right."

The phone buzzed once more. This time it was the police calling. "Did you get a report about the murder of two engineers in the vicinity of Sodom? Please come to the mortuary. I'll wait for you there."

At the hospital a male nurse led us through the yard to a small barracks. It smelled of disinfectants and decomposed bodies.

"Here they are," the man said.

One of them had his eyes open. They had no one to close their eyes, I said to myself. Their bodies were pierced with automatic bullets, and their intestines were hanging out of the wounds in their bellies. I was shocked by the sight of these young men, killed because some lunatic Jordanians felt they had to murder some Israelis.

I returned from a two-hour flight over the Negev mountains. From above, I saw the wonderful map of the Negev, with its wadis that curved like living branches, with its hills and dry mountains that seemed to be carved out of olive wood.

My phone rang. "Come to my office, Captain Judith." It was the voice of my boss.

"UN observers wish to hand over to an Israeli representative a citizen of Israel who infiltrated into the Gaza district. It sounds rather strange, because an Israeli would have to be insane or a criminal to go to the Egyptians. I order you to send the field security sergeant to bring back the escapee as quickly as possible."

"It's more likely the man was kidnapped," I ventured an opinion. "Your order will be carried out at once."

In the afternoon, a middle-aged man, short and bent, in wrinkled clothes, was brought in.

"How are you after your escape to the Egyptian paradise?" I asked.

"I am hungry, lady officer. I've had no food since yesterday," he pleaded.

I ordered a meal for him.

"Will I be released?" he asked.

"If you will answer all my questions truthfully, we will see. What is your name and where do you live?"

"I am Shrag from Tel Aviv. I was working in the vicinity of a camp in the south. I hoed trees in the citrus grove. When I came near an olive tree, with branches that reached down to the earth, an Arab in khaki came out of the tree. He threatened me with a revolver and led me inside the branches. There, another Arab with binoculars was watching the entrance to the camp. He wrote down in a notebook the number of every car that went in or came out. They kept me till dark and ordered me to go with them. They tied my eyes, but I know that we walked about three hours. When we came to an Arab village, they untied my eyes and gave me bread and water. Then came a jeep and took me to the police building in Gaza. I appeared before an officer who spoke Hebrew and English. He was trying to convince me that I had infiltrated Egyptian territory, but I was sly enough not to agree. I said I was kidnapped by the Egyptian soldiers. I saw some writing on the walls in English, 'bloody Jew' and some swastikas, so there must have been some Nazis there. I was taken to prison. Every Arab spat on me, and they made fun of me. I sat there three days. Today they called me and took me to the Israeli border. Lady officer, would you notify my wife that I am here, in safety?" He looked at me with entreating eyes.

I rested after the man was sent home. I drank a cup of strong coffee and smoked a cigarette. Before me, on the desk, were telegrams, reports, invitations, information . . . stacks of paper!

In the mess hall one officer invited me to a party. I refused. Another invited me to a cinema. I really wanted to see a movie, but I had to refuse. "You don't have time for your own pleasures. No one will give you a medal for working day and night," he said.

When I finished my job in the Negev, I returned to the command. Moshe Dayan was no longer there. Joe, my boss, had a grin on his face when he saw me. "Oh, so you're back! You didn't transfer from artillery to intelligence after all, did you? And how was your combat job in the Negev? What I need now is an officer to train the reserves."

"I want a month's furlough," I said. "I have learned a great deal about the Negev. I know its problems and shortcomings. Now I long for the desert, for its hills and plains."

"You haven't changed one bit, Judith. You are still obsessed with the desert."

"Have you seen the environs of Beersheba, with the young eucalyptus trees, the tall grasses and wild bushes, and the purple and yellow iris in bloom? This territory is exciting. It is beautiful and magnificent."

Joe shook his head. "If you want a furlough, go to the desert, pitch a tent, and write poems." He signed for my furlough.

In my uncle's house I found a note from Hagai. "Judith, come to a meeting in Buddha's house. We want to start a kibbutz in the Negev. We hope you'll be with us."

I thought for a minute. Yes, I would go and look into it.

22

When I entered Buddha's house, I found everyone seated around a table. Clouds of cigarette smoke seemed to reach up to the ceiling.

Hagai was speaking. *"Haverim* ('friends'), since we are planning to organize a new settlement, we want to know what each one intends to do there, and if there are any questions we will discuss them now. Buddha, you begin."

I was seeing Hagai for the first time since his discharge from the army. The former major, much appreciated by the intelligence corps, was now wearing a simple khaki shirt, open at the neck. Always there was that timid smile, the lowered eyelids.

Buddha, tall, rather wild-eyed, with dark hair that was beginning to gray at the temples, gave the impression of being an intellectual snob. He straightened his shirt, thrust forward his chin, glanced at all the faces around him, and began. "I am employed in the main office of the Ministry of Agriculture, and I have several projects I would like to put into practice. They would be important not only for our kibbutz but for the whole community. I have made many experiments in the Negev and my first request will be to build new terraces to stop the flash floods. Second, I will propose that the old Nabataean terraces be repaired. 'Turn again our captivity, O Lord, as the streams in the south. They that sow in tears shall reap in joy . . .' "

"And what if there is a drought for seven years and the rains do not make floods?" asked Arontzu, a man with strong features and red cheeks.

Buddha looked at him as if he belonged in a mental institution. *"Haverim,"* Buddha banged with his fist, 'wait with your questions till I finish. Besides, we don't build a kibbutz for only one year. If there is a drought—we wait. We will be in an area that has about four inches of rain per year. If I remember correctly, in the time of the Nabataeans there was more rain, perhaps sixteen inches. 'Look at the fields, their vineyards, their wheat, how they had a warm bath from the rain water . . .' "

"Oh, cut out your quotations. We all know them by heart, Buddha," interrupted Yoram, a former sergeant major in intelligence.

"Don't interrupt me, *haverim!* Third, I have a plan to build a dam, and fourth, I am interested in botany and in ecology. I'll come every Friday and spend the Sabbath with you. I also have some experience in cooking—"

"Perhaps you have some experience in dishwashing," laughed Yoram. Buddha sat down, shrugging his shoulders.

"If you don't mind, I'll take my turn," said Dani, a young soil specialist, blond and blue-eyed, of medium height but with a sinewy body and broad shoulders. "I'll devote my time to studying the soil crust of the whole area. I am employed by the Hebrew University. They will send their experiment crews and I will work with them. I want to find out what can grow here with irrigation, and without. I'll also work on meteorological information. I am working with the professors of botany and ecology—"

"Excuse me, Dani, what does ecology mean? Buddha also mentioned it," someone asked.

"That is the branch of biology that deals with the relationship between living organisms and their environment. The professors I work with will come to our settlement and they will be the link between us and the Ministry of Agriculture."

Spardek Ben Yaakov had a fine face with deep-set eyes. "I am trained in growing fruit trees. I had nurseries and orchards. I am also interested in every plant that can grow in the Negev. The professor I work for is a specialist in dewfall. I will measure the dew and perform experiments."

Arontzu, a former sergeant of scouts in intelligence, was next. "For

our kibbutz, which will begin with two military tents and two tin barracks, we will build, as soon as possible, three wooden barracks, and
the agricultural buildings, like sheds and chicken houses and so on. We
want a residential building. Tomorrow we will consult with Judith
about security. I would like to be in charge of construction, but don't
forget my hobby is scouting, and I'll do that occasionally."

Rafi stood up. He was tall and slim, and there was a hint of sarcasm
in his intelligent and sensitive face. He came from Germany, had
served in the British army and then as sergeant major in intelligence.
He was pedantic and a bit stubborn. "I will be a simple laborer and
will do whatever work the manager assigns to me. I can take care of
the accounts, but that will be a sideline. I'll listen to classical music. In
my free time I will go for walks and read books," he continued. When
all of us burst out laughing, Rafi made a wry face and sat down.

I took my turn. "I have been appointed *maaz*—military commander
—of this place. You all know that we work during the day and guard
at night. I will need your help in this work of vigilance. We will be a
lone settlement in an unsettled area. I will inspect our surroundings
with my commander—I am still in the army—and we will look for
roads, for caves, for the presence of infiltrators from the neighboring
countries, Egypt and Jordan. As for guard duty, we will talk about that
when we get there."

"I will be your corresponding secretary, if there is no one else for
that job," said Hagai.

I observed him again. What an odd and unpredictable man he was!
Always restless. Sometimes overzealous, at other times indifferent.
Sometimes very complicated, at other times so simple. Yes, he was a
real "character," complex, strange, and eccentric. He was speaking
again. "We have convinced the Jewish Agency and the military com-
mand. Now, I'll have the simple task of asking for the promised budget.
We will open a bank account and make contact with the Ministry of
Agriculture. We will also benefit from the salaries of Dani, Buddha,
Judith, and Spardek. Elkana will earn something with the truck. I hope
we will have enough for our daily bread.

"I am now speaking for those who haven't taken their turn. Yoram,
my old sergeant major in intelligence, will be our work manager. He
will also learn sheep raising because I believe we will receive some
imported sheep. One scientist promised to give us ten sheep for breed-

ing. A Bedouin sheikh promised to start us off with ten goats. Zvi, who is not present—he is a former sergeant of cavalry and is an expert on machinery—will drive our tractor. Zeev, who isn't here either, works as a mechanic in Haifa. I think he should take charge of our generator. You must know that we will have to live with kerosine lamps, without electricity or refrigeration, and whoever doesn't wish to lead such a primitive life, make up your mind right now." The smile on his face turned into ironic laughter. "Judith, you will have to be our nurse. You know first aid, and you will have to get all your supplies from the pharmacy of Kupat Holim ('Care of the sick of Histadrut' the Organization for Jewish workers). That's all."

First a crimson vermilion light and then a dark red-scarlet sunset illumined the darkening sky. The hills cast oblong shadows. The last car started its engine. After that raucous noise, quiet descended on the new settlement. It was situated on a wide plateau and was named, on May 15, 1952, Sde Boker ("field of herdsmen"). In the center of the plateau were set up two canvas military tents and two tin barracks. A light green tractor, a gray truck, and a black water tank constituted our equipment for life in the arid desert.

I called Barbara to help me prepare supper. She was a graceful, dark-haired girl, full of life and joy, who looked like a biblical beauty. In the tin barracks that served as a kitchen stood three kerosine Primus stoves. We lighted them and placed the large kettle on them. There was one big table and, for illumination, a kerosine lamp. The groceries were piled up against the wall. From the sack of bread, we prepared sandwiches and served them with boiling hot tea.

"Haverim," Hagai stood up and said solemnly, "we are now in the place we have chosen. I propose that we drink wine for the success of our kibbutz, for our health and good luck, and for the conquest of the desert!"

We all stood up, waited silently until our glasses were filled. *"Lehayim!"* Each lifted his glass, clinked it with his companions, and drank.

"Haverim, now our work manager will read the list of assignments for tomorrow."

Yoram, a serious fellow with strong opinions, who had miraculously survived the holocaust in Warsaw, read off all the assignments.

In my mind's eye I was seeing Moshe Dayan, how he had touched my shoulder and said, with a sharp look and an earnest smile on his resolute face, "When a new settlement is formed, all kinds of troubles and problems can be expected. Can I be sure that you, as *maaz,* will watch over everything and everybody?" And how I had replied seriously, "Yes, you can." And how he shook my hand vigorously, saying, "I wish you the best of luck!"

I now got up to read my list of guards. "The last one on guard will light the Primus and put the kettle on before I get up. *Haverim,* each of you must guard cautiously and bravely. If you see anyone who is unknown to you, ask, 'Who is there?' or, in Arabic, *'Min hada?'* If there is no answer and no other means of stopping the intruder—shoot."

Later we lit a bonfire and, to the accompaniment of accordions and mouth organs, we sang songs about soldiers of the demolition platoons, about a soldier killed in the Negev, about the valiant troops of the Palmach, and "My Beloved Is Mine and I Am His." We danced the national dances until after midnight, while our armed guards walked around the camp, peering into the darkness.

When it was my turn to stand guard, I felt cold in my cardigan and battle dress. The moon was sinking to the horizon. In its pale, silvery light the plateau seemed ghostly. The distant hills looked like high walls somewhere in space.

The air was full of strange voices. I heard the piercing chirrup of birds. Then some high-pitched screeching. A few moments of silence, broken by a howling whine. Silence, then again . . . With sudden alarm, brought on by the unknown sounds of the unknown desert at night, I thought: Will we be attacked? Shot? Murdered? We didn't mean to disturb the calm and serene life of the desert, but we had brought our human habits, our accordion music, our songs. Perhaps they disturbed the tranquility that the nomads had built for thousands of years. I gripped the wooden handle of my submachine gun and laughed into the cold night air. We were armed. We knew the infiltrators. We had weapons and knew how to use them. Nevertheless, deep inside I felt an undefined fear that someone would be careless or fall into a trap, but I drove away these disturbing thoughts.

"It is insane to go to a desert kibbutz, to the end of the world," said my uncle. "It may be good for idealists, but not for you." How little he understood that here I had found a challenge even greater than the army. In the army everything was done by order of the commander. Here I would work under my own command, on my own responsibility and leadership.

A noise attracted my attention. It was a shrill, vibrant twang, quick and sharp. It stopped, then started again. It must be the laughing hyena, I thought, and how strange to hear the yaps of a four-legged beast instead of the shot from a two-legged foe!

". . . and one young shepherdess was killed by infiltrators in Kibbutz Sde Boker. Relatives will be notified when the investigation is completed . . ."

Eleven o'clock at night. It was the last news bulletin. What should I do now? Something dull and painful stabbed at my heart. Barbara . . . that must be Barbara! She herded the animals . . . the sweetest girl I ever knew. And I was not even there, but here in Tel Aviv, and it was night.

She had come out as I waited for a car, that morning, and asked me to light her cigarette. "Why did you take a book, Barbara? You should have taken a rifle, for security," I said. She smoothed her hair, arranged her flowered kerchief becomingly, and smiled. "Well, I didn't. Besides, I wouldn't know how to shoot even if I were attacked." I wagged my finger at her. I should not have let her go, but it was so near the settlement, and how could I have foreseen what would happen?

The fact that I didn't even know how she was murdered tormented me and didn't let me sleep. I kept pacing the floor, smoking, thinking, until just before sunrise I finally slept from exhaustion. The bell rang. It was Zvi, with a car. "You heard what happened. Get dressed quickly. We are going to Jerusalem." We drank our coffee in silence.

After the funeral I went to Beersheba. Why had this happened? Why had they had to kill a shepherdess in order to steal twenty sheep and goats? Something was behind their action. One of them shot two bullets into her back as she was reading. Even a rifle wouldn't have saved her . . . Her mother approached me, leaning on a cane, her face composed but full of pain. "Judith, you were the last one to see Barbara. Did she say anything to you? Please tell me."

"She didn't say anything. She only asked me for a light," I said, feeling bitter and embarrassed before Barbara's parents, because she was dead and I was alive. Later, we saw Barbara's body wrapped in our blue and white flag.

I was waiting for a personal interview with my commander. In my numerous excursions through the territory I had come upon a deserted cave, with clothes and cooking utensils. Tobacco seedlings grew beside it, and a fireplace contained many dry twigs. Did the infiltrators use this cave? Or was it used by Egyptian intelligence? I had reported this to the army.

"*Shalom,* Judith," said the commander. "I sympathize with Sde Boker, mourning its first murder."

"Its first . . . Do you think there will be more?" I asked.

"Who knows? Some kibbutzim have had many murders. Some only one."

"I reported to the army about the infiltrators in our vicinity, but nothing was done."

"I regret it very much, but the army cannot protect settlements from such incidents. I cannot accuse anyone of negligence in this matter, not even you. You cared well for your comrades, didn't you? No one could have foreseen this. As I see it, your settlement has too few members, and who would want to join you at the end of the world in such an unsafe locality. I would advise you to take a Nachal company ('Young Fighting Chaluzim'), but only the commander of the South Front can decide about that."

I came away with a heavy heart. I would look into this, and see that no one without arms, or who didn't know how to use them, went anywhere!

"I don't believe a single word that the sheikh of Azazme told you," I said, "He is a clever liar. Such twaddle! He knows about the tracks they left, and when he said that they escaped through the Way of Kings toward Jordan, he was simply lying. He knows that the murderers killed the girl not just to steal the animals, but for fun—to kill a young Jewish girl! They wanted to show us that we cannot live quietly in the desert."

"But the sheikh knows the situation and the people, and he fought with our army," said someone.

Hagai smiled sadly. "If you don't believe a word he says, you must have your reasons."

"Oh, I have. They escaped with the animals, but they are connected with the Azazme tribe. They are regular infiltrators from Egypt. But what good is all this! Barbara is dead and nothing can help her. We must make sure that no one else gets killed. If I find anyone acting irresponsibly, I will have him court-martialed! Don't forget, we are still under the army and wartime orders."

I took my rifle and walked toward the fresh wind and the low white clouds. I saw in my mind's eye the morose and sullen face of Sheikh Azazme, hiding his incomprehensible smile under his thick black graying moustache and his thin tight lips. No, I didn't trust him. I remembered how Bambi, a happy Palmach fellow who had joined our settlement a month after we got here, returned from a patrol in which the sheikh took part. "The patrol found a child," related Bambi, "only five years old, a boy, in a filthy garment, barefooted and trembling. The sheikh said to me, 'Would you like to kill the boy?' and I said no, I would never do such a thing. He wanted to shoot the child, but I stopped him. He wanted to prove his faithfulness to the Israeli state by murdering a helpless child. I don't trust him. He is a sly devil."

I felt as though I were back in Hitler's Europe.

New candidates joined our settlement; Ahuva, our nurse, was my roommate. She was an intelligent girl from Beer-Tuvia who had finished a military nurse's course. I was released from my first-aid job. Then there was Joshua with his wife Nechama and their child. He was a former member of Lehi who had been banished to a prison in Africa when caught by the British.

It was early dusk and the clouds, still crimson in the west, had already turned to dark turquoise blue in the east. It was time to go into the kitchen. I lighted the petrol lamps. In the mess hall I turned on the battery radio. A Brahms concert was coming in from Jerusalem, and I listened with pleasure. Ahuva came in, a towel on her arm. "I am going to shower, Judith. Want to come with me?"

"Go ahead," I said, "my turn will come later."

When the salad was prepared and the tea kettle boiling, I went outside. The hills were gradually disappearing into their deep shadows. What secrets were they hiding? A fine mist was in the air. The imperturbable calm and tranquillity of the desert were broken only by the sound of the classical music.

Suddenly a light appeared. A car was approaching from the direction of Beersheba. Who could be coming, and why did it come so fast? Now it was pitch-dark, for the darkness descended in a few seconds here. Without slowing down, the car turned into the yard and stopped in front of the kitchen porch. It was an army truck, and someone jumped out and ran to the door. The second door was opened, and they carried someone out. "Wounded, shot," ran through my mind, and I rushed toward them.

"Bambi is wounded," shouted the driver. "Where shall we take him?"

"Here, into the mess hall," and I ran to open the door, to bring a mattress, and to send for Ahuva. She was the only one who had a key to the emergency chest. I hastened to Bambi. I saw his handsome life-less face, with its dark beard. His eyes were closed, his mouth moving a little. I unbuttoned his jacket and saw coagulated blood on the right side.

Ahuva came running, her dressing gown only partly buttoned. She looked at Bambi, quickly opened the emergency chest, and took out a gauze bandage. I looked at Bambi's face. His speech was unintel-ligible. His breathing was weak. I heard a hoarse moan, a rattle, and then it stopped. He breathed no more. "He is dead, Ahuva," I said. "I heard his death rattle." She took his pulse. "I don't feel any pulse. But let's do what we are supposed to. The doctor will see him later." And we bandaged him with a gauze bandage over the two wounds on his chest. "Judith, fill a few bottles with warm water, he is cold," she said to me.

"It was in a wadi almost four miles from Sde Boker," began the driver of the truck. "We saw a distant fire. Then we heard some shots. Bambi was sitting next to me. He took out his pistol, opened the door, stood on the step, and fired several times. The fire was returned and Bambi was hit. He fell out of the car. I stopped, jumped out, and picked him up. He was unconscious. I reversed and headed for Sde Boker. There were stones on the road but I sped through them. I was afraid of an ambush. How I got over the big rocks I don't know, but here I am. How is Bambi?" and he raised his sweating, strained, and excited face.

I did not reply for a moment, then said, "We must send Bambi to a doctor. The nearest one is in Beersheba. Will you go? Ahuva will accompany you, and two fellows from the settlement, with rifles and grenades, will go along."

We went out to the truck. Bambi was lying on an improvised bed. His face was pallid, lifeless, dead. To myself I said, "Good-bye, Bambi! What a loss for Sde Boker, you, such a fine fellow. I admired your singing, your tales and war stories, your dancing. And now, when there is no war and supposedly no danger, we have to stand at attention at the graves of our friends!"

I went to see the commander of the Southern Front. Many disturbing thoughts were running through my mind—pity and anger and sorrow that the bullets had to find Barbara's heart and Bambi's lungs. If these were simply unfortunate accidents—but no, behind these murders were the Arab thugs, killing from the top of a hill, or from the next wadi. An Arab killed an Israeli—"Allah will bless him!" They never appeared face-to-face with an Israeli, but shot from behind rocks, unseen.

"Commander, I am asking for reinforcements, not for an army patrol, but for a good firm unit of Nachal. We are only fifteen kibbutz members now."

"Who asked you to the end of the world?" the commander asked wryly. "Did you think that Robinson Crusoe and his man Friday could have gotten more crazy men and women to join them?"

"Why not? It is true we went into the desert, but you don't really think we were crazy! Why, I could see a blossoming desert, a flourishing settlement! If not for the Arab bandits who kill, we would be in no trouble."

The commander smiled bitterly. "I remember how I began my life in this land. It was 1929. The year started with terrible incidents— Jews were killed in Hebron, Zfat, Jerusalem. I volunteered for kibbutz life. I also thought of being close to the land. We created the Haganah, but many of my friends were killed. For no reason, only because they were Jews, and because they founded settlements that worked. At that time we had the British and the Arabs. Now we are Israelis, and yet our settlements are still exposed to murders, minings, thieving, and other crimes. But I want to help Sde Boker. I'll give you a Nachal company, and I don't want to hear of another murder."

It was now the summer of 1953. Sde Boker had acquired some sheep and goats. A Nachal company had joined us. The grazing situation was hopeless because of the drought. Everything was parched.

At a meeting, I spoke up. *"Haverim,* I've been *maaz* for a year and have cooked for all of us. There are enough girls here now to take over my work. I would like to become the shepherdess. I want to rest, to herd the animals in the hills, to stand guard, and to have time to think a bit."

After a noisy discussion I was released from my former jobs and became a shepherdess. I was happy with the early rising. I milked the goats and sheep. Then, with my rifle and bandoliers, I led them into the hills. While the animals grazed slowly on the dry, parched grass, I had time to think and meditate. I could view in perspective the past few years, the war, which had shaken me to my very depths, the actions with the partisans that had ended in my imprisonment. I visualized the various people I had encountered during those years and felt that I must write a book relating all my experiences. I remembered every member of my family, the sights of Auschwitz. How could I go on living without recording all this? I had seen the destruction of our people in Europe, and our fight for independence here. I was living in our restored ancestral land. Yes, I must write it all down. . . . I looked up at the very blue sky of the desert, and in my mind was inscribed indelibly every meeting with people, good and bad, brave and cowardly; my experiences in prison and in the concentration camps; and how it felt to be free and independent. I must.

One day I was appointed to herd the animals at Kibbutz Hanegev, north of Beersheba.

"Eytan, come here. I have a letter for you," I called to a blue-eyed fellow with a blond lock hanging over his forehead.

He ripped open the envelope and read the contents with visible excitement. "I am so happy. We are going!" he shouted and performed a little dance.

"You are going where, Eytan?" I asked

"Oh, it's a secret. You are our former *maaz*—" and he stopped, as if he had said too much.

He packed quickly, said good-bye, and was off.

A week later I heard the news bulletin: "Five Israelis were killed in Jordanese territory. The bodies will be picked up in Eilat."

I was shocked and appalled. Were these the curious adventurers who went to see Petra—a Nabataean capital carved in red stone, with its temples and tombs, in the region of Edom—and were these sights worth a human life? What a waste! I knew that the Jordanian army was situated in that region, and that it abounded with the fiercest Bedouins. If they learned that Israelis were about to visit Petra, they would know how to kill them.

Eytan, son of a farmer, veteran of the Harel division of the Palmach, who had fought for Jerusalem, and Arik, son of a farmer, scout for the Palmach, and three girls gave their lives for a look at Petra.

23

It was July 19, 1953. In the hot sun and torrid air I climbed the hills with my herd. Sometimes a strong wind blew from the west, but when it stopped it was stiflingly hot. As the sun reached its zenith, the ewes huddled together, their lowered heads hidden. Only their fat rumps and their dirty brown-white wool backs were visible. The black goats grazed on the slopes among the sandstones and dry bushes, seemingly unmindful of the scorching heat.

I sat down in the shade of some huge boulders, loosened the bandolier around my waist, put down my rifle half carelessly. No enemy would appear—it was too hot. Besides, I had a good view of the wadi from my perch.

I looked up at the whitish blue sky through my sunglasses and saw the blinding rays of the sun. My watch pointed to one o'clock. In another half hour the relief would be here. Our shepherds would come to take over, and we would go home . . . to the kibbutz, with its shade, water, and relaxation.

In front of me was the tail of the mule and its two hind legs, running rhythmically. Then, a jolt. The field road was bumpy. Another rock, another jolt, then the main road. Now it was smoother going. I took the reins from the Nachal soldier, stood up in the wagon, and drove the mule at a gallop until we reached the mess hall. Here the wagon turned with a flourish and stopped.

I jumped down, shook the dust out of my headgear, and saw three men standing. One was Dani, the other Zvi, and the third a stranger, tall, broad shouldered, deep chested, wearing an open shirt.

Here is a man, I said to myself, different from any I have met. He seemed to be in his element here. There was something about his appearance that made me wonder. . . He is sure of himself, this stranger. He has the look of belonging in this environment. But who knows whether he will stay? . . . Nevertheless I wanted to meet him. But first I wanted to shower, eat my meal, dress and comb my hair, and then be introduced.

At the table I sat with some boys from Nachal and listened to their conversation.

"The stranger is an American," said Sami, the carpenter. "He knows horses, sheep, beef cattle. He came because he is interested in sheep raising."

"He is from the air force. He was in Nirim to see how they grow beef cattle," said Fuad.

"He speaks only English," said another. "He has been talking only to Dani, and they went to Dani's museum, to see the cobras and the scorpions, and Dani's samples of soil."

Quickly I returned to my room. A white blouse with red polka dots, white shorts, white shoes. When I looked into the mirror I was satisfied. White looked well with my bronzed skin. I stopped at Dani's door and knocked.

Dani opened the door. "Judith, come in."

I saw the stranger sitting on the bed. He wore an open sport shirt that showed his muscles. There was a manly, straightforward look in his face. He looked me over, as a man might evaluate a mare on the market, scrutinizing me from my legs to my bronzed shoulders and arms, stopping at my face.

Dani said, "Ed, I want to introduce our shepherdess. She was formerly the commander of this place. Judith, this is a man from the American army, on furlough. He is a horse breeder who has worked with beef cattle and sheep."

In my mind I could see this young man riding a horse, with a holster on each side, wearing a large cowboy hat, and the cattle running before him.

We shook hands. I could feel his strong grip and responded in kind. "Sit down, Judith," and he made room for me near him.

I nodded and sat down. Our eyes met. His searching look seemed to ask, "Who are you?" He pleased me, and I asked, "Ed, is this your first time in Israel?"

When I finally returned to my room, I looked at my watch. It was 4:30 A.M. Through the window came the scarlet light of the rising sun. My roommate sighed in her sleep and turned from side to side.

I undressed quickly and lay down. I could not shake off the fascination of Ed's personality. How surprised I had been to hear him— an assimilated American—say, "I know where my homeland is. It is here."

After supper, we had sat around a bonfire. I discovered that we were talking like old friends. The men opened a bottle of cognac and offered it to Ed, but he said, "I don't drink." And when he was offered a cigarette, he also refused. How strange!

He told me a little about his boyhood. At fourteen he had left his parents' home for the docks, attending evening high school at the same time. Later, he went west. There he worked as a cowboy and lumberjack, and lived in a Mormon village for a time. Then he traveled with a former paratrooper. He bought a stallion, and together they wandered through the western states, breeding horses. They were true friends, sharing everything—poverty as well as joy—like brothers. I could imagine them riding through mountains and valleys, two strong, handsome men.

Ed impressed me as a man who had seen a great deal, who had worked among all kinds of people, and who knew how to size up a man . . . and also a woman. He liked poetry, and cowboy songs, both sad and happy ones, and he pleased me. Why, I wondered. Was it his face, his tall stature, his frankness, his charm? He seemed to fit into our environment perfectly. He was tough and strong.

"My beloved is mine and I am his . . ." I could hear the words that we sang around the bonfire. It was from the Song of Songs and I repeated to myself, "I charge you, O daughters of Jerusalem, if ye find my beloved, that ye tell him that I am sick of love. . . ." Was I truly in love with Ed? From my first sight of him and our first conversation?

An inner voice answered yes. I smiled, turned to the wall, covered my head to shut out the morning light.

Someone was sitting on my bed and shaking me. "Wake up, Judith, wake up."

I was not fully awake and tried to get to sleep again. "Judith, you have slept enough. I want you to get up and go with me to Beersheba. I have to leave."

Now I was fully awake and got up quickly. I reported to the manager that I would be back at noon.

And then he was gone. Only the touch of his hand on my shoulder remained. I stood alone, isolated in the Beersheba bus station. Buses honked noisily. People pushed and rushed by.

"Is he gone forever?" I asked myself.

"A letter for you, Judith," said Rafi, grinning broadly. "It must be from Ed."

I took the letter, read the return address, and walked slowly to my room, my heart pounding.

Ed wrote that he hadn't forgotten me. I could almost see him through the envelope!

Time passed and our correspondence brought us closer together. I had to go to him! I would go to Europe, marry him, and when he was free we would come back here. The trip to Europe, particularly as Ed's unit was stationed in Germany, troubled me. Europe awakened very bad memories, but the thought and the dream of Ed—big, strong, captivating Ed—became intense.

I sat in the express train between Marseilles and Paris. With every mile I was nearer to my "objective." From the window I saw a gray November view: French villages with red-tiled roofs, white churches, thick forests, orchards naked of leaves. It was drizzling. A fog covered the whole area, but in my heart the sun was shining.

A sleepy mood hung over the compartment, but I kept repeating to myself, "You are going to see Ed . . . you are lovesick, but it will not be long now. You will meet him and then everything will be all right."

I hardly remember how the train stopped in Paris and how I was overwhelmed by that big city, after a year and a half of desert life. When I walked out on the boulevards, I saw people of every race. The noise was terrific—cars, people shouting, people hurrying, running into the Métro, women rushing through the streets, boys shouting the news —but all this did not interest me until I received the telegram: "Coming 8:20 A.M. Gare de l'Ouest. Ed."

Now he was coming, I said to myself as I switched off the lamp. He would come and I would see him and read in his eyes whether my dream was to come true.

I awoke at six. My hotel was near the station. The dark, drizzling dawn came into the room. I looked out of my window—dark gray houses, with rain dripping from their roofs, and beyond, fog. Cars went by with their lights on, pedestrians were hurrying, each with his umbrella. No, this sight was not for me! Before dressing, I put my clothes on the bed: a black suit, lilac-colored jersey, high-heeled black shoes. Dressed in my best, I took a raincoat, covered my head, said, *"Au revoir, monsieur!"* to the receptionist, and stepped out into the street. I entered a coffee house, ordered coffee and a croissant. How could I eat? Didn't I realize that I was about to see the man whom I had chosen for life? Should I be apprehensive, or think it over again? Perhaps I was mistaken? But an inner voice assured me, "You are right . . . he is coming . . . you will meet him . . . and it is to be forever, forever, forever. . . ."

With a platform ticket, I stood before the closed gate. One minute more. Only half a minute. The gate opened and the waiting people dragged me forward. I saw the incoming train. Then I saw him! He was in a blue air force uniform, carrying a blue suitcase, tall, straight, with a military bearing. At last he saw me! He put down his suitcase and caught me in his arms.

"Ditta!"

"Ed!"

He lifted me up and our lips met.

When he put me down, he asked, "Where is there a restaurant and a washroom? I'd like to wash up, and we want breakfast." He took time to look me up and down, then said, "You look different. I remembered you as you were in Sde Boker. You, in a black suit!" and he laughed. "In my memory you were wearing white shorts and a white blouse with red dots."

"You look different, too," I said. "I remember you in jeans and a blue cowboy shirt."

As we were having breakfast, Ed became serious. "Ditta," he said, stirring his coffee, "now we are together again. Let's talk about getting married as soon as possible. Then you can come to live with me."

He placed his service cap on a chair. I saw his eyes, his face, his broad shoulders, and I longed for him. And in his face, I read the same dream that was in mine.

It was my birthday and we walked on the streets of Paris. We came upon a woman flower vendor with a big display of flowers, red, white, and yellow roses, purple violets, pink and white and violet asters, and even orchids—white, lilac, and purple. Ed said, "Ditta, let's stop. Choose your flowers."

I looked at the flowers thoughtfully. Roses—they were too aristocratic for my birthday. Orchids—they were a tropical flower, quite a stranger to me. I liked the violets. They brought to mind quiet forest glades, they had the scent of spring, of growing grass. I took two bunches, in their heart-shaped leaves, and smelled them. I smiled at Ed and said, "Thank you for these violets. They suit my birthday as nothing else could."

When we arrived at Sde Boker everyone greeted us. The Ben-Gurions had come to live there. Paratroopers guarded their wooden barracks house. A barrel was shining on its roof—the first sun-heater in Sde Boker.

First I met Pola Ben-Gurion. She was like an older *havera* of the kibbutz, and very friendly. Fluent in several languages—Hebrew, Russian, English, and Yiddish—she had a broad knowledge of life, was simple and unassuming, and showed an interest in the personal lives of all members of the kibbutz.

Pola invited us to come and meet her husband. We were asked into the library, where the walls were covered with books in many languages. Then BG came in. On his weather-beaten face I noticed his thick, bushy eyebrows. His hair was white. Observing his face, I thought: In this man is embodied the Israeli decisiveness, its achievements, its iron will, and its vision.

BG was interested to know how Ed had come to Israel, about his family, about his work.

When I asked him if he and his wife would be willing to take my parents' place and give me away in marriage, BG replied, "We will be glad to do it for all who wish to be wed here and settle in Sde Boker."

The wedding was set for January 12, 1954. It was early in the morning. The women were busy decorating cakes and making sandwiches. When I offered to help, they chased me away. Pola was the boss of the kitchen. "I know all about making parties," she said.

I went out for a walk with Ed. It was a clear day. The green bushes and the fresh growing grass stood out among the stones. We stopped, silently, in front of the stone that marked the spot where Barbara was killed. It was quiet. The sun came through the stratus clouds. We turned and walked to the end of the plateau. I wanted to show Ed the King's Way—the road that leads from Sinai to Israel, that has been used by caravans for numberless centuries. The dry sandstone mountains and the arid valley, in the winter sun, were magnificent.

"Ed, now you see why I like this desert, don't you?"

When we returned to the yard, the guests had begun to arrive. Pola called the other bride and me into a room, where we dressed and where the women arranged our bridal veils and our bouquets of flowers.

The two grooms were taken to another room.

My relatives came in to see me and all my friends greeted me. The rabbis were one and a half hours late, but Pola said, "When the rabbis are late there is nothing to worry about, so long as the bridegrooms are here."

I thought about my parents. They had not lived to lead me under the canopy. My uncle and David BG would escort Ed. Pola and my cousin Freda would take the place of my mother. I don't remember the details. Pola and Freda came for me. I picked up my bouquet of white carnations, looked into the mirror, adjusted my veil, and was led out.

In the yard I saw the dark red wedding canopy, the many guests. There was a flutter of excitement.

Under the canopy stood Ed, wearing a hat. His white shirt was open at the neck and he wore no tie. BG and my uncle were at his side. Pola and Freda led me seven times around Ed and then stopped near the man who was to be my husband. I saw tears in my uncle's eyes, and I myself was not far from crying.

The rabbi said the prayers, the cantor sang his song. I heard Ed say in Hebrew, *"Harei at mekudeshet . . ."* I saw BG's lower lip tremble a little. Ed stood perfectly still. Now I was Ed's wife. Forever! Ed crushed the wine glass with his foot.

Mazel tov rang out all around us as everyone came forward to congratulate us. I kissed so many men and women. . . . I shook so many hands . . . I heard BG repeat the old admonition, "Be fruitful and multiply and replenish the earth."

There was a big wedding party. I remember cutting the bride's cake with the roses on top.

Later I walked over to Ed. "Let's leave. Let's go where we will be alone, where we can celebrate our holiday . . . and my victory."

Was this a victory for me? I asked myself, and words tumbled out of me. "If my parents could have been here, they would have been very happy. When I think of what I have survived, I am happy. I have my victory over my enemies, over everything that stood in my way. And now you are my husband and you will believe in me. . ."

Ed listened quietly to my outpouring, and the expression on his face said, "This is the truth. I met you . . . and I love you!"

And the winter sun caressed us with its tender rays.

EPILOGUE

This branch has to be cut, and this one, too. But this twig is part of the main stem and should be trimmed only. The sun warms my back. I look at the trees and the luxuriant growth of grass. The tree is dormant in winter, sprouts and blossoms in the spring, bears fruit in the fall. Thinking about this renewal of life, a surge of memories rushes through my mind, as I look into space.

It is now 1965. Twenty years after the Allied victory. Eleven years after my marriage. Nine years after my heart operation. For six years we have been living in the village of Orot. It is more than twenty years since I escaped from the march to Mauthausen, and soon it will be eighteen years since I came to Israel. And twenty-two years have passed since I was a prisoner in Auschwitz, and it will be twenty-six years since Germany attacked Poland.

These memories stir me. I smile to myself bitterly that I can remember all that the girl called Judith Strick survived, with the exact dates. I can see before me, as if it happened yesterday, the scenes, the events, the people, the prisons and concentration camps, the Red Army, the IZL, the Israeli Defense Force, the kibbutz . . . and how a good wife follows the good husband when he wants to leave the kibbutz and go to a village.

I turn around. Before me I see our one-story house with its red tile roof shining in the sun. Nearby is the chicken house and the barn. The cows are grazing on Rhodes grass. And I am happy! I am glad that we have enough bread on our table. Every morning I can say, Thank God, I am alive another day!

And I think about the external force that reigns over our lives. I laugh. I was never an atheist, though I did not speak to God through prayer books, but always believed in an external force. I could have died in Auschwitz and no one would even have known my name. But I was preserved to see the Germans say *kaput*. And in Vienna I saw the last German SS man crumple to the ground. That made me happy . . . and also unhappy . . . but it is now forgotten. It happened so many years ago.

I should wake from my dream and prune the trees. Instead, I recall how my dearly loved father—whose favorite I was—would take me to the greenhouse to buy flowers. Before me would stand a row of hyacinths, pink, yellow, white, and purple, and I was allowed to choose anything I wanted. Then my father would also buy some tea roses for me. I shall never forget this, so I grow hyacinths and tea roses, and when they bloom and their scent permeates the air I give my thoughts to my dear father.

And when I am alone I speak to God and thank him that I did not die when they operated on my heart. The postoperative crisis was like another nightmare. And then I think of Ed. His care and devotion during the months that followed made life swell again in my body and mind.

I have no complaints. I was happy to risk my life fighting for what I believed to be right, and I am happy to live in dignity with the man I love.